1 MONTH OF FREE READING

at

www.ForgottenBooks.com

By purchasing this book you are eligible for one month membership to ForgottenBooks.com, giving you unlimited access to our entire collection of over 1,000,000 titles via our web site and mobile apps.

To claim your free month visit:
www.forgottenbooks.com/free982969

* Offer is valid for 45 days from date of purchase. Terms and conditions apply.

ISBN 978-0-260-89528-8
PIBN 10982969

This book is a reproduction of an important historical work. Forgotten Books uses
state-of-the-art technology to digitally reconstruct the work, preserving the original format
whilst repairing imperfections present in the aged copy. In rare cases, an imperfection in
the original, such as a blemish or missing page, may be replicated in our edition. We do,
however, repair the vast majority of imperfections successfully; any imperfections that
remain are intentionally left to preserve the state of such historical works.

Forgotten Books is a registered trademark of FB &c Ltd.
Copyright © 2018 FB &c Ltd.
FB &c Ltd, Dalton House, 60 Windsor Avenue, London, SW19 2RR.
Company number 08720141. Registered in England and Wales.

For support please visit www.forgottenbooks.com

Illinois State University
BULLETIN 1970 1971
GRADUATE CATALOG

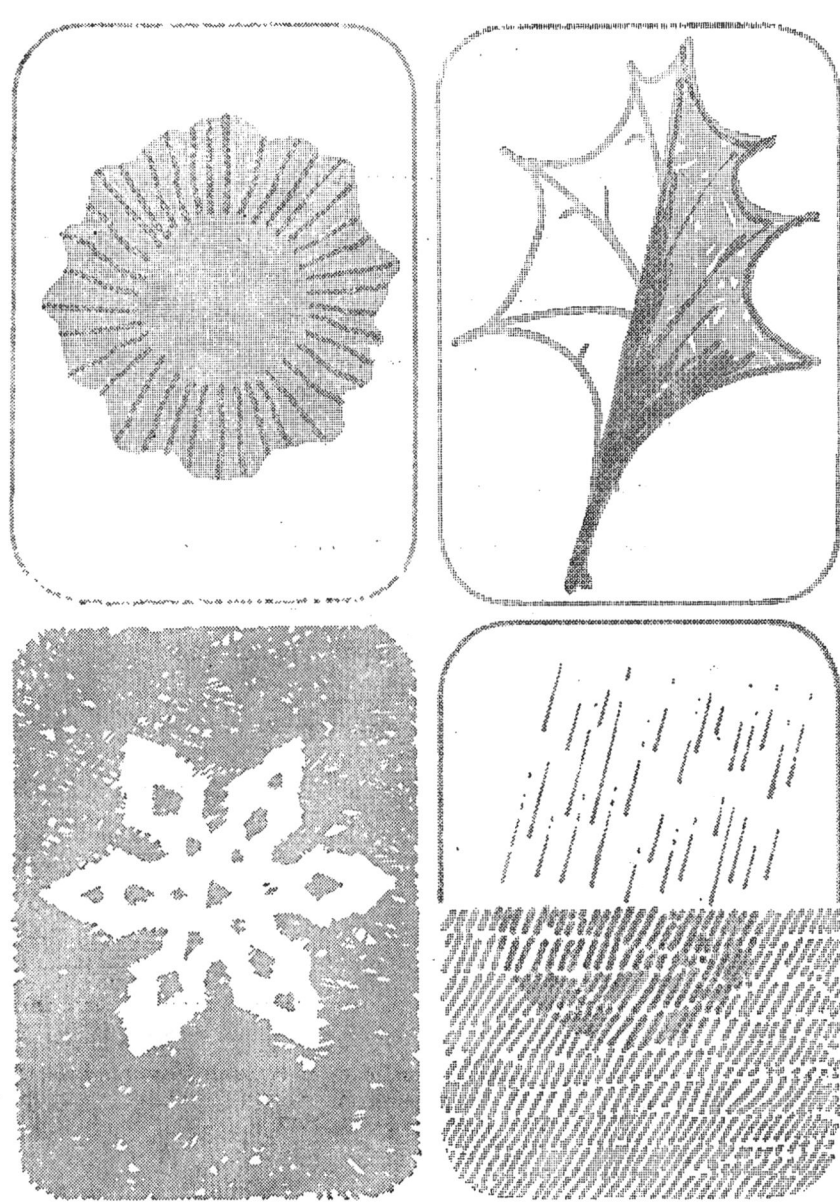

STATE OF ILLINOIS—Land of Lincoln
RICHARD B. OGILVIE, Governor

Table of Contents

- 3   University Calendar
- 4   Board of Regents
- 5   Administrative Officers and Graduate Council
- 6   The University
- 6   The Graduate School
- 7   Admission
- 11   Costs and Living Accommodations
- 14   Assistantships, Scholarships, Financial Aids, and Employment
- 15   Student Life and Services
- 17   Fields of Study and Degrees Granted
- 18   Master's Degrees
- 22   Specialist in Education
- 24   Doctor of Philosophy and Doctor of Education
- 27   Academic Procedures and Regulations
- 29   Graduation
- 29   Departments and Course Offerings
- 133   Faculty
- 144   Index

Volume 68, Number 340 (January, 1970)

Published six times per year monthly in January, March, November, December, and semi-monthly in February.

Entered as second class matter at the post office at Normal, Illinois, under the Act of Congress of August 24, 1912. Acceptance for mailing at special rate of postage provided for in section I-103, Act of October 3, 1917.

University Calendar

1970, SUMMER SESSIONS

June 15	Opening of and registration for eight-week summer session. Last day to apply to departments to take comprehensive examinations.
June 19	Last day for late registration and course changes.
June 24	Last day to apply for graduation in August.
July 10	Foreign language examinations.
July 11	Masters' comprehensive examination, 8 a.m.-12 noon.
July 24	Last day to drop a course.
July 28	Last day to file theses in library for August 7 graduation.
August 6-7	Final examinations for eight-week session.
August 10	Opening of post-session: classes begin, 2 p.m.

1970, FIRST SEMESTER

September 14	Registration for late afternoon, evening, and Saturday courses according to a published schedule.
September 14-17	Registration according to a published schedule.
September 18	Classes begin. Last day to apply to departments to take comprehensive examinations.
September 26	Last day for late registration and course changes.
October 2	Foreign language examinations.
October 23	Last day to apply for graduation in January.
October 31	Homecoming.
November 25	Thanksgiving vacation begins, 11 a.m.
November 30	Thanksgiving vacation ends, 8 a.m.
December 18	Last day to drop a course.
December 18	Christmas vacation begins after scheduled classes.

1971

January 4	Christmas vacation ends, 8 a.m.
January 9	Masters' comprehensive examination, 1-5 p.m.
January 20	Last day to file theses in library for January 30 graduation.
January 21-27	Final examinations for first semester.

1971, SECOND SEMESTER

February 1	Registration for late afternoon, evening, and Saturday courses according to a published schedule.
February 1-4	Registration according to a published schedule.
February 5	Classes begin. Last day to apply to departments to take comprehensive examinations.
February 13	Last day for late registration and course changes.
March 5	Foreign language examinations.
March 12	Last day to apply for June graduation.
April 2	Spring vacation begins after scheduled classes.
April 13	Spring vacation ends, 8 a.m.
May 8	Masters' comprehensive examination, 1-5 p.m.
May 14	Last day to drop a course.
May 31	Memorial Day holiday.
June 2	Last day to file theses in library for June 12 graduation.
June 3-9	Final examinations for second semester.
June 12	One-hundred-twelfth Annual Commencement.

1971, SUMMER SESSIONS

June 21-August 13	Eight-week summer session.
August 16	Opening of post session.

Board of Regents

Gordon H. Millar (Rock Island) ....Chairman
Loren M. Smith (Rockford) ....Vice Chairman
Franklin G. Matsler (Springfield) ....Secretary
Mrs. Thomas D. Masters (Springfield)...........Assistant Secretary-Treasurer

Appointed Members
1967 - 1971

J. Robert Barr..Evanston
Guy E. Cornwell...Chicago
Kenneth W. Lund...Oak Park

1967 - 1973

Percy L. Julian..Oak Park
Mrs. Thomas D. Masters..Springfield
Anthony Varese..McHenry

1969 - 1975

A. L. Knoblauch..Roseville
Gordon H. Millar...Rock Island
Loren M. Smith...Rockford

Ex-officio Member

Ray Page, Superintendent of Public Instruction.....................Springfield

---

Franklin G. Matsler, Executive Secretary..........................Springfield

Illinois State University is governed by the Board of Regents. The Board consists of ten members, nine appointed by the Governor for terms of six years and the Superintendent of Public Instruction who is ex-officio.

Officers of the University

The Presidency

President .... Samuel E. Braden
Vice President of the University and Dean of Faculties .... Richard R. Bond
Vice President of the University and Dean of
    Administrative Services .... Eric H. Johnson
Vice President of the University and Dean of
    Student Services .... Richard E. Hulet

Instructional Officers for Graduate Programs

Associate Dean of Faculties and Director of the
    Summer Session .... Francis B. Belshe
Dean of the Graduate School and Chairman of the
    Graduate Council .... Arlan C. Helgeson
Associate Dean of the Graduate School .... David L. Wheeler
Dean of the College of Applied Science and Technology .... Charles B. Porter
Dean of the College of Arts and Sciences .... Milton Greenberg
Dean of the College of Business .... Robert V. Mitchell
Dean of the College of Education .... Henry J. Hermanowicz
Acting Dean of the College of Fine Arts .... Richard L. Desmond
Dean of Admissions and Records .... Wilbur R. Venerable
Director of University Extension and Field Services and
    Assistant Director of the Summer Session .... Francis R. Brown
Director of Research Services and Grants .... Eric R. Baber

Members of the Graduate Council

Admissions Committee

Barbara C. Hall .... (1973)
Brigitta J. Kuhn .... (1972)
Douglas Poe .... (1971)
Joe W. Kraus .... (1970)
Fred D. Kagy .... (1970)

Membership Committee

Alton J. Bjork .... (1973)
Kenneth A. Retzer .... (1972)
Anthony E. Liberta .... (1971)
Eric R. Baber .... (1970)
Richard Allen .... (1970)

Curriculum Committee

Bernard J. McCarney .... (1973)
Paul F. Mattingly .... (1972)
Dale B. Vetter .... (1971)
Gary C. Ramseyer .... (1970)
Helen M. Cavanagh .... (1970)

Research Committee

Jack A. Ward .... (1973)
Robert L. Crist .... (1972)
Robert C. Duty .... (1971)
Elwood F. Egelston .... (1970)
John L. Frehn .... (1970)

The University

Illinois State University is located in the City of Normal, which, together with the adjacent City of Bloomington, forms a community of over 60,000 people. The cities lie in central Illinois, approximately 125 miles from Chicago.

Founded as the Illinois State Normal University in 1857, the University was the first state institution for higher education in Illinois and the second school for teacher education to be established west of the Allegheny mountains.

The adjacent east and west campuses of the University comprise an area of approximately 200 acres. An additional 450 acres are taken up in a university golf course and the university farm. About forty buildings house the classrooms, laboratories, library, offices, gymnasia, and residence halls of the University. A map of the campus is found on the inside cover of this catalog.

Currently the University enrolls nearly 15,000 students and offers a wide variety of graduate and undergraduate programs through its colleges of Applied Science and Technology, Arts and Sciences, Business, Education, and Fine Arts.

The University is governed by the Board of Regents of the three Regency Universities in Illinois.

The Graduate School

The University began offering graduate work in 1943, when it introduced master's degree programs in several departments. Graduate work has expanded gradually since that time, with doctoral work being introduced in 1962.

Today the Graduate School offers master's degree work in more than thirty academic fields and professional education areas and offers a sixth year, Specialist in Education, degree in Educational Administration. Doctoral programs are offered in Art, Biological Sciences and Educational Administration.

It is the chief aim of the Graduate School to provide an atmosphere in which competent students may join a qualified faculty in extending their fields of knowledge, and where they may share experience in research leading to professional improvement and scholarly achievement.

ACCREDITATION

Illinois State University is accredited on the master's level by the North Central Association of Colleges and Secondary Schools and the National Council for Accreditation of Teacher Education. Its doctoral programs were granted preliminary accreditation by the North Central Association in June, 1964, and its sixth year and doctoral programs in educational administration were granted provisional accreditation by the National Council for the Acreditation of Teacher Education in 1966. The University holds institutional memberships in the American Council on Education, the American Association of Colleges for Teacher Education, and the Council of Graduate Schools in the United States.

LIBRARY RESOURCES

The collections of the University Library include 420,000 cataloged books and 130,000 U.S. Government publications, a total of 550,000 volumes. Many thousand additional publications are available in miniature in 20,000 reels of microfilm and 250,000 microcards and sheets of microprint. The Map Collection contains

140,000 maps and other cartobibliographic items and a record collection of 5,000 phono-records of music and literature is available.

The Library's associate membership in the Center for Research Libraries makes the resources of that 2,000,000-volume collection available for members of the faculty and graduate students. A teletypewriter in Milner Library links the Library with more than a hundred research libraries throughout the country, and a courier service brings books from the University of Illinois Library twice weekly.

SEMESTER PLAN AND SUMMER SESSIONS

The University operates on the semester plan and provides, in addition to its fall and spring semesters, two summer sessions—one session of eight weeks and a post session of one, two, or three weeks.

During the post session, which follows the eight-week summer session, a student may register for a one, two, or three-hour course. One-hour courses continue for one week, two-hour courses for two weeks, and three-hour courses for three weeks.

Limited student teaching and internship facilities are available during the eight-week summer session for those who are qualified.

A graduate student may register for eight semester hours during the eight-week summer session. Nine hours may be taken with permission of the Dean of the Graduate School.

The *Summer Bulletin* is issued annually and may be obtained by writing to the Director of the Summer Session. The bulletin contains information on the cost of attendance, the schedule of classes, and special features of the summer session, such as the Educational Conference, Educational Exhibit, short courses, and workshops.

EVENING, SATURDAY, AND EXTENSION CLASSES

In addition to courses offered during the regular school day, late afternoon, evening, and Saturday classes are offered during the regular school year. These courses carry residence credit.

Selected graduate courses are offered each year in various extension centers. Not more than six semester hours of graduate extension work may be used in meeting requirements for a master's degree. Inquiries concerning extension courses should be directed to the Director of University Extension and Field Services.

Admission

WHO MAY APPLY

A student who has completed his work for a bachelor's degree, or who will do so within one semester, at a college or university that is accredited by the appropriate regional accrediting association, may apply for admission to the Graduate School. While conditional admission may be granted to a last semester senior, only those who have received a bachelor's degree will be permitted to register. Under certain conditions, however, seniors may be permitted to begin graduate work. See page 9.

APPLICATIONS AND CREDENTIALS

All students who wish to take work for graduate credit must submit a formal application for admission to the Graduate School. This includes students who have graduated from, or are attending this University. It applies also to those who wish to take university extension courses for graduate credit. Application forms and instructions are available from the Office of the Dean of Admissions and Records, Hovey Hall.

WHEN TO APPLY

A prospective student at the master's level should file his application, and arrange for official transcripts to be sent, at least three weeks before the date of registration. Filing at a later date may delay registration. (Under special circumstances the Dean of Admissions and Records may approve applications tentatively, pending receipt of official transcripts or action by the committee on admissions. Conditional admission will not be granted for short courses or post session.)

Applicants for admission to specialist and doctoral programs are encouraged to apply as early as possible. Two months should be considered as the minimum period between filing of applications and registration.

MEDICAL EXAMINATION

Each student who takes more than six semester hours during a regular semester and every graduate assistant or fellow who accepts a waiver of fees, regardless of the number of semester hours for which he registers, is required to file a University physical examination form with the University Health Service. The examination must be made at the student's expense. It must be made by a physician licensed to practice medicine in the state of residence. A report of the findings of a chest x-ray or skin test for tuberculosis, done within the year, must be a part of this examination. Forms are available from the University Health Service.

RE-ADMISSION OF FORMER STUDENTS

Graduate students who wish to return to the University after a lapse of one semester or more should apply for re-admission through the Office of Admissions and Records at least seven days prior to the beginning of registration for the session which they wish to attend. A student who has attended another college or university during his absence from the campus should request that institution to send a transcript of his work to the Office of Admissions and Records at this University.

ADMISSION OF NON-DEGREE STUDENTS

The University admits two types of students who are eligible to take graduate work for graduate credit. These are (a) students in degree programs and (b) non-degree students.

A student in a degree program follows a program that, if successfully completed, leads to a degree. A non-degree graduate student may take graduate courses, but he has not been approved to work toward a degree.

A non-degree student who later wishes to work toward a degree must make application for admission to a degree program in the Office of Admissions and Records. He must meet the regular entrance requirements for a degree program. In the meantime, there is no guarantee that courses taken while he is a non-degree student may be used in meeting the requirements for a degree.

Credits earned by a non-degree student are recorded and are available for transfer. But such credit may not be used in meeting the requirements for a degree at Illinois State University unless the student is regularly admitted to a degree program as noted above. If the student is admitted, he may then request that earlier work be considered in meeting requirements. In approving such a request the University will consider the quality of the work and the requirements of the curriculum in which the student is enrolled.

A non-degree student may register for courses for which he has the prerequisites, unless such registration is restricted by the Dean of the Graduate School.

ADMISSION TO MASTER'S PROGRAMS

An applicant for a program leading to the master's degree is considered on the basis of his academic record and other criteria that may include examinations, interviews, and letters of recommendation. Tests for admission are described below.

An applicant with a superior academic record may be admitted directly to a degree program. No student is admitted to a degree program who does not have at least a 2.6 grade point average (on a scale in which $A = 4$) in his last sixty hours of undergraduate work. A student who does not meet this standard but whose academic record and Graduate Record Examination scores give promise of high performance may be given a probationary period of enrollment as a non-degree graduate student. In considering an applicant for any curriculum, there may be departmental requirements in addition to the general requirements of the University.

When an applicant is approved, the departmental adviser will indicate any courses that may be required to remove undergraduate deficiencies. The adviser also may specify certain graduate courses which will be required in addition to those listed in the catalog. The adviser will designate which, if any, of these courses may be used in meeting requirements for the degree.

A senior in good standing at this University may begin graduate work during the semester or summer session in which he completes the requirements for the bachelor's degree, if he otherwise qualifies for a degree program. During a semester he may not register for more graduate credit than the difference between fifteen hours and the number of hours required to complete the bachelor's degree. During the summer session he may not register for more graduate credit than the difference between eight hours and the number of hours required to complete the bachelor's degree. It is understood that graduate credit may be received for graduate courses only if requirements for the bachelor's degree are completed during the semester or summer session in which the student begins graduate work. This opportunity is also extended to last semester seniors of other universities who find it possible to take graduate work at this University while completing requirements for the bachelor's degree on their own campuses. Interested students should write to the Dean of the Graduate School for further information.

ADMISSION TO SPECIALIST AND DOCTORAL PROGRAMS

A student seeking admission to a specialist or doctoral degree program must present letters of recommendation, and must take qualifying examinations before being admitted to the program. He may be required to come to the campus for an interview. Tests for admission are described below.

Admission of an applicant to a specialist or doctoral program will take account of personal and professional qualifications as well as scholastic records and measurement of academic ability. Admission involves approval by the department as well as the Graduate School.

TESTS REQUIRED FOR ADMISSION

Master's Programs

All students seeking admission to master's degree programs must submit scores on the Aptitude Test of the Graduate Record Examination. They should also submit scores on the Advanced Test of the Graduate Record Examination if tests are available in their fields of study. Arrangements for taking the Graduate Record Examination can be made locally in the Test Service Office, 109 Moulton Hall, or by writing to Educational Testing Service at either Box 955, Princeton, New Jersey, 08540, or 1947 Center Street, Berkeley, California, 94704.

Specialist and Doctoral Programs

All students seeking admission to specialist and doctoral programs must submit scores on the Aptitude Test of the Graduate Record Examination and the appropriate advanced test. Information concerning this examination may be obtained at testing centers, or by writing to Educational Testing Service at either Box 955, Princeton, New Jersey, 08540, or 1947 Center Street, Berkeley, California, 94704. Local students may take the test at ISU. An English usage test is also required. Arrangements for taking this test, either locally or at other testing centers, can be made by writing to the Test Service Office, 109 Moulton Hall, Illinois State University.

English Examination for International Students

Illinois State University requires that students from non-English speaking countries, who seek admission to the Graduate School, must take the "Test of English as a Foreign Language." Students wishing to take this examination should write to TOEFL, Education Testing Service, Princeton, New Jersey, 08540. They will be informed as to testing centers nearest their homes and the dates on which the examination will be offered. Following completion of the examination they should ask the Educational Testing Service to send test scores to the Graduate School, Illinois State University, Normal, Illinois 61761.

ADMISSION TO TEACHER EDUCATION PROGRAMS

Students who have been admitted to the Graduate School and who wish to take work leading to certification for public school positions in Illinois should send transcripts of their past work along with a check for ten dollars, to the State Teacher Certification Board, 212 East Monroe Street, Springfield, Illinois 62706, requesting an evaluation for the particular certificate in which they are interested. They should also complete an application form in the office of the Dean of the College of Education, so that they can be assigned an adviser to assist them in planning a program to meet requirements specified by the State Certification Board.

All students seeking to complete certification requirements at Illinois State University must meet university standards for teacher education programs, which include an acceptable academic record and sufficient credits in a suitable teaching field where student teaching assignments are possible. Eventual assignment to student teaching must be approved by both the head of the academic department in the field in which the student plans to teach, and the Head of the Department of Professional Laboratory Experiences.

Graduate students who already hold certification for teaching but are seeking certification on a different level, such as supervision, will be advised as to procedure in their respective departments.

Costs and Living Accommodations

The average cost for board, room, fees, and textbooks for an Illinois resident approximates $1300 for the school year of 36 weeks. The fees below are subject to change.

APPLICATION FEE

An application fee of $15 (check or money order) must accompany the application for admission.

FEES—RESIDENTS OF ILLINOIS

The following fees are due on registration day. Students are not admitted to classes until fees have been paid.

Each Semester

For students who register for more than six semester hours:

*Registration Fee	$ 97.50
Activity and General Service Fee	41.50
**Student Insurance	9.00
University Union fee	11.00
Recreational facilities fee	9.00
	$168.00

For students who register for six semester hours or less:

Registration fee per hour	$ 15.00
General Service Fee	12.50

Eight-Week Summer Session

For students who register for more than three semester hours:

Registration fee	$ 48.75
Activity and General Service fee	16.00
Student Insurance	4.50
University Union fee	5.00
Recreation facilities fee	4.50
	$ 78.75

For students who register for three semester hours or less:

Registration fee per hour	$ 15.00
General Service fee	8.00

---

* Graduate Assistants and Fellowship holders, see page 14.
** This was the charge for the second semester, 1969-70. The rate is subject to change.

Post Session and Short Sessions

Registration fee per hour..........................$ 15.00
(Activity, student insurance, University Union, and recreational facilities fees are not charged)

Auditors

Fees for students who take courses as auditors, without credit:

Registration fee per hour..........................$ 15.00
Maximum charge for a semester................... 97.50
Maximum charge for eight week summer session...... 48.75

Other Fees and Expenses

Graduation fee ....$ 15.00
    Must be paid before published deadline.
Late registration fee 10.00
    Charged after scheduled registration period.
Change in program fee............................ 5.00
    Charged during late registration period.
Transcript of record ....$ 1.00
    Transcripts are issued only when all obligations have been met.
Locker and towel fee for students in physical education courses ($2.00 refunded when padlock is returned) $ 3.00

STUDENT HEALTH AND ACCIDENT INSURANCE

Each student is assessed a fee to purchase a health and accident insurance policy. This policy provides for 100% payment of the first $500 of reasonable hospital expenses and 80% of such expense above $500. It covers 80% of the reasonable expense for a surgeon or certain physicians fees other than those for surgery. There is also an allowance for consultation and ambulance fees. The maximum amount payable for any one accident or sickness is $10,000.

Those students who can produce evidence of equal or better coverage may apply for a refund of the insurance fee by contacting the Office of University Insurance. Application must be submitted within ten days following registration.

Coverage for a student's spouse and children may be obtained at an additional cost in the Office of University Insurance if applied for within ten days after registration.

Each student may exercise an option to continue this insurance during the summer months even though he is not enrolled in the University. The insurance must be purchased at the Office of University Insurance at the end of the school year and no later than the June commencement date.

Claim forms and brochures explaining the coverage are available in the Office of University Insurance.

FEES—OUT-OF-STATE STUDENTS

A student who is not a resident of Illinois pays the non-resident registration fee indicated below. All other fees are the same for non-residents.

A student under 21 years of age is considered a non-resident if his parents are not legal residents of Illinois. A student over 21 years of age is considered a non-resident if he is not a legal resident of Illinois at the time of registration. The Dean of Admissions and Records is responsible for applying out-of-state fees.

Each Semester

Non-resident registration fee, more than six
semester hours $358.00
Non-resident registration fee, six semester
hours or less, per hour......................... 54.00

Eight-Week Summer Session

Non-resident registration fee, more than three
semester hours $154.00
Non-resident registration fee, three semester
hours or less, per hour......................... 46.00

REFUNDS

If a full-fee student withdraws officially from the University by the date given below, the Registration and Student Insurance fees are refunded. Other fees are not refunded except that $15.00 of the Activity and Service fee ($4.50 for students who registered for six or fewer semester hours) will be refunded.

Specifically, no refund of fees will be made after June 22, 1970, for the eight-week summer session, September 21, 1970, for the first semester, and February 8, 1971, for the second semester.

For all short sessions and the post session, no refund of fees will be made after the first day of the session.

LIVING ACCOMMODATIONS

Inquiries regarding housing should be addressed to the Office of University Housing.

On Campus

Current room and board rates in residence halls for men and women are $510 per semester. The University provides all room equipment and linens. Personal towels, blankets, and bedspreads are provided by the student.

Married student housing facilities include 122 one-bedroom and 70 two-bedroom unfurnished apartments. One-bedroom units rent for $75 per month, two-bedroom units, $90 per month.

The University reserves the right to increase current rates if necessary at the beginning of any semester or summer term with the understanding that adequate notice will be given.

Off Campus

A rooming agreement, defining terms on which rooms are rented, is completed by all students and householders when space is reserved in University-approved off-campus homes. Lists of available housing are maintained in the Housing Office.

Rates for rooms vary from $8.50 to $12 per week. Meals secured in the community average $25 per week. In some homes, cooking privileges are available.

Assistantships, Scholarships, Financial Aids, and Employment

Graduate assistantships are available in most of the departments of the University. In addition, assistantships are granted to men and women who serve as counselors in the University residence halls. In each instance, the graduate assistant is assigned responsibilities that contribute directly to his professional career.

Graduate assistants are exempt from payment of the registration fee. They are required, however, to pay all other fees regularly assessed full-time graduate students.

The National Defense Education Act provides for a loan for graduate students not to exceed $2,500 per academic year. This loan is based on proven financial need as determined by the Financial Aids Office through the appropriate application. The loan recipients who enter the teaching field upon their departure from the University may be eligible to cancel one-tenth of the loan amount per year of teaching, up to a maximum of 50% of the loan. Special Education teachers are allowed forgiveness of 100% of the loan at the rate of 15% per year of teaching. Recipients who teach in areas where there is a high concentration of low income families are allowed forgiveness of the loan at the rate of 15% per teaching year. There is no interest on these loans as long as the student remains in school, and 3% interest following departure from school.

The Illinois State Guaranteed Loan Program, which was initiated in 1966, makes it possible for graduate students to borrow up to $1,500 per academic year. This loan is less need, and more convenience oriented than the Federal Loan Program. There is no interest on the loan while the student remains in school, and 7% interest following departure from the University. The Office of Student Financial Aids can provide additional information and application procedures.

A limited number of tuition scholarships are available for foreign students.

The undergraduate catalog lists other scholarships and grants, some of which may be available to graduate students.

A general loan fund is available for graduate students, from which they may borrow at no interest a sum not to exceed $150. Information concerning this fund may be obtained from the Office of Student Financial Aids.

FOR VETERANS

Federal Benefits

Veterans or dependents of veterans who believe that they may be eligible for benefits should contact the Office of Student Financial Aids, Hovey Hall, either by mail prior to registration or in person soon after their arrival on campus.

State Military Scholarships

During any semester or summer session a veteran may avail himself of the provisions of the State Military Scholarship Law, provided he has an honorable discharge and was a resident of the state of Illinois at the time of his induction. These scholarships, which cover four years of registration and activity fees at the state supported universities only, are administered through the Office of Admissions and Records. Work under a State Military Scholarship must be completed in a six-year period and a leave of absence must be requested if a scholarship is not used in consecutive semesters.

PART-TIME EMPLOYMENT

There are possibilities for part-time work for both men and women on the campus and in the community. Information may be received from the Financial Aids Office.

Student Life and Services

STUDENT LIFE...ISU

STUDENT LIFE . . . ISU is the official handbook of University policies and regulations set up by student-faculty boards and by faculty and administrative agencies and officers, under the authority of the Board of Regents governing Illinois State University.

The students, faculty, and staff of Illinois State University constitute an academic community. As guides for individual action within this community the University affirms the Standards of Conduct, the Fundamental Rights of Students and the General Regulations as enunciated in STUDENT LIFE . . . ISU. Each member of the community should—when appropriate opportunities occur—reaffirm and communicate these statements, pointing out to those whose behavior is in violation of them that membership in this community implies adherence to them.

STUDENT SERVICES

The purpose of Student Services is to assist the student in making a satisfactory adjustment to University life and to realize fully his potential as a college student. Although all the members of the administration and the faculty are involved in counseling, the Student Services staff is specifically assigned this area of responsibility. Included is the staff of the Dean of Student Services office, counselors in residence halls, the Health Service, and other specialized services. Counseling relating specifically to academic matters is provided in the classrooms, in the departmental offices, and in the offices of the Dean of Faculties.

HEALTH SERVICE

The University Health Service is maintained by and is an integral part of Illinois State University. Because good health is an essential for success as a student or teacher, the Health Service is concerned directly with promotion of good physical and mental health among university students.

The Health Service, located in Fairchild Hall, includes an infirmary. In addition to services which are educational or preventive in nature, the University physician is available for consultation during office hours regarding any health problem a student may have.

Each student who takes more than six semester hours during the semester is eligible for health service and is required to have a University physical examination form on file with the Health Service before entering the University. A student who takes more than 3 hours during the summer session also is eligible for health service but is not required to have a physical examination.

PSYCHOLOGICAL COUNSELING SERVICE

The Psychological Counseling Service, located in Fairchild Hall, is available to students who would like assistance with educational, personal, social, and vocational matters. In addition to providing counseling for students in the University, the Counseling Service provides training experiences for graduate students in clinical, counseling, and school psychology.

VETERANS SERVICES

The Director of Student Financial Aids is Director of Veterans Services. His office advises veterans on the provisions established by the federal government. In order that the proper forms may be executed, the veteran should write to the Director of Veterans Services before he registers.

For details regarding financial aid, see the section on Assistantships, Scholarships, Financial Aids, and Employment.

CULTURAL OPPORTUNITIES

The University Union serves as a center for student activities, social and cultural. Lectures, entertainments, and art displays by faculty, students, and off-campus persons are presented in this building.

Undergraduate organizations on the campus present many programs of aesthetic, dramatic, and musical nature. There are also student forensic and athletic events.

The Entertainment Board brings to the campus each year nationally known musicians, dancers, lecturers, and stage personalities. It also sponsors the Arts Theatre, featuring American and foreign film classics.

Civic organizations in Bloomington-Normal provide many musical and dramatic events.

Illinois Wesleyan University, located in Bloomington, presents additional cultural opportunities through its faculty, students, and off-campus personalities and groups.

BUREAU OF APPOINTMENTS

The University maintains an active program of placement for graduates and alumni and endeavors to keep constantly informed regarding the requirements of schools, businesses and governmental agencies.

The Bureau makes an effort to follow up graduates in order to assist them to positions of responsibility commensurate with their experience and success in the field. All graduates who desire to secure professional and financial advancements should each year bring their credentials up to date in the Bureau of Appointments.

ALUMNI OFFICE

Through the Alumni Office, the Alumni Association, and ISU area clubs, former students maintain contact with one another and the University. The Alumni Office keeps records of over 24,000 alumni on file and also serves as headquarters for alumni when they are on the campus. *The Register*, published four times a year, and *The Statesman*, published twice a year, are sent to all alumni.

The Association plans Founders' Day, class reunions, the annual alumni luncheon at commencement, and also many homecoming activities.

THE UNIVERSITY FOUNDATION

The Illinois State University Foundation is a tax-exempt, not-for-profit corporation, organized under the laws of the State of Illinois. The purpose of the

Foundation is to invite and receive gifts, bequests, grants, and other contributions consistent with the purpose of ISU.

Gifts received by the Foundation are used to support scholarships, fellowships, and faculty research, and to provide equipment and special purpose buildings not likely to be provided by Legislative appropriations. Because the University must use state funds primarily for additional classrooms and laboratories, and for faculty salaries, the support which the University Foundation can generate from individuals, from industry, from private organizations, from foundations, and from government agencies provides the margin of excellence needed to ensure that Illinois State University will continue to be a creative and progressive force in higher education.

Alumni and other friends of the University who seek further information about the purpose of the Foundation, or concerning ways in which they may make contributions to the Foundation, should confer with Harold Wilkins, Executive Vice-President of the ISU Foundation.

Fields of Study and Degrees Granted

*College of Applied Science and Technology

Health and Physical Education	M.A., M.S., M.S. in Ed.
Home Economics	M.A., M.S., M.S. in Ed.
Industrial Technology	M.A., M.S., M.S. in Ed.

*College of Arts and Sciences

Biological Sciences	M.S., M.S. in Ed., Ph.D.
Chemistry	M.S., M.S. in Ed.
Economics	M.A., M.S.
English	M.A., M.S., M.S. in Ed.
French	M.A.
Geography	M.A., M.S., M.S. in Ed.
History	M.A., M.S., M.S. in Ed.
Latin	M.A., M.S. in Ed.
Mathematics	M.A., M.S., M.S. in Ed.
Physical Sciences	M.S., M.S. in Ed.
Physics	M.S., M.S. in Ed.
Political Science	M.A., M.S.
Psychology	M.A., M.S.
School Psychology	M.A., M.S., M.S. in Ed.
Social Sciences	M.A., M.S., M.S. in Ed.
Sociology	M.A., M.S.
Spanish	M.A., M.S. in Ed.
Speech	M.A., M.S., M.S. in Ed.
Western European Studies	M.A.

*College of Business

Business (Accounting and Business Administration)	M.A., M.S.
Business and Business Education	M.A., M.S., M.S. in Ed

College of Education
- Educational Administration — M.A., M.S., M.S. in Ed., Spec. in Ed., Ed.D., Ph.D.
- Elementary Education — M.A., M.S., M.S. in Ed.
- Guidance and Counseling — M.A., M.S., M.S. in Ed.
- Reading — M.S. in Ed.
- Secondary Education — M.S. in Ed.
- Special Education — M.A., M.S., M.S. in Ed.
- Supervision — M.A., M.S., M.S. in Ed.

*College of Fine Arts
- Art — M.A., M.S., M.S. in Ed., Ed.D.
- Music — M.A., M.S., M.M., M.M.Ed.

* Students may complete programs for secondary or college teaching in these colleges, in addition to "straight" master's programs. See pages 19, 20.

Master's Degrees

CREDIT REQUIREMENTS

Master's degrees are offered in the fields indicated above. The minimum credit requirement for the degree is 32 semester hours. A student may elect one of two alternate plans for the degree. He may elect to do a thesis for which he may receive from four to six hours of credit in Independent Research 499, or he may elect to do 32 hours of coursework and take a comprehensive examination. He may not present credits in Independent Research 499 toward the degree unless his thesis is completed and approved for deposit in the University Library.

In the arts and science master's programs, including those for college and secondary teaching, a student must present, exclusive of Independent Research 499, at least 12 of the 32 hours in courses numbered at the 400 level, eight hours of which must be in his major field. A total of at least 16 semester hours of work must be in the major field (counting courses at the "300" level and above). Remaining credits may be in such related fields as the student's adviser recommends, with the exception that in the teaching programs certain courses in education and psychology are specified.

A student should check carefully with his adviser the departmental requirements for master's degrees, since the above regulations indicate only minimums set by the Graduate School.

GENERAL DEGREE REQUIREMENTS

Degrees offered are listed with each department's offerings. Students should note any special requirements in their respective fields.

Master of Arts

The Master of Arts degree is awarded to a student who has completed an appropriate program, as designated in this catalog, provided he meets the following requirements: The student must have earned credit for a minimum of two years of a foreign language at the college level, or must demonstrate a reading knowledge of a foreign language. In some departments this must be French or German (see departmental regulations). He also must have earned a minimum of 32 semester hours of credit in the humanities and social sciences, in addition to work in foreign language. These requirements in foreign language, humanities, and social sciences, may be met by satisfactory work at either the graduate or undergraduate level.

Master of Science

The Master of Science degree is awarded to students who complete requirements for the degree as designated in the departmental offerings in this catalog.

Master of Science in Education

The Master of Science in Education degree may be awarded to students who have met the requirements of one of the graduate programs in professional education in the University.

Master of Music and Master of Music Education

Requirements for these degrees are listed in the section devoted to the Music Department.

COLLEGE TEACHING PROGRAM REQUIREMENTS

This program is designed for students desiring an internship experience and a basic seminar concerning the nature of college teaching. Students should register for Internship-Seminar in College Teaching 491, a course offered jointly by the Department of Education and the major department, and for Education 474, Seminar in College Teaching.

Students planning to teach in junior colleges requiring certification may need to take work beyond the 32 hours required for the degree. They should obtain information as to the certification rules of the state in which they desire to teach, in order to include the necessary courses in their programs. The University offers several courses concerned with the junior or community college.

SECONDARY TEACHING PROGRAM (for certified teachers)

This master's program for secondary teachers assumes that the student will have completed undergraduate work for certification, and it is designed to provide a master's degree in the student's discipline, with appropriate professional electives. Students needing to meet certification requirements should plan to take such additional courses in education-psychology as will satisfy certification requirements in the states in which they desire to teach.

A student in the master's degree program for secondary teaching must take Education 475, Introduction to Research, or an approved alternate course offered by his own department. In addition he must select six hours from the following courses:

> Measurement and Evaluation in Education 387   (3)
> Curriculum Theory 476   (3)
> A graduate course in historical, social, or philosophical
>   foundations of education
> Introduction to Guidance 360   (2)
> Independent Study in Education 331   (1-3)
> Advanced Educational Psychology 416   (3)

The remainder of the coursework is taken in the student's major department.

Students should note requirements listed with departmental offerings in this catalog and should consult advisers concerning their programs.

SECONDARY TEACHING PROGRAM (for liberal arts graduates)

This program, leading to a Master of Science in Education degree, is designed to encourage and enable selected students who hold a liberal arts bachelor's degree from an accredited college to earn a professional master's degree while qualifying for a regular secondary teaching certificate in Illinois.

RESIDENCE REQUIREMENTS

A candidate for a master's degree must spend at least one full term in residence in order to qualify for the degree. A full term may be interpreted as one semester, with a class load of 8-15 hours, or a summer session with a class load of from 6-8 hours.

TIME LIMITS

All graduate credit used in meeting requirements for the degree must be earned within a period of six years.

TRANSFER AND EXTENSION CREDIT

On approval of the Dean of the Graduate School, a student holding a bachelor's degree from this University may present a maximum of eight semester hours of graduate credit from another college or university for use in meeting the requirements of the master's degree. A student who holds a bachelor's degree from another college or university may present a maximum of six semester hours of graduate credit earned at another college or university. A student who plans to take courses elsewhere is advised to have such work approved in advance to make sure that the courses are appropriate for his curriculum at Illinois State University.

Not more than six semester hours of graduate extension work may be applied toward the master's degree. Correspondence courses are not accepted toward a master's degree. Forms for requesting transfer of credit may be obtained in the Graduate Office, Hovey Hall.

ACADEMIC ADVISERS

Each student has an academic adviser to assist him in planning his work. This adviser should be consulted regarding the sequence of courses, the selection of electives, and the option of thesis or comprehensive examination.

If a student follows a curriculum of specialization in a subject-matter field, the head of the department concerned is his academic adviser unless another faculty member has been appointed by the head of the department. This plan applies to all secondary and college teaching curricula, also elementary education with departmental specialization. In other curricula, other academic advisers have been appointed.

An advisory committee is appointed for each student who writes a thesis. This committee is responsible for directing the thesis project, recommending the student for admission to candidacy for the degree, and conducting the final examination.

If a student chooses the option of a comprehensive examination, his academic adviser has the responsibility of recommending him for admission to candidacy and conducting the final examination.

PROGRAM APPROVAL REQUIRED

At registration, each student's program should carry the approval of his academic adviser. If a program does not have such approval there is no assurance that the courses can be used in meeting the requirements for the degree.

ADMISSION TO CANDIDACY

To be admitted to candidacy for the master's degree the student must file a Plan of Study with the Dean of the Graduate School. This is done on forms obtained in his departmental office. At the time of filing, all deficiencies must be removed and the candidate must meet the requirements of the University regarding scholarship (page 28). Normally the student applies for admission to candidacy when he has completed approximately half of his work toward the master's degree. He must do so before the beginning of the semester or summer session in which he expects to receive his degree. The Plan of Study must indicate whether the student has selected the comprehensive examination or the thesis option. If the student is offering a thesis as part of his work for the degree, his thesis proposal (see below) must have been approved by the Dean of the Graduate School.

THESIS

A student electing the thesis option must register for from four to six hours of 499, Independent Research for the Master's Thesis as approved by his adviser. To register for 499 he must have filed an approved Research Proposal. No grade will be given for the course but credit will be entered on the student's record at the time his approved thesis is deposited in the University library. No credit for 499 may be offered for the master's degree by a student who does not complete a thesis.

A thesis is written under the direction of an advisory committee. The chairman of the advisory committee must be a member of the department representing the student's major field. This chairman is appointed by the head of the department or the academic adviser. The second member of the advisory committee is appointed by the department head, following a joint recommendation by the student and the chairman of the advisory committee. A student must be admitted to a degree program in the Graduate School before a thesis committee can be appointed.

The title, scope, and design of each proposed thesis must be approved by the Dean of the Graduate School. This approval must be received before a student may apply for admission to candidacy. In order to allow time for review, the student is required to file his Proposal for Research with the Dean of the Graduate School early in the semester preceding the one in which he expects to receive the master's degree. Forms for submitting the proposals are available in the Graduate Office.

There is no assumption of uniformity in thesis research. For example, a student may propose a creative project in art or music. In each instance, however, the completed project must meet approved standards of scholarship in the chosen field of study. In each instance there must be evidence of ability to think logically, to gather and organize material, to draw and defend conclusions, and to present the results of the foregoing procedures in a creditable manner.

THESIS CONSULTANT

A thesis consultant approves all theses for the Graduate School before they are officially accepted. The student is urged to consult the thesis consultant of the

Graduate School as soon as he has completed a preliminary draft of the first part of his thesis and has received approval of this draft by his thesis committee. At this time the thesis consultant will counsel the student regarding problems such as those related to format, footnotes, illustrations, and the use of language.

Before a thesis is deposited in the Library, it is the responsibility of the thesis consultant of the Graduate School to examine the materials and to make sure that the report is neatly and correctly typed; is free of technical errors in format, footnoting, and bibliography; is suitable for binding; and reflects credit upon the University and its graduate program. If the form of the thesis is not thus approved, the student must make whatever corrections are necessary and submit the materials again.

A descriptive note or annotation of not more than thirty words and an abstract of not more than three hundred words must be approved by the advisory committee and must accompany the thesis when it is filed in the Library.

After approval by his committee members and the thesis consultant for the Graduate School, the student must file two unbound examination (carbon) copies of his thesis in his departmental office at least one week (seven days) before he takes his oral examination. It is the student's responsibility to retrieve these examination copies shortly before his oral examination. His adviser has the responsibility of notifying members of the department and the Graduate School office that the copies have been made available for examination and he will also notify them of the time and place of the oral examination.

Following the examination the student must file the original copy and the second copy of the approved thesis, with any corrections suggested by his orals committee, unbound, in the University library. To be eligible for graduation a student must deposit his thesis in the library at least ten days before the end of the semester. Theses filed after that date will be credited toward graduation the following semester or session.

A thesis manual may be purchased from the University Textbook Service.

EXAMINATIONS

An examination, oral, written, or both, must be taken by each student before he receives the master's degree. This examination covers the graduate work which the student is presenting for his degree. The time, place, and nature of the examination are determined by the student's advisory committee if he selects the thesis option. The comprehensive examination is the responsibility of the department.

Specialist in Education

PROGRAM REQUIREMENTS

ADMISSION

A student seeking admission to a program leading to the Specialist in Education degree must present letters of recommendation and must take qualifying examinations before being admitted to the program. He may be required to come to the campus for an interview.

Admission of an applicant to a specialist degree program will take account of personal and professional qualifications as well as scholastic records and measurement of academic ability. Admission involves approval by the department as well as the Graduate School.

While the specialist program is a complete program and is usually terminal, a person completing a specialist degree is not precluded from entering a doctoral program. He should not expect to be able to transfer all his specialist course work to a doctoral program, however, since some work appropriate to the one degree will probably not be appropriate to the other. Similarly a doctoral candidate may not expect to abandon his program and accept a specialist degree as compensation for a partially fulfilled program.

ACADEMIC ADVISERS

The head of the department, with the approval of the Dean of the Graduate School, appoints an academic adviser for each student admitted to a specialist degree program. If the student is pursuing a minor field of study, as well as a major field, the adviser, in approving the student's program, should obtain the advice of the department representing the student's minor field. At the time of each registration, the academic adviser files copies of the student's program with the heads of departments concerned and with the Dean of the Graduate School.

CURRICULUM

A student selecting the specialist degree must select a major field of study, and a supporting program approved by his academic adviser, the Dean of the Graduate School, and the Department directly involved.

TRANSFER AND RESIDENCE

A student seeking the specialist degree may petition to transfer, from another institution, not to exceed six semester hours of graduate credit beyond the master's degree. The Dean of the Graduate School must approve all transfer credit used in meeting the requirements for the specialist degree.

A student seeking the specialist degree must, after receiving a master's degree, complete at this University the equivalent of at least one academic year of graduate work. This must include one semester in which he is in residence; or one summer in which he is in residence for eleven consecutive weeks. A student is considered to be in residence when he devotes a major part of his time to graduate study and research on the campus.

A student will not be considered in residence while he is employed full-time.

Extension courses may not be used in meeting requirements for the specialist degree.

TIME LIMITATIONS

The specialist degree is not granted on the basis of a student having successfully completed a certain number of courses, but upon evidence of his scholarly attainment as demonstrated especially by examinations and competence in research.

Although course credit is not the primary basis for granting the specialist degree, a student is not eligible to take his final examination until the latter part of the session in which he is completing thirty semester hours of work beyond the master's degree. More than two semesters may be necessary to complete all requirements for the degree.

All work for the specialist degree must be completed within six calendar years after the student begins work beyond the master's level. If the student does not complete his work within this time, he may be required to take additional examinations, or additional course work, or both, in order to continue in the specialist program.

ADMISSION TO CANDIDACY

A student seeking the specialist degree may be admitted to candidacy after: (a) removal of any deficiencies assessed at admission, (b) approval of his proposal for research, and (c) approval by his academic adviser of a plan of study leading to the specialist degree.

RESEARCH

A student seeking the specialist degree is required to complete a research project that gives evidence of his scholarly attainment and capacity for independent investigation appropriate to the degree.

The Dean of the Graduate School appoints the student's research committee, which includes his academic adviser. The topic and research design must be approved by the Dean of the Graduate School and the department representing the student's major field. The entire committee shares the responsibility for the research project although the academic adviser may work more directly with the student.

FINAL EXAMINATION

The Dean of the Graduate School appoints a committee which is responsible for the final examination. This examination may be oral, written, or both. The committee includes the student's academic adviser, as well as other members of the graduate faculty.

Doctor of Philosophy and Doctor of Education

PROGRAM REQUIREMENTS

ADMISSION

A student seeking admission to a doctoral degree program must present letters of recommendation, and must take qualifying examinations before being admitted to the program. He may be required to come to the campus for an interview.

Admission of an applicant to a doctoral program will take account of personal and professional qualifications as well as scholastic records and measurement of academic ability. Admission involves approval by the department as well as the Graduate School.

ACADEMIC ADVISER

The head of the department, with the approval of the Dean of the Graduate School, appoints an academic adviser for each student admitted to a doctoral program. The adviser is responsible for approving the student's program of courses with the advice of departments representing, when applicable, both major and minor fields. Normally this function is assumed by the chairman of the student's dissertation committee after that committee has been named. At the time of each registration, the academic adviser files copies of the student's program with the heads of departments concerned and with the Dean of the Graduate School.

REQUIRED COURSES AND FIELDS

A doctoral student may select both a major and a minor field (or fields) of study. The selection of minor field (or fields) must have the approval of the Dean of the Graduate School and the department directly involved. A minor field may, under certain circumstances, be in the same department as a major field.

RESIDENCE

A doctoral student, after completing work for a master's degree or its equivalent, must complete at least four semesters of resident graduate work, including at least two consecutive semesters in full-time residence at this University. Work in summer sessions may not be used in meeting this requirement of two consecutive semesters. A student is considered to be in full-time residence when he devotes a major portion of his time to graduate study and research on the campus.

A student will not be considered in residence while he is employed full-time.

Extension courses may not be used in meeting requirements for the doctor's degree.

TIME LIMITATIONS

The doctor's degree is not granted on the basis of a student having successfully completed a certain number of courses, but upon evidence of his scholarly attainment as demonstrated especially by examinations and competence in research.

All work for the doctorate, including the dissertation, must be completed within eight calendar years after the student begins work beyond the master's level. If the student does not complete his work during this time, he may be required to take additional qualifying examinations, or additional course work, or both, in order to continue in the doctoral program.

LANGUAGE REQUIREMENTS FOR THE Ph.D.

All candidates for the Ph.D. must meet appropriate standards in oral and written English. In addition the general requirement for the degree is a reading knowledge of two foreign languages chosen from French, German, Russian, or other approved languages. In some fields the native language of a foreign graduate student may be offered in fulfillment of a foreign language requirement.

In all cases the department involved shall furnish evidence of its approval of a student's choice of language as containing a substantial body of knowledge pertinent to his field of inquiry and may furnish evidence that the candidate has proficiency in that language.

By petition, the student may substitute a more advanced knowledge of one language for a reading knowledge of two. In either case the Department of Foreign Languages has the responsibility of certifying that the language requirement has been met. A reading examination is given from an article or book in the candidate's field. The use of a dictionary is permitted. Advanced knowledge of a single foreign language is demonstrated by skills sufficient to give and to comprehend lectures in the field of specialization, to respond to questions relating to the specialization as well as to read the language without the aid of a dictionary. Language examinations are given according to a schedule published in the annual calendar.

The Graduate School permits the substitution of other research tools or competencies for one of the two foreign language requirements, where such substitutions are particularly appropriate to the field involved. Departmental alternatives are described with departmental offerings in this catalog.

RESEARCH TOOLS FOR THE Ed.D.

Ed.D. candidates who are not required to offer foreign languages as research tools, are expected to have developed other competencies appropriate for doctoral candidates in their fields. These may involve proficiencies in such areas as statistics, measurement and evaluation, research techniques, and experience in field survey work or special course work.

As is the case with ability to use a foreign language, some research skills may be the product of undergraduate and early graduate work. The concern of the Graduate School is that the doctoral candidate be able to understand the research work of leading scholars in his field, that he master the processes which will enable him to do productive research himself, and that he be able to report his research findings clearly to others.

PRELIMINARY EXAMINATION AND ADMISSION TO CANDIDACY

A doctoral student may be admitted to candidacy after: (a) meeting the foreign language requirement or alternate approved program, (b) passing a comprehensive preliminary examination, and (c) receiving approval of the dissertation topic.

The comprehensive preliminary examination is written or written and oral. It covers both major and minor fields. It also is concerned with the student's professional competence and his ability to undertake independent research.

The Dean of the Graduate School appoints the examining committee which includes the student's academic adviser and a representative of his minor field (or fields).

DISSERTATION FOR THE Ph.D. AND Ed.D.

The doctoral candidate is encouraged to select a dissertation topic early in his work and to plan his course work with the advice of his dissertation committee. The Dean of the Graduate School appoints a dissertation committee of not less than three members, the chairman of which acts as the student's academic adviser. The topic of the dissertation must be approved by the Dean of the Graduate School as well as this committee. The entire committee shares responsibility for the dissertation although the chairman may work more directly with the student.

The dissertation for the Ph.D. must involve independent research and an original contribution to knowledge. While the dissertation for the Ed.D. may meet the above requirements it is customary to allow greater flexibility in the Ed.D. dissertation, so that it may, for instance, involve the application of existing knowledge or theory to a practical educational problem or situation.

The dissertation must be approved by the dissertation committee, as well as the final examination committee appointed by the Dean of the Graduate School. This committee represents the University at large.

The student is not required to have the dissertation printed. He will be required to pay the expense of microfilming for distribution by University Microfilms. The University may publish part or all of the dissertation.

REGISTRATION FOR DISSERTATION WORK

A candidate for the doctorate who has completed coursework must register for Research 490 or a similar course recommended by his department during the semester or summer session in which he takes his final oral examination and in any semester or summer session in which he holds an assistantship or fellowship, or in which he wishes to use University facilities.

FINAL EXAMINATION

The Dean of the Graduate School appoints a committee which is responsible for the final examination. This examination may be oral, written, or both, and is concerned with more than the dissertation topic. The committee includes the student's academic adviser, as well as other members of the graduate faculty.

Academic Procedures and Regulations

THE GRADING SYSTEM

Grades

The grades with their value in grade points are as follows:

A	(Passing)	4 grade points per semester hour
B	(Passing)	3 grade points per semester hour
C	(Passing)	2 grade points per semester hour
D	(Passing)	1 grade point per semester hour
F, WF	(Failing)	No grade points per semester hour
I	(Incomplete)	No grade points per semester hour
WX, WP	(Withdrawal)	No grade points per semester hour
DE	(Deferred)	No grade points per semester hour

A, B, C, or D will be recorded for work which has been given a passing grade.

F will be given to (1) Students who withdraw from a course at any time without official permission; (2) Students who are in a course all semester but who fail to make a passing mark.

Withdrawals

WX, WP, or WF will be given to students who have received official permission to withdraw from a course. WX is given if the student withdraws before the quality of the work can be determined; WP, if the student is passing at the time of withdrawal; and WF, if failing. Official permission to withdraw from a course will not be given after the fourteenth week of a semester or the sixth week of a summer session.

Specific final dates for withdrawals during the two semesters of the academic year are published in the class schedule booklet for each semester. Specific dates for withdrawals during the summer session are published in the Summer Session Bulletin. In a case involving prolonged illness, a student may be permitted to withdraw at a later date if such withdrawal is recommended by the University Health Service.

For withdrawals from courses students should report to the Registration Office, 110 Moulton Hall. After the period during which program changes are made, a student must have a conference with the instructor of any course from which he is planning to withdraw. This conference must be held prior to the granting of official permission to withdraw from a course. All students who wish to withdraw from the University should first report to the office of the Dean of Student Services. In case of accident or illness which would make withdrawal in the regular way impossible, a letter sent to the Graduate Dean explaining the situation will be sufficient, providing that library card and any borrowed volumes are returned.

If a student withdraws from a class or from the University during the semester without arranging officially with the Registration Office his withdrawal will be considered unofficial after three weeks of absence or by the close of the semester (whichever is the shorter period of time), unless justifiable reason for extension of time is accepted by the Dean of the Graduate School.

Incompletes and Deferred Grades

An I (incomplete) will be given a student who is doing passing work but who, because of illness or other justifiable reasons, finds it impossible to complete the work by the end of the semester or session. The student must be in class to within three weeks of the close of the semester or one week of the summer session, and the quality of his work must be such that he can complete it through special assignments and examinations. Incompletes should be cleared during the next semester or session a student is in school and must be cleared before one year has elapsed. A deferred grade (de) is usually given in research courses leading to a thesis or dissertation if the work is not completed by the end of the semester or session.

A student expecting to graduate at the end of any semester or session should be sure to have incompletes cleared in the office of admissions and records at least three weeks before the end of the semester in order to give adequate time for his records to be cleared for graduation.

ACADEMIC LOAD

Twelve hours is the usual load for a graduate student during the semester. The maximum academic load for graduate students is fifteen semester hours.

In the eight-week summer session, the maximum load is eight semester hours.

A fully employed person may not enroll for more than one course, nor for a total of more than four hours, during any semester.

If a student holds an assistantship, his academic class load is adjusted accordingly.

SCHOLARSHIP AND OTHER REQUIREMENTS

A student must have at least a B average at this University in order to be admitted to candidacy for a degree. For graduation a B average is also required. The Dean, in consultation with the student's adviser, may ask a student whose work is unsatisfactory to discontinue graduate work or grant him a probationary period in which to bring his work up to required standards. A student who fails to bring his total record up to a B average during the probationary period will not be permitted to register for further graduate work.

Transfer credit must carry a grade of B or better if it is to be used in meeting requirements for a degree. Courses completed at this University with grades below C may not count toward a degree, but these grades are counted in computing the average. If a graduate student repeats a course, both grades are counted in computing the grade-point average.

The last course or courses before graduation must be completed with this University.

It is the student's responsibility to make a formal request for the transfer of any credit which he proposes to use in meeting requirements at this University.

The Council may deny admission to the University, or registration at any time, or admission to candidacy for the degree, upon the basis of unsatisfactory scholarship, or what in their judgment is unfitness for teaching on physical, moral, mental, or emotional grounds.

AUDITOR

A student may register as auditor, attending class without participation and without credit. Registration must have the approval of the instructor. Registration as an auditor is performed separately through the Office of the Registrar. The auditor fee is indicated in the section on cost. Students who are registered for seven or more hours for credit may audit courses free of charge.

Graduation

A student must apply for graduation in the Graduate Office, 310 Hovey Hall, before the deadlines specified for each session in the calendar in this catalog. At the time application is made, the graduation fee of $15 must be paid.

COMMENCEMENT

Degrees are conferred and diplomas awarded after the close of each semester, at the end of the eight-week summer session, and after the post session. Commencement is held once each year in June. Participation is voluntary. Graduate students who expect to complete degree requirements prior to June commencement may participate in June commencement. Those who will finish their degree requirements after June commencement, in the summer session or post session, may participate in the June commencement during the next academic year.

Departments and Course Offerings

SEMESTER PLAN

The University operates on the semester plan. The value of courses, is therefore, in terms of semester hours. A semester hour is assigned for a fifty-minute period of lecture or discussion for a semester of 18 weeks. For laboratory two fifty-minute periods are necessary for a semester hour.

COURSE NUMBERING SYSTEM

This Graduate Catalog contains courses numbered 300 to 599

300–399 Advanced undergraduate and graduate courses. Open to juniors, seniors, and graduate students.

400–499 Graduate courses.

500–599 Courses limited to advanced graduate or doctoral students.

TEACHING STAFF

The members of the teaching staff of each department are listed in the departmental sections which follow. The entire faculty for the Graduate School is shown in a section after **Departments and Course Offerings.**

Accounting

(See Business)

Anthropology

(See Sociology-Anthropology)

Art

Chairman of the Department: Fred V. Mills.   Office: Centennial Building, West 203

Teaching Staff: G. Barford, H. Boyd, R. Freyberger, W. D. Hartley, F. L. Hoover, T. Malone, F. Mills, E. Niemi, M. Rennels, C. L. Steinburg, H. Stumbo, N. Towner, V. Vint, K. Holder, K. Knoblock, T. Mather, R. Small, M. Stack, A. Sweet.

The department offers work leading to the following degrees: M.A., M.S., M.S. in Ed., and Ed.D. General University requirements for degrees are described elsewhere in this catalog.

ART EDUCATION

Master's degree programs with a concentration in Art Education require a minimum of 32 hours including the following courses: Art 321, 401, 497 and a graduate course in art history. Both programs require the completion of a thesis in art education or the option of a comprehensive examination.

In addition, for the M.A. degree with a concentration in Art Education, the student must select a minimum of two courses from the following: Art 403, 411, 412, and 421. He is also required to have 10 or more hours in areas of interest within the field of art, art education, education or allied areas; however, no fewer than 4 hours of these must be in art education or education.

For the M.S. degree with a concentration in Art Education the student must select no fewer than six hours in art education of which one course must be from the following: Art 403, 411, 412, and 421. In addition he must elect six hours in one of the following: art history, ceramics, jewelry, painting, printmaking, sculpture, and textiles.

ART HISTORY AND AESTHETICS

The master's degree program in Art History and Aesthetics may lead to either the M.A. or the M.S. degree. The program will be developed in consultation with an adviser from the Art History or Aesthetics area. Each program is designed with the individual student's strengths and interests in mind.

ART STUDIO

The master's degree program in Art Studio may lead to either the M.A. or the M.S. degree. These degrees are offered in advanced ceramics, design, drawing, jewelry, painting, printmaking, sculpture and weaving. The program will be developed in consultation with an adviser from the major studio area. Each program is designed with the individual student's strengths and interests in mind.

DOCTOR OF EDUCATION DEGREE IN ART

Doctoral students may choose either Theory and Practice of Art Education or Studio Practice as a major field of specialization. Students selecting Studio Practice as a major are expected to take work in more than one studio area and must pursue one area in depth. The minor may be one of these areas if it has not been chosen as the major. It may also be in art history or in a field outside the Department of Art. In some cases a minor incorporating two fields is acceptable.

The sequential procedure leading to the degree is as follows:
a. admission to advanced graduate standing in the Department of Art.
b. a tentative advanced graduate study program planned in consultation with assigned adviser
c. a Degree Program Interview (for final approval of degree study program)
d. Qualifying Examinations following completion of approximately two-thirds of the planned course requirements.
e. approval of the dissertation topic by the student's committee
f. admission to doctoral candidacy
g. completion of terminal degree requirements within *five years* of the date on which candidacy was granted.

The department reserves the right to keep examples of original work produced by graduate students for its permanent collection of student art work.

COURSES

321 PHILOSOPHY OF ART   3 sem. hrs.
An introduction to the history of aesthetics and criticism with an emphasis upon the development of independent philosophical inquiry.

324 ADVANCED JEWELRY AND SILVERSMITHING   2-6 sem. hrs.
Special problems in jewelry and silversmithing. May be repeated. Prerequisite: Art 224.

327 ADVANCED CERAMICS   2-6 sem. hrs.
Special problems in ceramics. May be repeated. Prerequisite: Art 227.

331 ADVANCED DRAWING   1-3 sem. hrs.
Special problems in drawing. May be repeated. Prerequisite: Art 114.

332 ADVANCED SCULPTURE   2-6 sem. hrs.
Special problems in sculpture. May be repeated. Prerequisite: Art 232.

340 ADVANCED WEAVING   2-6 sem. hrs.
Special problems in weaving. May be repeated. Prerequisite: Art 240.

345 ADVANCED GRAPHICS 2-6 sem. hrs.
Special problems in graphic arts. May be repeated. Prerequisite: Art 245.

351 SPECIAL PROJECTS IN ART 2-6 sem. hrs.
Special projects in art or art education chosen by the student for special investigation with the approval of the instructor. A student may enroll in this course for credit more than once if the material covered is not duplicated.

361 ADVANCED PAINTING 2-6 sem. hrs.
Special problems in painting. May be repeated. Prerequisite: Art 262.

370 CONTEMPORARY ART 2 sem. hrs.
Development of modern movements in painting, sculpture, architecture, and industrial design in Europe and America.

373 INDIAN ARTS OF MIDDLE AMERICA 3 sem. hrs.
Arts of the indigenous people in the area between the northern boundary of Mexico and the southern boundary of Panama. Emphasis upon pre-Columbian periods including Olmec, Mayan, Zapotec, Aztec and related cultures. The place of Indian arts today with special reference to the Cuna Indians of the San Blas Islands.

375 RENAISSANCE ART 3 sem. hrs.
General influence determining the art product in Italy, Germany, Holland, England, and Flanders; related arts. Sources and readings for research. Chronological survey of artistic evidence in architecture, sculpture, painting, and the minor arts.

381 ART IN THE UNITED STATES 3 sem. hrs.
A survey of the development of painting, sculpture, industrial design, and architecture in the United States with an emphasis upon twentieth-century trends.

401 HISTORY AND PHILOSOPHY OF ART EDUCATION 3 sem. hrs.
A study of the historical and philosophical foundations of art education.

402 STUDIES IN ART EDUCATION 2 sem. hrs.
Problems in art education from the point of view of research and experimentation. Development of instructional methods and materials, and means of testing their validity.

403 ORGANIZATION OF PUBLIC SCHOOL ART PROGRAMS 2 sem. hrs.
Problems relating to the development and administration of total public school art programs in communities of different sizes.

411 ART IN ELEMENTARY SCHOOLS 3 sem. hrs.
Art program from kindergarten through the sixth grade: content, methods, and teaching materials. The role of art in the total curriculum.

412 ART IN SECONDARY SCHOOLS 3 sem. hrs.
The art program at the junior, senior high, and junior college levels: content, methods, and teaching materials. The role of art in the total curriculum.

421 PROBLEMS IN TEACHING ART IN HIGHER EDUCATION 2-5 sem. hrs.
Opportunity for observation, participation, and teaching at the college level. Assignments are made with the approval of the department chairman at least two months prior to registration.

422 COLLEGE PROGRAMS IN ART 2 sem. hrs.
Planning and administration of college and university art programs.

425 PSYCHOLOGY OF ART 3 sem. hrs.

A survey of philosophical and psychological studies of the creative individual; art appreciation and production, and the art product; consideration of social and educational implications.

444 PROBLEMS IN STUDIO WORK 2-6 sem. hrs.

Individual study and direction in creative activity. May be repeated.

451 SPECIAL PROJECTS IN ART 2-6 sem. hrs.

Special project in art or art education chosen by the student for investigation with the approval of the instructor and the head of the department. A student may enroll in this course for credit more than once if the material covered is not duplicated.

471 PRIMITIVE ART 3 sem. hrs.

Art of preliterate cultures in several parts of the world and the culture traits, complexes, and institutions associated with them.

482 CONTEMPORARY PAINTING 3 sem. hrs.

Backgrounds for twentieth-century painting. Major movements in modern painting: Impressionism, Post-Impressionism, Dada, Surrealism, social consciousness, Regionalism, Abstract Expressionism. Painting Today.

483 CONTEMPORARY ARCHITECTURE 3 sem. hrs.

Backgrounds for twentieth-century architecture. New materials and techniques. The European group. Oud, Le Corbusier, Gropius, and van der Rohe. The Americans: Richardson, Sullivan, and Wright. The International Style. The American home today.

491 INTERNSHIP-SEMINAR IN COLLEGE TEACHING IN ART 3 sem. hrs.

Credit for the course is given in Education (see Education 491).

499 INDEPENDENT RESEARCH FOR THE MASTER'S THESIS 1-6 sem. hrs.

A student electing the thesis option must take from four to six hours of 499. A proposal for research must be on file before registration for this course is approved by the student's adviser. While registration beyond six hours may be permitted for the convenience of the student, he may not count more than a total of six hours of 499 among the 32 required for the master's degree.

597 RESEARCH SEMINAR 1-6 sem. hrs.

Introduction to bibliography, methods of scholarly research and the critical evaluation of research in the field. May be repeated by more advanced students who desire direction and constructive criticism as they pursue research problems.

599 RESEARCH IN ART Variable credit

Research involving the gathering of data to form the basis for the doctoral dissertation. Approval of the chairman of the department is required.

Biological Sciences

Head of the Department: R. Omar Rilett.   Office: Science Building 206

Teaching Staff: D. Birkenholz, H. Brockman, L. Brown, W. Brown, R. Chasson, T. Chuang, J. Cralley, W. Daniel, E. Dilks, D. Fensholt, K. Fitch, J. Frehn, C. Hardiman, H. Hetzel, H. Huizinga, D. R. Jensen, A. Liberta, J. L. Martens, L. Mentzer, A. Merrick, O. Mizer, E. Mockford, M. Nadakavukaren, D. Pittman, E. I. Rhymer, R. O. Rilett, W. Starrett,* J. Tone, J. Ward, D. Weber, R. Weigel, E. Willis.

The department offers work leading to the following degrees: M.S., M.S. in Ed., and Ph.D. Master's degree students are required to take the following courses: 300 and 301—Readings in the Biological Sciences and 304—Seminar in Biology. University requirements for the M.S. and Ph.D. degrees are described elsewhere in this catalog.

A student working toward the Ph.D. degree in Biology may concentrate his studies in the following areas: botany, genetics, microbiology, physiology, or zoology.

Ph.D. LANGUAGE REQUIREMENTS

General language requirements of the Graduate School apply. With the approval of the Departmental Graduate Curriculum Committee, the Head of the Department may permit the substitution of psychology 440 and 441 OR Mathematics 350 and 351 for one of the two foreign language requirements. The student is required to earn a grade of A or B in both of the courses in the sequence he selects.

COURSES

300 and 301   READINGS IN THE BIOLOGICAL SCIENCES   Each 1 sem. hr.
Readings of classical and modern biological literature.

302   HISTORY OF BIOLOGY   3 sem. hrs.
A study of the great biologists emphasizing their contributions to the development of the biological sciences. Lecture.

303   NATURAL SCIENCE FOR ELEMENTARY TEACHERS   3 sem. hrs.
Present-day developments in science in relation to instruction in elementary schools. Content, activities, and approach involved in teaching an integrated science program at various grade levels. Lecture and laboratory.

304   SEMINAR IN BIOLOGY   1 sem. hr.
Staff members, guest speakers and graduate students will discuss their current research at these seminars. All seniors and graduate students in the department are expected to participate each semester, but credit is given once only.

305   SPECIAL PROBLEMS IN BIOLOGY   1-3 sem. hrs.
Special work in fields represented by the research interests of the staff. Assignments depend upon the student's interest and background. Projects must be approved by the staff member and the head of the department.

306   REGIONAL AND AREA STUDIES   1-9 sem. hrs.
An intensive study of particular lands, environments, cultures, and peoples. May be given in cooperation with other departments, on or off the campus. The areas to be studied, participating departments, and credit hours available in the several departments will be announced each time the course is offered.

---

* Illinois Natural History Survey

318 LABORATORY TECHNIQUES 2 sem. hrs.
Preparation of permanent microscope slides of plant and animal tissues and special techniques for whole mounts, plastic embedding, plastic injections, and nerve preparations. Lecture and laboratory.

319 GENETICS 4 sem. hrs.
Data and concepts of genetics from Mendel to today. Lecture and laboratory. Prerequisite: Twelve semester hours of laboratory courses in biological sciences, or consent of instructor.

320 PLANT PATHOLOGY 4 sem. hrs.
Systematics, morphology, life-cycles, and control measures for organisms causing plant diseases. Lecture and laboratory.

331 TAXONOMY OF VASCULAR PLANTS 4 sem. hrs.
Plant classification with emphasis on native and naturalized species. Lecture and laboratory.

332 TAXONOMY OF NON-VASCULAR PLANTS 4 sem. hrs.
Plant classification with emphasis on the evolution of the algae, fungi and bryophytes. Lecture and laboratory. Prerequisite: Biological Sciences 122.

333 COMPARATIVE PLANT MORPHOLOGY 4 sem. hrs.
Comparative morphology of vascular plants emphasizing morphogenesis. Lecture and laboratory. Prerequisite: Biological Sciences 123.

334 INTRODUCTORY MYCOLOGY 3 sem. hrs.
Morphology, taxonomy, and evolution of the fungi. Lecture and laboratory.

340 ADMINISTRATION OF SCHOOL HEALTH 3 sem. hrs.
Administration and organization of school health programs and health education programs. Lecture.

342 INTRODUCTION TO BIOCHEMISTRY 4 sem. hrs.
See Chemistry 342.

360 SANITATION 4 sem. hrs.
Microbiology as applied to community water supplies, waste disposal, swimming pools, foods and their distribution, and stream and air pollution. Lecture and laboratory. Prerequisite: Biological Sciences 260.

365 PHYCOLOGY 4 sem. hrs.
Taxonomy, morphology, anatomy, and physiology of the algae with special emphasis on species common to Illinois. Lecture and laboratory. Prerequisite: Biological Sciences 122.

381 APPLIED HUMAN ANATOMY 4 sem. hrs.
Study of the human body with emphasis on the musculo-skeletal and nervous systems. Designed for students who will teach physically handicapped children. Lecture and laboratory. Prerequisites: Biological Sciences 182 or Health and Physical Education 182.

382 THE EYE—A LABORATORY AND CLINICAL STUDY 2 sem. hrs.
Anatomy and physiology of the eye. Lecture and laboratory supplemented by clinical demonstrations on the detection and care of eye disorders. Prerequisite: Biological Sciences 182.

383 PARASITOLOGY 4 sem. hrs.

Morphology, life histories, and host-parasite relationships of arthropod, helminth, and protozoan parasites. Lecture and laboratory.

385 PHYSICAL DEFECTS—SURVEY AND REHABILITATION 3 sem. hrs.

Physical defects of handicapped children and procedures used in rehabilitation. For those preparing to teach special classes of physically-handicapped children. Lecture and laboratory. Also offered as Health and Physical Education 385. Prerequisite: Biological Sciences 381.

390 EVOLUTION 3 sem. hrs.

Environmental, behavioral and genetic mechanisms involved in the processes of evolution. Lecture and discussion. Prerequisite: Biological Sciences 319 or consent of instructor.

391 ENTOMOLOGY 4 sem. hrs.

Anatomy, physiology, and embryology of insects. Lecture and laboratory.

392 EMBRYOLOGY 4 sem. hrs.

Comparative embryology of the vertebrates with emphasis on avian and mammalian embryos. Lecture and laboratory. Prerequisite: Biological Sciences 192.

394 PROTOZOOLOGY 4 sem. hrs.

Survey of the Phylum Protozoa, emphasizing morphology, physiology, reproduction, and taxonomy. Lecture and laboratory.

395 BIOLOGY OF THE LOWER VERTEBRATES 4 sem. hrs.

The biology of fish, amphibians, and reptiles. Lecture and laboratory.

396 BIOLOGY OF THE HIGHER VERTEBRATES 4 sem. hrs.

The biology of birds and mammals. Lecture and laboratory.

401 ADVANCED ECOLOGY 4 sem. hrs.

Advanced study of physiological and behavioral adaptation and response of organisms to environmental factors. Prerequisites: Biological Sciences 201, courses in physiology and genetics.

402 AQUATIC BIOLOGY 4 sem. hrs.

Ecological study of streams, ponds, and lakes, and the interrelationships of the plants and animals in these habitats. Field trips to varied aquatic habitats and aquatic field stations in the area are included. Lecture and laboratory.

404 SEMINAR IN THE TEACHING OF BIOLOGY 1 sem. hr.

Techniques and aids for biology teaching in secondary schools and junior colleges. Students will be required to participate in the activities of the seminar by giving reports, preparing demonstration materials, or illustrating special teaching materials.

416 CELLULAR PHYSIOLOGY 5 sem. hrs.

A study of fine structure and physiochemical properties of the cell. Topics considered include: Ultrastructure and functions of cell organelles, thermo-dynamic principles pertaining to metabolism, enzyme properties, and active transport. Lecture and laboratory. Prerequisite: Consent of instructor.

417 CYTOLOGY 4 sem. hrs.

Organization of cells with emphasis on the relationships between structure and function. Lecture and laboratory. Prerequisite: Biological Sciences 319.

418 ELECTRON MICROSCOPY 4 sem. hrs.

Preparation, staining, embedding and sectioning procedures, negative staining and vacuum evaporation techniques, preparation of specimen support membranes, photographic methods, use of the electron microscope and introduction to electron optics. Lecture and laboratory. Prerequisite: Consent of Instructor.

419 ADVANCED GENETICS 4 sem. hrs.

Recent developments in genetics including topics of genetic recombination, gene structure and function, mutation, and gene regulation. Lecture. Prerequisite: Biological Sciences 319 or consent of instructor.

420 SEMINAR IN GENETICS 1 sem. hr.

Topics in various fields of genetics. Subjects will vary from semester to semester. This course may be repeated for credit with consent of the department head. Prerequisite: Biological Sciences 319 or consent of instructor.

421 CYTOGENETICS 4 sem. hrs.

Correlation of cytology with genetics. Lecture and laboratory. Prerequisites: Biological Sciences 319 and 417.

425 RADIATION BIOLOGY 4 sem. hrs.

Interactions of radiation at the molecular, cellular, organismic, and population levels. Lecture and laboratory. Prerequisites: Calculus, biochemistry or cell physiology, organic chemistry, physics, and genetics.

426 SPECIAL TOPICS IN PLANT PHYSIOLOGY 2 sem. hrs.

Lectures in selected areas of plant physiology: water and mineral relations, carbon and nitrogen metabolism, plant growth and development. Course may be repeated for credit. Prerequisite: organic chemistry.

428 ENZYMOLOGY 3 sem. hrs.

Mechanism of action, isolation and characterization, biosynthesis, and kinetics of enzymes. Lecture and laboratory. Prerequisite: Biochemistry, calculus, or consent of instructor.

433 PLANT ANATOMY AND HISTOLOGY 3 sem. hrs.

Origin, development, and structure of tissues in vascular plants. Lecture and laboratory. Prerequisite: Consent of instructor.

440 EPIDEMIOLOGY 3 sem. hrs.

Principles related to the incidence and control of epidemic diseases. Etiology, pathogenesis, host response, identification, and diagnostic procedures. Lecture. Prerequisite: Biological Sciences 260.

450 ADVANCED STUDIES IN SPECIALIZED FIELDS 1-4 sem. hrs.

Intensive study of recent developments in such fields as biochemistry, biophysics, biomathematics, biological oceanography, ecology, ethology, reproductive and developmental biology, invertebrate zoology, parasitology, and systematics. The field covered in this course will vary according to the interests and needs of the students and the availability of instructors or visiting professors. Provided different material is covered, the course may be taken for credit more than once. Lectures and laboratories when appropriate.

464 ADVANCED MYCOLOGY 3 sem. hrs.

Isolation, culturing, physiology, and ultrastructure of fungi. Lecture and laboratory. Prerequisite: Biological Sciences 334 or consent of instructor.

466 MICROBIAL PHYSIOLOGY   5 sem. hrs.

Fundamental concepts and techniques of bacteriology. Anatomical, nutritional, and metabolic properties. Microbiological assays. Prerequisites: Biological Sciences 260 and chemistry through quantitative analysis and organic. Lecture and laboratory.

467 MICROBIAL GENETICS   5 sem. hrs.

Heredity in microorganisms and the viruses as a branch of microbiology. Lecture and laboratory. Prerequisites: Biological Sciences 260 and 319 and quantitative analysis and organic chemistry or consent of instructor.

480 HISTOLOGY   4 sem. hrs.

Microscopic anatomy of cells, tissues, and organs of vertebrates. Lecture and laboratory.

481 SENSORY PHYSIOLOGY   3 sem. hrs.

Structural and functional aspects of the sensory systems. Topics considered include photoreception, chemoreception, action potentials, hearing, sensory pathways and associated brain centers. Lecture and laboratory. Prerequisite: Biological Sciences 482 or 483, Biophysics, or consent of instructor.

482 MAMMALIAN PHYSIOLOGY   4 sem. hrs.

The physiology of muscular, nervous and circulatory organ systems. Lecture and laboratory. Prerequisite: Course in vertebrate anatomy and organic chemistry, or consent of instructor.

483 MAMMALIAN PHYSIOLOGY   4 sem. hrs.

The physiology of the respiratory, excretory, digestive and reproductive systems. Lecture and laboratory. Prerequisite: courses in vertebrate anatomy and organic chemistry, or consent of instructor.

484 HUMAN DEVELOPMENT AND BEHAVIOR   3 sem. hrs.

Basic genetics, developmental biology, physiology, and endocrinology for students in education, psychology, health and physical education, and special education.

485 ENDOCRINOLOGY   4 sem. hrs.

Endocrine glands of vertebrates and invertebrates emphasizing the function of selected hormones. Lecture and laboratory. Prerequisite: Biochemistry.

486 ETHOLOGY   4 sem. hrs.

The behavior of animals under natural conditions as interpreted through comparative studies and experimentation. Lecture and laboratory. Prerequisite: two semesters of college zoology.

487 HUMAN GENETICS   3 sem. hrs.

Gene action, population genetics, biochemical genetics, mutation genetics, and practical applications of genetics with primary emphasis on man. Prerequisite: Biological Sciences 319.

491 INTERNSHIP-SEMINAR IN COLLEGE TEACHING IN THE BIOLOGICAL SCIENCES   3 sem. hrs.

Credit for the course is given in Education (see Education 491).

492 ADVANCED EMBRYOLOGY   4 sem. hrs.

Concepts of embryonic fields, differentiation, evocation, competence, and regeneration. Laboratory exercises to demonstrate fundamental mechanisms of development in the amphibian and chick. Lecture and laboratory. Prerequisites: Biological Sciences 319 and 392.

493 BIOPHYSICS 3 sem. hrs.
The application of principles of physics to biological problems. Attention will be given to: electromagnetic radiation, optics and microscopy, radioactivity, and bioelectric potentials. Lecture and laboratory. Prerequisites: Calculus, general physics, and chemistry, or consent of instructor.

495 COMPARATIVE ANIMAL PHYSIOLOGY 4 sem. hrs.
A comparative study of the physiology of the organ systems with emphasis on invertebrates. Topics considered include osmotic balance, nutrition, nitrogen excretion, respiration, metabolism, endocrine mechanisms, excitation and contractibility, and bioluminescence. Lecture and laboratory. Prerequisites: invertebrate zoology and organic chemistry, or consent of instructor.

497 RESEARCH SEMINAR 1-6 sem. hrs.
Introduction to bibliography, methods of scholarly research and critical evaluation of research. Must be taken by first year graduate students in the secondary curriculum unless the department requires Education 475. May be repeated by more advanced students who desire direction and constructive criticism as they pursue a special research problem.

499 INDEPENDENT RESEARCH FOR THE MASTER'S THESIS 1-6 sem. hrs.
A student electing the thesis option must take from four to six hours of 499. A proposal for research must be on file before registration for this course is approved by the student's adviser. While registration beyond six hours may be permitted for the convenience of the student, he may not count more than a total of six hours of 499 among the 32 required for the master's degree.

590 RESEARCH IN THE BIOLOGICAL SCIENCES Variable credit
Research involving the gathering of data to form the basis for the thesis required for the Ph.D. Approval of the head of the department is required.

Botany

(See Biological Sciences)

Business

Dean of the College of Business: Robert V. Mitchell. Office: Turner Hall 211-B

The faculty of the College of Business offers programs leading to the M.A., M.S., or M.S. in Ed. degrees. The Master's program in Business is administered in the Department of Accounting and in the Department of Business Administration, while the Master's programs combining Business and Business Education are administered in the Department of Business Education. Candidates for the master's degrees should consult with the head or chairman of the department in which the particular program is administered to determine the specific requirements for the degree. The graduate faculty of all three departments in the College offer graduate courses which may be a part of a student's program.

DEPARTMENT OF ACCOUNTING

Head of the Department: Raymond W. Esworthy. Office: Turner Hall 210-C
Teaching Staff: R. Esworthy, J. Hallam, J. Rich, T. Secoy, R. Tussing.

COURSES

330 GOVERNMENTAL ACCOUNTING 3 sem. hrs.

Procedures, accounts, and reports of governmental agencies; the solution of problems embracing the practical application of fund accounting and the interpretation of financial reports of various government units. Prerequisite: 5 semester hours of accounting.

331 COST ACCOUNTING 3 sem. hrs.

Elements of production costs, including materials, labor, and overhead or burden; the job-cost, the process-cost, and the standard cost systems; the solution of problems embracing the practical application of costing methods, formulas and standard costs. Prerequisite: 9 semester hours of accounting or consent of the department head.

332 ADVANCED COST ACCOUNTING 2 sem. hrs.

Consideration of current accounting problems involving cost-volume-profit analysis, capital budgeting, relevant costs, and other advanced cost accounting topics related to management decisions. Prerequisite: Accounting 331.

333 INCOME TAX PROCEDURE 3 sem. hrs.

Federal income tax provisions affecting individuals and business enterprises, and problems involved in tax computations. Prerequisite: 6 semester hours of accounting.

334 ADVANCED TAX PROBLEMS 3 sem. hrs.

Intensive examination of federal taxation procedures affecting corporations, partnerships, estates and trusts. Examination of gift and social security taxes. Prerequisite: Accounting 333 or consent of department head.

335 AUDITING 3 sem. hrs.

Nature of audit evidence, basic audit techniques, audit practices and procedures, professional ethics, audit reports. Prerequisite: 12 semester hours of accounting.

360 BUSINESS DATA PROCESSING 3 sem. hrs.

Business data processing involving the fundamental characteristics of mechanical and electronic systems and their application to business. Prerequisite: 6 semester hours of accounting.

361 BUSINESS SYSTEMS ANALYSIS FOR COMPUTER PROGRAMMING 3 sem. hrs.

Systems planning, coding, and programing for the digital computer as it is used in business for data processing. Includes instruction and laboratory work on the IBM 360 Data Processing System, and some instruction on other types of computers. Symbolic languages will be used for the programing of common data processing applications such as: payroll, inventory control, expense analysis, and financial statements. Prerequisites: Accounting 360 or consent of department head.

366 ADVANCED BUSINESS DATA PROCESSING 3 sem. hrs.

Development of problem formulation, flowcharting, coding, testing, executing and documenting, using a compiler-level computer language. Discussions of disk systems, tape systems, and operating systems as applied to business problems. Prerequisite: Accounting 360 or consent of department head.

367 COMPUTER APPLICATIONS FOR BUSINESS DECISION MAKING 3 sem. hrs.

Application of the principles of dynamic mathematical techniques, and the utilization of accounting data in the solution of business problems. Principal techniques applied will be linear and integer programing, queuing-line problems, construction of models, and the structure of business games. Prerequisite: 9 semester hours of

Accounting, including 360; 12 semester hours of Business Administration, including 270 and/or Mathematics 250 or consent of department head.

430 ADVANCED ACCOUNTING THEORY 4 sem. hrs.

Fundamental concepts of accounting theory: their nature, structure, history, and development. Relationship and application to current accounting problems. Prerequisite: 15 semester hours of accounting or consent of department head.

431 INCOME DETERMINATION 4 sem. hrs.

A critical analysis of income including concepts, measurement, reporting, and social significance. Attention given to current unsettled issues related to revenue recognition and cost expirations. Prerequisite: 430 or consent of department head.

435 ADVANCED AUDITING 4 sem. hrs.

A critical analysis of auditing standards and procedures, the relationship of trends and developments of the accounting profession to the practice of auditing, including the examination of current professional literature. Prerequisite: Accounting 335, or consent of the department head.

468 COMPUTER-BASED MANAGEMENT INFORMATION SYSTEMS 3 sem. hrs.

Designing of management information systems, modules and their integration into an overall computer-based management information system for business. Prerequisites: Accounting 360 and 361, or consent of head of the department.

470 ADVANCED STUDIES IN SPECIALIZED FIELDS 2-4 sem. hrs.

Recent developments in accounting, data processing and information systems. May be taken for credit more than once, provided different material is covered. Prerequisite: 15 semester hours of accounting or consent of department head.

497 ACCOUNTING RESEARCH AND REPORTS 2-4 sem. hrs.

Research methodology, bibliography, reporting techniques, sources of reference materials. Individual practice in conducting and reporting on specific research projects. Prerequisite: 15 semester hours of accounting or consent of department head.

499 INDEPENDENT RESEARCH FOR THE MASTER'S THESIS. 1-6 sem. hrs.

A student electing the thesis option must take from four to six hours of 499. A proposal for research must be on file before registration for this course is approved by the student's adviser. While registration beyond six hours may be permitted for the convenience of the student, he may not count more than a total of six hours of 499 among the 32 required for the master's degree.

DEPARTMENT OF BUSINESS ADMINISTRATION

Acting Chairman of the Department: C. Richard Decker.   Office: Turner Hall 210-E

Teaching Staff: C. R. Decker, T. Dunfee, A. Fletcher, D. Hakala, H. Koepke, J. Meador, R. Mitchell, H. E. Reese, T. Shin.

COURSES

311 FUNDAMENTALS OF LIFE AND HEALTH INSURANCE 3 sem. hrs.

General consideration of personal and business risks. Principles of life and health insurance and their applications. Prerequisite: Bus. Ad. 141 or consent of department chairman.

312 FUNDAMENTALS OF PROPERTY AND LIABILITY INSURANCE 3 sem. hrs.

Principles of property insurance with fundamental application to individuals, risk in fire, marine, bond, and casualty areas. Prerequisite: Bus. Ad. 141 or consent of department chairman.

322 INTERNATIONAL FINANCE 3 sem. hrs.

International payments, structures and functions, international credit markets, investments, and institutions. Prerequisite: Business Administration 257 is recommended.

324 CAPITAL INVESTMENT DECISION 3 sem. hrs.

Theory of capital management, application of principles of capital investment to the measurement of costs and returns, the evaluation of risks, the determination of capital structures, and the allocation of capital by the firm. Prerequisite: Business Administration 220 and 270.

330 BUSINESS IN A LEGAL ENVIRONMENT 3 sem. hrs.

An examination of the economic, business and social values or forces which cause law related to business activities to change and adapt. Prerequisites: Business Administration 141 and 142 or consent of instructor.

340 PRODUCTION MANAGEMENT 3 sem. hrs.

Principles and techniques of management as they apply specifically to the production of physical goods. Production planning and control, methods analysis and work measurement, inventory control, quality control, and plant location and layout. Prerequisite: Business Ad. 253, and 270 (or Mathematics 250), or consent of department head.

341 GOVERNMENT REGULATION OF BUSINESS 3 sem. hrs.

A survey of current government regulation of business including analysis of the constitutional foundation of governmental regulation, the means by which such regulation is effected, and the substantive rules that comprise such regulation. Specific areas covered will include the current regulation of mergers, monopolies, pricing practices, advertising, food and drugs, securities, unfair trade practices, and administrative regulation of specific industries including public utilities and transportation. Prerequisite: Economics 101 is recommended.

346 INVESTMENTS 3 sem. hrs.

Introduction to the appraisal of securities and the management of investment funds, essentially from the viewpoint of the individual investor. Stresses principles of value determination and risks association with various types of securities, including bonds, preferred stocks, and common stocks and their use in portfolios. Coverage includes government securities, industrials, utilities, and financial institutions.

355 CONSUMER BEHAVIOR 3 sem. hrs.

A study of the nature and determinants of consumer behavior. The influence of sociopsychological variables including motivation, learning, personality, small groups, social class, demographic variables and culture on the formation and change of consumers' attitudes, consumption and purchasing behavior. Prerequisite: Business Administration 255 is recommended.

357 RETAILING 2 sem. hrs.

Organization and operation of retail stores and service establishments of various types with some consideration of the application of the content to distributive education and general business subjects of the high school. Whenever feasible, the local business community will be used as a laboratory for the observation and analysis of retailing practice. Prerequisite: Economics 101 or Bus. Ad. 252.

358 MARKETING MANAGEMENT 3 sem. hrs.

The development and evaluation of the marketing plan. Emphasis on the role of the marketing executives in the integration and synthesis of the marketing processes used to increase the profitability of manufacturers and distributors of consumer and industrial goods. Includes analysis of actual and hypothetical cases. Prerequisite: Bus. Ad. 255.

359 MARKETING RESEARCH 3 sem. hrs.

The nature and scope of marketing research. Research design, specific marketing research procedures, and the research report. A marketing research project will be conducted. Prerequisites: Bus. Ad. 255 and 270 or Mathematics 250.

370 ORGANIZATIONAL BEHAVIOR AND ADMINISTRATION 3 sem. hrs.

An analysis of business organizations. The focus is on organization structure and the processes of motivation, perception, communication, coordination and change. Research and theory of individual and group behavior is used in examining administrative problems within business organizations. Prerequisite: Bus. Ad. 253 is recommended.

371 DECISION THEORY 3 sem. hrs.

Behavioral and quantitative factors that enter into business decision making. Major emphasis on quantitative methods of making decisions under conditions of uncertainty. Prerequisite: Business Administration 270.

406 READINGS IN MANAGEMENT 2 sem. hrs.

Selected readings from the literature of general management, including recognized classics in the field and other significant contributions of both theoretical and technical nature. Prerequisite: 15 semester hours in business administration and/or accounting.

410 CONSUMER BUSINESS PROBLEMS 2 sem. hrs.

Application of business knowledge to the solution of practical problems of the consumer. Emphasis on class and individual problem solving in the areas of personal finance and investment involving a consideration of interacting economic forces and technical business operations.

412 LEGAL ASPECTS OF BUSINESS DECISIONS 2 sem. hrs.

Brief consideration of legal reasoning as the developmental process of law, followed by a comprehensive presentation of how legal problems are resolved in the course of organization, operation and termination of business enterprises. Prerequisite: Bus. Ad. 141 and 142 or consent of department chairman.

420 FINANCIAL MANAGEMENT 3 sem. hrs.

Analysis of financial problems of business enterprises and the formulation of financial policies. Financing of current operations and long term capital needs, income management, and expansion policies. Prerequisite: Bus. Ad. 257.

457 PROBLEMS IN RETAIL STORE MANAGEMENT 2 sem. hrs.

Investigation and critical discussion of problems frequently encountered in managing a retail store, with special attention given to the small store. Principles and procedures of store management developed as they relate to the cases chosen for analysis. Visits to stores and participation by selected store managers in group discussions are regular parts of the course.

460 PERSONNEL MANAGEMENT 3 sem. hrs.

Organization and administration of the personnel program in business and governmental institutions. Principles and procedures relating to selection, placement, and training of employees, and to the maintenance of employee morale and efficiency.

Administration of employee services, wage and salary programs, and negotiation with organized labor. Analysis of actual business cases.

470 PURCHASING POLICIES AND PROCEDURES 3 sem. hrs.

Purchase of materials, supplies, and equipment as a major business function. Organization for purchasing, internal requisitioning, and stock control. Basic procurement principles, processes, and problems in industrial, governmental, and institutional organizations. Actual business cases analyzed.

480 SEMINAR IN MANAGEMENT 3 sem. hrs.

Intensive analysis of management principles and practices as they apply to financial and risk management, marketing management, office management, personnel management, and production management. Case studies of both real and hypothetical business organizations will permit individual research by students in various phases of management theory and practice.

499 INDEPENDENT RESEARCH FOR THE MASTER'S THESIS 1-6 sem. hrs.

A student electing the thesis option must take from four to six hours of 499. A proposal for research must be on file before registration for this course is approved by the student's adviser. While registration beyond six hours may be permitted for the convenience of the student, he may not count more than a total of six hours of 499 among the 32 required for the master's degree.

DEPARTMENT OF BUSINESS EDUCATION

Head of the Department: Warren S. Perry   Office: Turner Hall 210-B

Teaching Staff: A. Condon, T. Martin, W. Perry, D. Scalamogna.

COURSES

320 PRACTICUM IN OFFICE MACHINES INSTRUCTION 2-3 sem. hrs.

Designed to serve as a "professional education" course for vocational teachers of office education programs (as described in Illinois State Plan for Vocational Education, Bulletin 182—Series B, Revised). Emphasis will be on recognition of the new ideas and clarification of the "how" and "why" of office machines, and on the application of demonstration teaching techniques and laboratory supervision. Prerequisite: Bus. Ed. 211.

321 PRACTICUM IN DATA PROCESSING INSTRUCTION 2-3 sem. hrs.

Designed to apply to the "professional education" needed for vocational teachers of "in-school" clerical programs, and to provide instruction and practice in teaching methodology to teachers of office practice, clerical practice, office machines, and business data processing. Emphasis will be on systems analysis and on the recognition of new developments in business data processing. Prerequisites: Accounting 360, and consent of department head.

361 PRINCIPLES OF BUSINESS EDUCATION 3 sem. hrs.

Stimulation of professional interest in business education and development of consciousness of professional responsibilities which should be assumed by business teachers through consideration of such topics as: development and present status of business education; professional organizations and publications; curriculum construction in business education; standards and evaluation in business subjects; facilities, equipment, and supplies; teaching aids; and development of favorable business community relations.

380 ORGANIZATION AND ADMINISTRATION OF COOPERATIVE VOCATIONAL AND DISTRIBUTIVE EDUCATION PROGRAMS 4 sem. hrs.

Provides the background education and the teaching techniques needed for the organization and administration of vocational office and distributive education in the cooperative part-time program involving coordinated work experience. Includes some discussion of in-school programs of distributive education. Prerequisite: Consent of department head.

381 DIRECTED OCCUPATIONAL EXPERIENCE FOR OFFICE AND DISTRIBUTIVE EDUCATION 4 sem. hrs.

One of the professional courses required by the Illinois Plan for Vocational Education as a part of the education of a teacher-coordinator of office or distributive education. It will also serve as six months credit in occupational experience for in-school teachers of vocational office or distributive education according to this state plan. Coincident with the course work, a student must execute a plan for the simultaneous acquisition of approved on-the-job experiences. Usually the course will be offered during the eight-week summer session. The actual time schedule for the class sessions and consultations with the instructor will vary with the types of jobs and job locations of the students.

400 SEMINAR IN BUSINESS EDUCATION 2 sem. hrs.

Consideration of business education problems of greatest concern to the group and to the individual students by means of class discussions, presentation of position papers, group discussions, and individual conferences.

402 ADMINISTRATION AND SUPERVISION OF BUSINESS EDUCATION 3 sem. hrs.

Fundamental concepts and techniques needed by administrators, supervisors, department heads, and teachers of business education in planning and carrying out realistic programs of business education in junior and senior high schools and junior colleges.

408 PROBLEMS OF OFFICE MANAGEMENT 3 sem. hrs.

Detecting, analyzing, and solving problems applicable to large or small offices. Principles of office organization, layout, and operation are discussed and applied to cases under consideration. Critical evaluation of office operations resulting from application of data processing systems. Individual and committee investigations are conducted, and selected office managers are called upon to serve as resource persons.

430 IMPROVEMENT OF INSTRUCTION IN BOOKKEEPING AND BASIC BUSINESS 3 sem. hrs.

Identification of objectives and course content of bookkeeping and accounting on the high school and college level, and the role of basic business education in the total school program. Instructional methods and techniques, planning units of instruction, instructional media and teaching aids, and evaluation of student achievement as they relate to bookkeeping and accounting, and the basic business subjects. Prerequisite: Teaching experience or student teaching.

440 IMPROVEMENT OF INSTRUCTION IN SECRETARIAL SUBJECTS 3 sem. hrs.

Secondary school subjects included are vocational typewriting, personal typewriting, shorthand, transcription, business English, and secretarial office practice. The instructor will draw from his own experiences, from those of the group, from the writings of authorities in the field, and occasionally from the ideas of visiting lecturers or demonstrators. Prerequisite: Teaching experience or student teaching.

450 IMPROVEMENT OF INSTRUCTION IN DISTRIBUTIVE EDUCATION
3 sem. hrs.

Organization, administration, and supervision of programs of distributive education, with emphasis on the cooperative part-time programs. Methods, materials, and equipment in teaching salesmanship, retailing, and other courses of training for distributive occupations.

491 INTERNSHIP-SEMINAR IN COLLEGE TEACHING IN BUSINESS EDUCATION 3 sem. hrs.

Credit for this course is given in Education (see Education 491).

497 INTRODUCTION TO RESEARCH IN BUSINESS EDUCATION 3 sem. hrs.

Critical evaluation of research in business education with emphasis on the application of findings to the improvement of instructional programs. Selection of a research problem, the use of the library, the analysis of related literature, the collection and statistical treatment of data, and the interpretation of findings of research. Research tools and types of research particularly applicable to both formal and informal research in business education.

499 INDEPENDENT RESEARCH FOR THE MASTER'S THESIS 1-6 sem. hrs.

A student electing the thesis option must take from four to six hours of 499. A proposal for research must be on file before registration for this course is approved by the student's adviser. While registration beyond six hours may be permitted for the convenience of the student, he may not count more than a total of six hours of 499 among the 32 required for the master's degree.

Chemistry

Head of the Department: Sol Shulman.   Office: Science Building 426

Teaching Staff: A Bond, R. Bunting, R. Duty, T. Edwards, G. H. Evans, J. Higgins, J. House, R. Hunt, T. Ichniowski, M. Kurz, L. Mukherjee, R. Reiter, B. Ryder, S. Shulman, J. Tsang.

MASTER'S DEGREE IN CHEMISTRY

The degrees of M.S. and M.S. in Ed. with a major in chemistry are offered for candidates who elect to follow a core program of courses prescribed by the department. For a master's degree in chemistry, the student must demonstrate a proficiency in the reading of French, German, Russian or other approved language. A thesis based on original research is required for a master's degree in chemistry. A thesis is optional, but is encouraged for the M.S. in Ed.

For the M.S. in chemistry, no graduate credit will be allowed for 360, 361, 362 and 363. Except in special circumstances, graduate credit for 360 and 361 is not applicable toward the M.S. in Ed. University requirements for master's degrees are listed elsewhere in this catalog.

Students wishing to complete an interdisciplinary degree between chemistry and physics should consult the physics program.

COURSES

315 INSTRUMENTAL METHODS OF ANALYSIS 2-3 sem. hrs.

A survey of instrumental methods of chemical analysis including electrometric, spectrophotometric and optical procedures. Prerequisite: Chemistry 215 or consent of instructor, Chemistry 362 or concurrent registration.

323 QUALITATIVE ORGANIC ANALYSIS 3 sem. hrs.

Identification of organic compounds with emphasis on modern spectrometric methods. Three class meetings per week including two three-hour laboratory periods. Prerequisite: Chemistry 320.

325 MODERN METHODS AND TECHNIQUES IN ORGANIC CHEMISTRY 2 or 3 sem. hrs.

Modern laboratory techniques associated with synthesis, quantitative analyses, distillations and chromatography. Organic literature searches will be stressed. Prerequisite: Chemistry 321 or equivalent.

342 INTRODUCTION TO BIOCHEMISTRY 3 sem. hrs.

Chemistry of the lipids, carbohydrates, nucleic acids, vitamins, enzymes; their degradation, formation, and associated energy changes in biological processes. Three class meetings per week. Prerequisite: Chemistry 232 or concurrent registration.

343 INTRODUCTION TO BIOCHEMISTRY LABORATORY 2 sem. hrs.

Application of biochemical principles and methods discussed in the introductory companion course, Chemistry 342. Two three-hour laboratory periods per week. Prerequisite: Chemistry 215, 342 or concurrent enrollment.

344 INTERMEDIARY METABOLISM 3 sem. hrs.

An introduction to metabolic sequences for the biosynthesis and degradation of biologically important compounds. Integrated systems and metabolic control. Prerequisite: Chemistry 342.

350 INORGANIC CHEMISTRY 3 sem. hrs.

A survey of modern inorganic chemistry including structure of inorganic compounds, coordination chemistry, non-aqueous solvents and selected inorganic reactions. Prerequisite: Chemistry 362 or concurrent enrollment.

351 INORGANIC PREPARATIONS 2 sem. hrs.

Preparation of typical inorganic compounds illustrating special and more advanced techniques. Six hours of laboratory and conference per week. Prerequisite: Chemistry 350 or concurrent enrollment.

358 RADIOCHEMISTRY 2 sem. hrs.

A survey of nuclear models, theories, and decay schemes. Application of radiochemical methods to elucidation of reaction mechanisms and molecular structure. Prerequisite: Chemistry 362.

360 PHYSICAL CHEMISTRY 3 sem. hrs.

First in a series of theoretical chemistry dealing with gases, liquids, solutions, thermochemistry, thermodynamics, chemical and phase equilibrium, kinetic theory, and chemical kinetics. Prerequisite: Chemistry 141 or 150; Physics 109 or 111; eight semester hours of chemistry or physics courses numbered 200 or higher; Mathematics 116.

361 PHYSICAL CHEMISTRY LABORATORY 1 sem. hr.

Laboratory studies of the derivations and applications of the principles treated in physical chemistry. One three-hour laboratory period per week. Prerequisite: Chemistry 360 or concurrent enrollment.

362 PHYSICAL CHEMISTRY 3 sem. hrs.

Continuation of Chemistry 360, including ionic equilibrium, conductance, electromotive force, photochemistry, spectroscopy, crystals, molecular theory. Prerequisite: Chemistry 360.

363 PHYSICAL CHEMISTRY LABORATORY 1 sem. hr.

Laboratory studies of the derivations and applications of the principles treated in physical chemistry. One three-hour laboratory period per week. Prerequisite: Chemistry 362 or concurrent enrollment.

380 TOPICS IN CONTEMPORARY CHEMISTRY 3 sem. hrs.

New concepts and recent developments in the fields of organic, inorganic, analytical, physical and biochemistry. May be repeated for credit. Prerequisite: Consent of instructor.

404 ELECTRONICS FOR SCIENTISTS 3 sem. hrs.

Circuits of scientific instruments, electronic principles, servo systems, comparison measurements, operational amplifiers, feedback control, digital circuits, transistors, and vacuum circuits. Two three-hour laboratories and one lecture per week. Prerequisite: Chemistry 315 or graduate status in physics.

410 ADVANCED ANALYTICAL CHEMISTRY 3 sem. hrs.

Advanced study of chemical analysis with emphasis on the fundamental principles of analytical chemistry. Lecture and laboratory. Prerequisite: Chemistry 315 or permission of instructor.

420 ADVANCED ORGANIC CHEMISTRY 3 sem. hrs.

An advanced study of organic chemistry with emphasis on stereoisomerism, conformational analysis, resonance, synthesis, elucidation of structure, heterocyclic and natural products chemistry. Prerequisite: Chemistry 320 or equivalent.

422 MECHANISMS IN ORGANIC CHEMISTRY 3 sem. hrs.

A critical examination of nucleophilic, electrophilic and free radical reaction mechanisms including the study of the stability and reactivity of carbanions, carbonium ions and carbenes. Hammett functions, kinetic isotope effects, aromaticity and carbon acidity will be integrated into the course. Prerequisite: Chemistry 320 and credit or registration in 360.

424 SPECIAL TOPICS IN ORGANIC CHEMISTRY 3 sem. hrs.

Lectures in selected topics of modern organic chemistry. Course may be repeated for credit. Prerequisite: Organic Chemistry 320 or equivalent.

440 SPECIAL TOPICS IN BIOCHEMISTRY 3 sem. hrs.

Advanced study in selected areas of biochemistry. May be repeated for credit in consecutive years as different topics are introduced. Prerequisite: Chemistry 342.

450 ADVANCED INORGANIC CHEMISTRY 3 sem. hrs.

Interpretation and discussion of the subject matter of inorganic chemistry from the viewpoint of modern theory. Prerequisites: Chemistry 350 and 362.

452 PHYSICAL INORGANIC CHEMISTRY 3 sem. hrs.

Study of theoretical factors related to the properties of matter, including symmetry elements, group theory, and the application of various instrumental techniques to the study of the structure of inorganic compounds. Prerequisites: Chemistry 315 and either 350 or 450.

460 QUANTUM CHEMISTRY 3 sem. hrs.

An introduction to the methods of obtaining exact and approximate solutions to the Schroedinger equation, and the use of these solutions in the description of atomic and molecular systems. Prerequisites: Chemistry 363 and Mathematics 340, or consent of instructor.

462 CHEMICAL THERMODYNAMICS AND INTRODUCTION TO STATISTICAL THERMODYNAMICS 3 sem. hrs.

An expansion of the introduction to chemical application of Thermodynamics given in Physical Chemistry 362, and an introduction to the methods and results of application of the theorems of statistical mechanics to molecular models. Prerequisites: Chemistry 363 and Mathematics 340, or consent of instructor.

464 CHEMICAL KINETICS 2 sem. hrs.

The collection and interpretation of data on chemical kinetics and the application of the results to the determination of the mechanisms of chemical reactions. Prerequisite: Chemistry 362 or consent of instructor.

490 RESEARCH IN CHEMISTRY Variable credit

Research involving the gathering of data to form the basis for the thesis. Open only to advanced graduate students. This course can be repeated for credit. Approval of the head of the department is required.

491 INTERNSHIP-SEMINAR IN COLLEGE TEACHING IN CHEMISTRY 3 sem. hrs.

Credit for the course is given in Education (see Education 491).

492 SEMINAR IN CHEMISTRY 1 sem. hr.

Survey of current work in chemistry both in pure research and in the application of newer theories of chemistry to the teaching of chemistry on the secondary and college levels. May be repeated for a total of 2 semester hours.

494 SEMINAR IN CHEMISTRY 1-2 sem. hrs.

Survey of current work in selected areas of chemical research. May be repeated for credit for a total of two semester hours.

499 INDEPENDENT RESEARCH FOR THE MASTER'S THESIS 1-6 sem. hrs.

A student electing the thesis option must take from four to six hours of 499. A proposal for research must be on file before registration for this course is approved by the student's adviser. While registration beyond six hours may be permitted for the convenience of the student, he may not count more than a total of six hours of 499 among the 32 required for the master's degree.

AUXILIARY COURSES

The following courses are not applicable to an advanced degree in chemistry.

300 BASIC CONCEPTS OF CHEMISTRY 3 sem. hrs.

Modern aspects of chemistry, with emphasis on recent developments in the area of atomic structure. Lecture and laboratory. Designed for teachers of elementary and junior high school science with limited background in the area of chemistry. Not open to students who have had one semester of college laboratory chemistry within the past ten years, or with first or second fields in chemistry, physics, or physical sciences. Prerequisite: Physical Sciences 100 or 205 or two years of teaching experience.

301 PROBLEMS IN THE TEACHING OF HIGH SCHOOL CHEMISTRY 3 sem. hrs.

A study of modern methods and problems confronting the teachers of chemistry. Involves a careful study of CBA, Chem Study, and regular high school chemistry. For teaching majors only. Prerequisite: 10 semester hours each of Physics and Chemistry.

302 INDUSTRIAL CHEMISTRY 3 sem. hrs.

Specific aspects of community and industrial problems. Includes trips to industries and research laboratories. Lectures and discussion periods involving related chemical and physical principles are coordinated with the field trip program. Gives a background in applied science as an enrichment for classroom teaching. Prerequisite: Twenty-two hours of physical sciences including one year of general chemistry, one year of general physics, and two 200- or 300-level courses in chemistry or physics.

305 GENERAL SCIENCE 3 sem. hrs.

Objectives of general science. Selection of subject matter, tests, texts, workbooks, equipment, and supplies will be considered. For teachers qualified to teach general science in the elementary, junior high, and senior high schools.

306 HISTORY OF CHEMISTRY 2 sem. hrs.

Development of chemistry from early times to the present. Prerequisite: 16 semester hours of chemistry.

308 CHEMICAL LITERATURE 1 sem. hr.

Introduction to chemical literature in journals, handbooks, abstracts, monographs, and patents. Problems requiring literature searches in all fields of chemistry. Prerequisite: Twenty semester hours of chemistry.

311 LABORATORY INSTRUMENTATION 3 sem. hrs.

Lecture-Laboratory. Instruments used in chemical analysis. Applications to qualitative and quantitative analyses will be stressed in the laboratory. Not open to chemistry majors or comprehensive majors—see Chemistry 315. Prerequisite: Ten semester hours of chemistry.

320 ORGANIC CHEMISTRY 3 sem. hrs.

Chemistry of organic compounds with emphasis on unifying mechanistic features of organic reactions. Prerequisite: Chemistry 230 or permission of department.

321 ORGANIC CHEMISTRY LABORATORY 2 sem. hrs.

Laboratory practice in newer techniques and methods of organic chemistry. Two three-hour laboratory periods per week. Prerequisite: Prior or simultaneous registration in Chemistry 320 or permission of the department.

Economics

Acting Head of the Department: Douglas Poe. Office: Schroeder 338

Teaching Staff: J. Bombelles, W. Harden, M. Hassan, J. Koch, B. McCarney, V. Owen, D. Poe.

MASTER'S DEGREE IN ECONOMICS

The Department of Economics offers work leading to the M.A. or M.S. degree. The student will ordinarily be expected to write a thesis for which he will receive 4 to 6 hours of credit. If he can demonstrate to the satisfaction of the Department Head that he has already done substantive writing in the discipline, he may elect to take 32 semester hours of course work and write a comprehensive examination in lieu of the thesis. Economics 440 and 441 are required of all master's degree candidates.

MASTER'S DEGREE IN THE SOCIAL SCIENCES

The department offers work jointly with the departments of history, political science and sociology-anthropology, leading to the following degrees: M.A., M.S., M.S. in Ed. The program is described under Social Sciences.

COURSES

306 REGIONAL AND AREA STUDIES 1 to 9 sem. hrs.

An intensive study of particular lands, environments, cultures, and peoples. May be given in cooperation with other departments, on or off campus. The areas to be studied, participating departments, and credit hours available in the several departments, will be announced each time the course is offered.

320 INDUSTRIAL ORGANIZATION AND PRICES 3 sem. hrs.

A theoretical and empirical analysis of the basic influences on industrial markets and industrial performance. Consideration is given to market practices, the role of competition, and related policy issues. Prerequisite: Economics 101.

331 INTERMEDIATE ECONOMIC STATISTICS 3 sem. hrs.

A study of various methods of collecting and analyzing economic data including estimation and decision theory, linear regression and correlation analysis. Prerequisite: Economics 230 or consent of instructor.

332 MATHEMATICAL ECONOMICS 3 sem. hrs.

The application of mathematics to economic problems and relationships. Should not be taken by students who have no previous background in mathematics. Prerequisite: Economics 230.

333 OPERATIONS RESEARCH 3 sem. hrs.

Quantitative techniques for economic analysis and decision making. Includes linear programming, input-output analysis, game theory, queuing theory with particular emphasis on applications to the theory of the firm. Prerequisite: Economics 230 or equivalent.

335 TRANSPORTATION 3 sem. hrs.

Development of railway, waterway, air, and highway transportation. Considerable attention is given to the major problems growing out of increased traffic and its regulation. Major emphasis on contemporary conditions and problems. Prerequisite: Economics 101.

340 INTERMEDIATE MICROECONOMIC THEORY 3 sem. hrs.

The theory of consumer behavior and of the firm and determination of prices of consumer goods, productive services, and capital goods. Considerable emphasis upon resource allocation. Prerequisite: Economics 101.

341 INTERMEDIATE MACROECONOMIC THEORY 3 sem. hrs.

Detailed examination of the theoretical basis of modern explanations of economic stability and relative shares in the national income. Prerequisite: Economics 101.

345 INTERNATIONAL ECONOMICS 3 sem. hrs.

Designed to give such basic aspects of the international economy as the reasons for trade, the terms of trade, and the adjustments necessary to achieve the highest possible plane of living. Particular emphasis on the tariff issue and the purposes and functions of the international financial institutions now extant. Prerequisite: Economics 101.

350 PUBLIC FINANCE 3 sem. hrs.

An attempt to discover criteria for determining (1) how much governments should spend and for what and (2) the economic and equity effects of different methods of obtaining government revenue. Prerequisite: Economics 101.

372 HISTORY OF ECONOMIC THOUGHT 3 sem. hrs.

Economic thought and theory from ancient to modern times. Emphasis on those ideas which influenced the economic development of western civilization. Prerequisite: Economics 101.

390 SELECTED STUDIES IN ECONOMICS 3 sem. hrs.

The field of study covered will vary each semester according to the interests and needs of the students and the availability of instructors. Provided different material is covered, the course may be taken more than once. Prerequisite: Economics 101.

400 SURVEY OF ECONOMIC PRINCIPLES 3 sem. hrs.

For mature students who need an understanding of the basic tools of economic analysis. Compresses into a single semester matters ordinarily covered in two semesters of Economic Principles. Enrollment is limited to graduate students who have had no more than one semester of previous study in economics.

405 THEORIES OF ECONOMIC DEVELOPMENT 3 sem. hrs.

Consideration of economic development theories and their implications for development policy to further economic growth. Prerequisite: Economics 205 or equivalent.

410 SOVIET ECONOMICS 3 sem. hrs.

Economic growth of the Soviet Union. NEP and economic planning. Examination of particular sectors of the Soviet economy. Pricing, decentralization, and economic reform. Prerequisite: Principles of Economics II, 101.

415 CONTEMPORARY MONETARY THEORY 3 sem. hrs.

Advanced study of the role of money in an economy. The effects of changes in the quantity of money and its velocity of turnover on employment, income, consumption, and price levels. A comparison of the flexible version of the quantity theory with the national income theory. Implications of these theories to monetary policy. Prerequisite: Economics 215.

416 CONTEMPORARY MONETARY POLICY 3 sem. hrs.

Current issues in monetary policy, the formulation of effectiveness, impact, organization, indicators, and problems of monetary policy, along with the instruments, goals, and policies of the central bank. Theoretical and empirical studies are reviewed. Prerequisite: Economics 215.

435 SEMINAR IN TRANSPORT AND PUBLIC UTILITY PRICING 3 sem. hrs.
Prerequisite: Economics 335 or 320.

440 ADVANCED PRICE THEORY 3 sem. hrs.

The theory of the firm, the consumer and the resource owner and the determination of prices under alternative market structures. Prerequisite: Intermediate Microeconomic Theory 340, or equivalent.

441 ADVANCED INCOME THEORY 3 sem. hrs.

National income analysis with emphasis on the contemporary theories of consumption, investment and interest, also consideration of the level, growth and fluctuations of national income. Prerequisite: Intermediate Macroeconomic Theory 341 or equivalent.

445 INTERNATIONAL ECONOMIC ANALYSIS 3 sem. hrs.

An analysis of the adjustments in the balance of payments among countries. The mechanisms through which income effects, price effects, and changes in commercial policy may restore equilibrium to the balance of payments of a country. The extent to which these forces are automatic or managed is also considered. Prerequisite: Economics 345.

450 THEORY OF PUBLIC FINANCE 3 sem. hrs.

Detailed examination of the various concepts of equity in taxation. Development of the theory of tax shifting. Consideration of various criteria for government spending. Evaluation of fiscal policy stabilization tools. Analysis of the burden, economic effects, and possibilities of retirement of the public debt. Prerequisite: Economics 350.

451 FINANCING STATE AND LOCAL GOVERNMENTS 3 sem. hrs.

Types of spending and possible sources of revenue for state and local governments; probable economic effects and administrative problems inherent in each.

470 SEMINAR IN THE PUBLIC FINANCE OF HIGHER EDUCATION 3 sem. hrs.

Prerequisite: Educational Administration 479, Economics 400, or permission of the instructor.

490 SEMINAR IN ECONOMICS 1-4 sem. hrs.

491 INTERNSHIP-SEMINAR IN COLLEGE TEACHING IN ECONOMICS 3 sem. hrs.

Credit for the course is given in Education (see Education 491).

492 GRADUATE READINGS IN ECONOMICS 1-3 sem. hrs.

For the graduate student who would benefit from a more specialized independent type of study adapted to his background and needs. To be taken by permission of the head of the department and the instructor involved.

497 RESEARCH SEMINAR 1-6 sem. hrs.

Introduction to bibliography, methods of scholarly research and the critical evaluation of research in the field. May be repeated by more advanced students who desire direction and constructive criticisms as they pursue special research problems.

499 INDEPENDENT RESEARCH FOR THE MASTER'S THESIS 1-6 sem. hrs.

A student electing the thesis option must take from four to six hours of 499. A proposal for research must be on file before registration for this course is approved by the student's adviser. While registration beyond six hours may be permitted for the convenience of the student, he may not count more than a total of six hours of 499 among the 32 required for the master's degree.

Education

Chairman of the Department: Leo E. Eastman.   Office: Edwards Hall 300

Teaching Staff: A. Bjork, W. Blake, E. S. Blankenship, C. Bunke, R. J. Cantlon, L. Carlton, J. Durham, L. Eastman, C. Edwards, R. Eiben, R. Halinski, R. Hendon, H. Hermanowicz, C. Hicklin, R. Holdridge, H. T. Jones, H. Knight, C. Kurth, D. Livers, R. Meyering, M. Miller, W. Miller, R. Moore, G. Ramseyer, D. Rhodes, C. Sherman, C. E. Streeter, M. Waimon, W. Zeller.

PROGRAMS OFFERED

Master's programs with advisement in the Department of Education are offered in Guidance and Counseling, Reading, and Supervision. University requirements for master's degrees are given elsewhere in this catalog.

EDUCATIONAL MEDIA

The master of science in education and the master of science degree programs in educational media are flexible so that a student can prepare himself for administrative, production, training or service positions in public or private schools, junior colleges, colleges and universities; or prepare himself for doctoral work in audiovisual, instructional technology, or educational media; or prepare himself for media positions in government, business and industry.

Students in the master of science in education degree will be required to take Education 475, Education 476, and one graduate course in the history, philosophy, or social foundations of education. In addition, 16 semester hours must be taken to complete a major in educational media. The remainder of the courses will be with the consent of the adviser.

The following courses or their equivalent are prerequisite to the program: Education 240 and Education 241 or Library 210 depending on the student's interest or needs.

GUIDANCE AND COUNSELING

The student may work toward a Master of Arts, a Master of Science, or a Master of Science in Education degree by fulfilling the requirements specified in this catalog. The following courses are required in all master's degree programs in Guidance and Counseling: Education 360, 460, 462, 463, 464 and Psychology 420. Additional courses are selected following recommendations of the adviser with reference to the following areas of specialization:

A. **Elementary School Guidance and Counseling.** Prepares counselors for elementary and junior high schools. Persons completing this program will be eligible for the Special Certificate in Guidance in the State of Illinois.

B. **Secondary School Guidance and Counseling.** Prepares counselors for secondary schools. Persons completing this program will be eligible for the Special Certificate in Guidance in the State of Illinois.

C. **Counseling in Higher Education.** Prepares counselors for junior and senior colleges, and student personnel workers for institutions of higher education.

READING

Requirements for an M.S. in Ed. with specialization in reading will vary somewhat depending upon the area or level of reading in which the graduate student plans to concentrate. However, all students are expected to have a common base of knowledge about reading processes, diagnosing reading difficulties, and providing desirable programs in reading. The Dean of the College of Education will assign students to the appropriate department for advisement. Advisement of students will depend upon their selection from among the three following areas of concentration:

A. **Clinical Reading.** Major emphasis upon diagnosis and educational accommodation of special cases of severe reading disability. Advisement: Head, Department of Special Education.

B. **Elementary School Reading.** Emphasis upon the roles of teachers and reading consultants in developmental reading program for elementary education. Advisement: Head, Department of Elementary Education.

C. **General, Secondary, and Higher Education Reading.** Developmental programs and general functions of reading specialists or consultants and the kinds of services provided in general, secondary, or higher education. Advisement: Head, Department of Education.

From 22 to 24 semester hours are required, including the following:

1. Ed. 475, 476, and one course in history or philosophy of education.
2. 15 semester hours of study from among the following reading courses as advised: 301, 303, 307, 401, 402, 405, 408, and 419.
3. Additional courses to complete the program requirements as advised.

SECONDARY EDUCATION (for liberal arts graduates)

The Master of Science in Education degree in Secondary Education at Illinois State University is designed to encourage and enable selected students who hold a liberal arts bachelor's degree from an accredited college to earn a professional master's degree while qualifying for a regular secondary teaching certificate in Illinois.

Applicants must have (1) a well-balanced background in general education; (2) a strong major in the high school teaching discipline in which he plans to be certified; and (3) no courses in professional education. They must be (1) eligible for a professional teaching certificate in Illinois; and (2) able to meet the admission requirements of the graduate school as stipulated in the current catalog.

Applicants will be screened carefully on the basis of (1) the quality and completeness of their undergraduate work; (2) their personal characteristics; and (3) their previous experience. Both recommendations and a personal interview may be required.

TWO OPTIONS

Option I is a 32 hour program, including a one semester internship, for those who choose to complete all the requirements for both a degree and a regular teaching certificate during a continuous 13 month period, which begins with a summer session, continues through the academic year, and concludes with the following summer session.

Option II is a 35-38 hour program for those who have secured a teaching position and who prefer to complete all the requirements during three extended summer sessions of 10 or 11 weeks or four regular 8-week summer sessions while teaching full time within the supervisory radius of Illinois State University.

Both of these programs must be initiated at the beginning of any regular summer session starting the third Monday in June. Both are minimum programs and students with deficiencies may require additional courses and time. At least 12 semester hours in each program must be taken from 400 level courses. The Master of Science in Education degree in Secondary Education is a non-thesis program but both options require a concluding one credit workshop and paper.

Additional information is available from the department.

SUPERVISION

While courses and advisement in this field fall mainly in the Department of Education, the Dean of the College of Education may assign students to advisers in other departments of the college for study of supervision in special areas.

The following courses are required in the Supervision curriculum, regardless of the specialization: Education 387, 437, 475, 476, 477, 478, and Educational Administration 481.

A graduate course is also required for all candidates in the Supervision curriculum from one of the following fields: History of Education, Philosophy of Education, or Social Foundations of Education.

If specialization is in Elementary Supervision, the additional course, Education 403, is required.

If specialization is in the Supervision of Student Teaching, the additional course, Education 497, is required.

Additional courses are to be selected following recommendations of adviser. Such courses may include those to be taken in other departments.

Students entering this curriculum should hold a teaching certificate. Students without teaching experience may be admitted to the program but will be expected to obtain such experience prior to admission to candidacy for the degree.

Persons completing this program will be eligible for a supervisory certificate in the State of Illinois.

COURSES

303 PRACTICUM IN UNIVERSITY READING STUDY CENTER 3 sem. hrs.

Those enrolled for the Practicum shall meet six hours each week. Through observation and participation, students enrolled in the practicum will learn the skills necessary for working in a reading-study center at the high school, junior college, and senior college level. The enrollment is limited to ten students with senior or graduate status. Prerequisite: Education 218 or 307 and permission of the instructor.

308 TEACHING ADULTS TO READ 3 sem. hrs.

The nature and needs of the population of reading programs for adults. Goals, techniques, content, and materials for the teaching of reading to adults. Prerequisite: One course in teaching of reading.

309 ADULT EDUCATION PROGRAMS 3 sem. hrs.

Instruction, direction, and administration of public school adult education. The adult learner, his needs and characteristics; facilites, staff, supervision and administration of adult education programs; the relation of public school adult education programs to other education programs under the sponsorship and direction of the public schools.

324 SELECTED STUDIES IN HISTORY OF EDUCATION 1-3 sem. hrs.

The field of study will vary according to the interest and needs of the students and the availability of instructors. Provided different material is covered, the course may be taken for credit more than once. Prerequisite: Education 335 or one upper level course in history or consent of the instructor.

326 SELECTED STUDIES IN PHILOSOPHY OF EDUCATION 1-3 sem. hrs.

The field of study will vary according to the interest and needs of the students and the availability of instructors. Provided different material is covered, the course may be taken for credit more than once. Prerequisite: Education 231, or one upper level course in Philosophy, or consent of the instructor.

328 THE SCHOOL AS A SOCIAL INSTITUTION 3 sem. hrs.

The utilization of social scientific concepts in the study of education. Emphasis on the organization and functions of the school as a social institution. Prerequisites: Completion of general education requirements in social science or consent of instructor.

330 MAN AND THE ANALYSIS OF EDUCATION 3 sem. hrs.

Introduction to the fundamental dimensions of foundational inquiry: historical, philosophical, social, and comparative foundations of education. Special emphasis on the relationship between selected views of man and their implications for education.

331 INDEPENDENT STUDY IN EDUCATION 1-3 sem. hrs.

Intensive, independent study on a problem or topic in education. The number of credit hours received depends upon the nature of the topic or problem studied. A formal written paper is required. Provided different subject matter is covered, the course may be taken more than once, but no more than six semester hours of cumulative credit may be earned. Prerequisite: Permission of the instructor and Head of the department.

332 EDUCATION IN THE INNER CITY 3 sem. hrs.

An introduction to the problems of educating students who reside in the inner city. Student characteristics, needed teacher attitudes and skills, instructional materials and techniques, and school and community programs are explored. Field trips will be taken to selected schools. Consultants from other departments of the University and from non-university agencies will be utilized. Prerequisites: Education 202, 203, 204 or 216 or consent of instructor.

333 THE JUNIOR HIGH SCHOOL 2 sem. hrs.

History of the institutional development of the junior high-middle school. Evolving philosophy, functions, and curricula as related to the characteristics and needs of early adolescents and the goals of public education. Schedule designs, instructional and guidance approaches, and the role of the informal curriculum at this level. Special problems and issues, and the evaluation and accreditation of junior high schools.

334 PUBLIC RELATIONS FOR EDUCATION 2 sem. hrs.

Study of basic methods and theories of public relations. Concentration on public relations in establishing and maintaining cooperation between the school and community. Special class projects include participation in a public relations conference, student investigations and reports in areas of interest, field trips, as well as lectures by guests representing communication media.

335 HISTORY OF EDUCATION 3 sem. hrs.

Development of European and American educational systems and programs. Emphasis on the historical perspective of modern educational problems.

336 INTRODUCTION TO COMPARATIVE EDUCATION 3 sem. hrs.

A comparative analysis of the major ideas and institutions of selected national systems of education. Emphasis on the investigation of problems relevant to developments in American education.

337 PROGRAMED LEARNING 3 sem. hrs.

Construction and evaluation of programed learning; critical analysis of learning theory as it relates to programed learning. Use of programed materials in the classrooms.

340 STATISTICS I 3 sem. hrs.

Basic statistics used in education and the behavioral sciences. Intensive study of frequency distributions, measures of central tendency and dispersion, and standard scores. Sampling error theory, simple hypothesis testing, correlation techniques, and regression analysis are also covered. The emphasis is on application and interpretation.

350 INSTRUCTIONAL PLANNING SEMINAR 3 sem. hrs.

A basic course in curriculum and instruction at the secondary level. Topics to be considered include purposes, curriculum, methods and evaluation. Study and practice will be given in constructing overviews, units, and daily lesson plans. For master's degree students in the internship program in teaching. Prerequisite: Consent of instructor.

360 PRINCIPLES OF GUIDANCE 2 sem. hrs.

Backgrounds, philosophy, and services in school guidance programs. Examination of the appraisal, informational, and counseling services. Emphasizes the role of the classroom teacher as well as the organization of guidance activities.

361 STUDENT PERSONNEL WORK IN HIGHER EDUCATION 3 sem. hrs.

Fundamental concepts, organization and administration of higher education student personnel work. Consideration given current problems of college students and the role of student personnel workers as generalist educators.

365 PRODUCTION OF INSTRUCTIONAL MATERIALS 3 sem. hrs.

Production of a variety of projected and non-projected materials for classroom use. Planning, evaluating, and organizing audiovisual presentations. Fundamental skills of preservation, compilation, adaptation, lettering, enlargement, reduction, duplication and production of audio materials will be demonstrated and laboratory practice will be provided. Prerequisite: Education 240.

366 ADVANCED AUDIOVISUAL PRODUCTION 3 sem. hrs.

Advanced topics and techniques of production, such as planning, storyboarding, scripting, photosketching, etch bleaching, and audiovisual synchronization. Laboratory practice in designing and producing material for individualized instruction, large group presentation and other multi-media configurations. Prerequisites: Education 365 and Education 240 or permission of instructor.

367 AUDIO PRODUCTION 3 sem. hrs.

Considers the theoretical aspects of audio production, as well as the selection, evaluation, production, operation and maintenance of audio devices and materials. Extensive laboratory practice in the use of all types of equipment and materials will be provided.

368 MOTION PICTURE PRODUCTION 3 sem. hrs.

Theory and practice in producing motion pictures. Considers production planning, treatments, storyboard, script writing, shooting, editing, titling and other technical problems of production.

387 MEASUREMENT AND EVALUATION IN EDUCATION 3 sem. hrs.

Basic principles underlying measurement and evaluation in education. Includes development, use, and improvement of standardized and teacher-made tests and self-rating devices. Stresses interpretation of test data and use of test results. Students may develop measurement and evaluation programs and undertake projects in their major fields. Appropriate for elementary, secondary and college levels.

399 STUDENT TEACHING 1-10 sem. hrs.

(See Professional Laboratory Experiences 399.)

402 RECENT RESEARCH IN READING 3 sem. hrs.

Analysis of recent research in reading at the elementary, secondary, and college levels together with its implications in the areas of modified practices in the teaching of reading, materials of instruction, and teacher preparation.

405 PSYCHOLOGY OF TEACHING READING 3 sem. hrs.

The study, analysis and investigation of psychological aspects of the act of reading.

406 ADVANCED SECONDARY SCHOOL READING 3 sem. hrs.

The role of the reading specialist in the secondary school; special provisions for meeting the reading needs of high school students; techniques and materials suitable for use in the secondary school; procedures for developing reading skills in the content areas. Prerequisite: One course in reading.

408 PRACTICUM IN READING FOR CLASSROOM TEACHERS 3 sem. hrs.

This course is designed to prepare classroom teachers to help pupils in regular classrooms to overcome their reading problems. Through observation and participation in classrooms, students will become acquainted with ways of diagnosing and correcting reading difficulties. Individual and group conferences with the instructor will be scheduled. Prerequisite: Education 307 or permission of the adviser.

419 SEMINAR IN READING 3 sem. hrs.

The content of the course will depend upon the needs and backgrounds of the students. Group and individual study of current practices, trends, and issues in reading will be employed.

424 EDUCATIONAL CLASSICS 3 sem. hrs.

Historic conceptions of education and their relevance to programs and practices today. Readings in the works of such leading educational thinkers as Plato, Locke, Rousseau, and Dewey. Prerequisite: One course in history or philosophy of education or consent of the instructor.

428 SEMINAR IN FOUNDATIONS OF EDUCATION 2-3 sem. hrs.

Intensive inquiry into the educational significance of problems generated by philosophical, social, or historical issues. Prerequisite: One graduate level course in the discipline appropriate to the study undertaken, or consent of the instructor.

430 WORKSHOP IN EDUCATION 2-6 sem. hrs.

For experienced professional workers in the field of education. Emphasis given to serving superintendents, principals, supervisors, and teachers who are presently responsible for some aspect of curriculum study and/or program improvement in their schools. Primary concern with analysis and solution of practical and on-the-job educational problems. Procedure: exact statement of problems for study; critical examination of the literature on research and existing practice in the problem to be followed by reports, discussions, and conclusions. Prerequisite: Teaching experience.

431 INDIVIDUALIZED FIELD WORK IN EDUCATION 2 or 3 sem. hrs.

In order to accommodate the individual needs of graduate students, a variety of direct experiences in working with elementary or high school students, public school curricula and staff, and/or community groups involved in public school programs are provided. Approval for selecting this course and arranging for individual field work must be made by the department head.

432 PHILOSOPHY OF EDUCATION 3 sem. hrs.

Social forces and schools of philosophical thought which have contributed to education and which are influencing current educational practices. To help the student achieve a functional educational philosophy applicable in his teaching situations.

433 THE AUDIOVISUAL DIRECTORSHIP 3 sem. hrs.

Principles of and practices in organizing and managing an audiovisual program in the individual school building and school system. Considers such problems as audiovisual services, facilities, finance, personnel, public relations and evaluation standards for all aspects of the program. Prerequisite: Education 240 or permission of the instructor.

434 AUDIOVISUAL RESEARCH 3 sem. hrs.

Critical analysis of selected research studies in audio-visual instruction, instructional communications and technology. Research methods and sources of data in major categories of media research. Prerequisites: Education 240, 475.

435 INSTRUCTIONAL SYSTEMS DEVELOPMENT 3 sem. hrs.

For teachers, media specialists, supervisors, and administrators. The systems approach calls for specific identification of an instructional problem; analysis of the resources and alternatives; and the synthesizing of theory, research findings, man, machines, ideas, and procedures toward an effective solution. Prerequisite: Consent of instructor.

436 MEDIATED INSTRUCTIONAL SYSTEMS 3 sem. hrs.

Advanced topics and techniques of planning and producing audiovisual instructional materials for self-instructional systems, dial-access systems, multi-screen projection systems. Extensive laboratory practice will be provided. Prerequisites: Education 366, 367, 368, and 435.

437 ANALYSIS OF TEACHING   3 sem. hrs.

For various school personnel, including prospective college teachers of education who are interested in methodical study of teaching behavior. Major research attempts in assessing teacher effectiveness and problems connected with such efforts. Descriptive studies and conceptual systems of teaching, their nature and possible uses.

440 STATISTICS II   3 sem. hrs.

The logic of statistical inference. An examination of the statistical techniques most commonly employed in research in education and the behavioral sciences. Topics included are interval estimation the t and f tests, chi-square, one factor analysis of variance, multiple regression, and non-parametric statistics. The emphasis is on application and interpretation. Prerequisite: Education 340.

441 EXPERIMENTAL DESIGN   3 sem. hrs.

The statistical principles of experimental design. Selection, analysis, and interpretation of the most widely employed designs are emphasized. Designs included are the simple randomized, factorial, repeated measures, randomized blocks, latin square, and analysis of covariance. Topics such as multiple comparisons, power and trend analysis are also covered. Prerequisites: Education 340, 440 (Statistics I and II).

450 COMPUTER APPLICATIONS IN EDUCATION   3 sem. hrs.

An examination and discussion of the variety of ways computers are or could be used in our public schools and colleges. Administration, instruction, research, storage of information, accounting and simulation. Prerequisite: Educational experience or consent of instructor.

460 GUIDANCE APPRAISAL   2 sem. hrs.

The administration and interpretation of appraisal techniques appropriate to the student's level of interest: elementary, secondary, or higher education. Special emphasis on student self-appraisal. Prerequisite or concurrent registration: Education 360.

461 ORGANIZATION OF GUIDANCE SERVICES   2 sem. hrs.

The activation, organization, administration, and utilization of guidance services. Selection of personnel, in-service education of the staff, evaluation of the program, and steps in the introduction of a comprehensive program are considered. Prerequisite: Education 360.

462 PRACTICUM IN COUNSELING AND GUIDANCE   3-6 sem. hrs.

Provides the prospective counselor with supervised experience in individual and/or small-group counseling. Experiences are provided appropriate to the student's level of interest: elementary, secondary, or higher education. May be repeated for credit for a total of six semester hours. Prerequisites: Education 360, 464, and permission of instructor.

463 THEORY AND PRACTICE IN GROUP COUNSELING   2-4 sem. hrs.

Participation in a group with associated study of interpersonal relationships through tapes, films, observation, and related reading. Also includes study of relevant theories of group counseling and interaction. May be repeated for credit for a total of four semester hours. Prerequisite or concurrent registration: Education 360.

464 THEORIES AND TECHNIQUES OF COUNSELING   3 sem. hrs.

Goals, methods, and procedures as seen from a number of differing theoretical positions. Emphasis on interpersonal dimensions of counseling interviews. Case material illustrating applications in a variety of counseling situations—schools, community, college and university, focusing on problems of personal-social, educational, and vocational adjustment.

465 VOCATIONAL COUNSELING 2 sem. hrs.

Acquiring and using occupational and educational information. Consideration of job requirements and training opportunities; developing occupational units; nature of vocational development.

466 JUNIOR COLLEGE COUNSELING 3 sem. hrs.

Problems and characteristics of counseling in community junior colleges. Prerequisites: Education 360 and either Education 472 or Junior College experience.

470 TEACHING IN THE COMMUNITY (Junior) COLLEGE 2 sem. hrs.

Techniques and methods of teaching on the community college level; problems of articulating the community college and the high school; special qualifications needed for the community college teacher; his preparation and training; the use of examinations, marks, and records; specific problems and methods of the classroom peculiar to the various teaching fields.

471 COMMUNITY (Junior) COLLEGE ADMINISTRATION 2 sem. hrs.

Introduction to the administration and organization of junior college. Relationships with boards of control, community, administrators, faculty, and students. Legal aspects, records, financial support, and public relations.

472 THE COMMUNITY (Junior) COLLEGE 3 sem. hrs.

History and development, functions, curricula, instruction and personnel problems in the community college. The community college is studied in relation to other units of the educational system.

473 SEMINAR IN THE COMMUNITY (Junior) COLLEGE 2 sem. hrs.

Specific problems related to the community college, such as problems of guidance and personnel work; sponsorship of out-of-class activities; improvement of instruction; and curriculum problems. The exact content of the course may vary from semester to semester. The problems will be selected, in part, according to the needs and interests of the students.

474 SEMINAR IN COLLEGE TEACHING 3 sem. hrs.

Designed to give prospective college teachers a general overview of the diversified responsibilities, obligations, and knowledge associated with collegiate teaching. Curricula of higher education, understanding of college students, and prevailing problems in collegiate education are stressed in the seminar. Extensive reading in the field of collegiate education is expected of each student in addition to research relevant to college teaching in his own field of academic specialization. Close cooperation is maintained with each student's major department.

475 INTRODUCTION TO RESEARCH 3 sem. hrs.

Selection of a research problem, collection of data, types of research, the research report, and use of the library in connection with the research problem. Elements of statistics are introduced. Emphasis is given to understanding and interpreting frequently used statistical concepts. Provides a background for the preparation of the thesis. Enables the student to become an intelligent consumer of the products of educational research.

476 CURRICULUM THEORY 3 sem. hrs.

The nature of curriculum theory and the sources of knowledge utilized in the formulation of curriculum theory. Critical analysis of major curriculum patterns that have emerged in American education. Approaches to curriculum study, revision, and evaluation.

477 SUPERVISION OF INSTRUCTION 2 sem. hrs.

Principles underlying the improvement of instruction through supervision. Emphasizes the following supervisory needs: (a) an understanding of the leadership role; (b) an understanding of recent research concerning pupils, including learning; (c) an understanding of group dynamics, and (d) an understanding of action research and its application. Techniques for giving the understandings practical application are considered. Means are proposed for the evaluation of pupils, teachers, supervisors, and supervisory practice.

478 SEMINAR IN SUPERVISION OF INSTRUCTION 3 sem. hrs.

Prerequisite: Education 477.

491 INTERNSHIP-SEMINAR IN COLLEGE TEACHING 3 sem. hrs.

For students in the college teaching programs. Observation and teaching in the student's major area, with other experiences appropriate to academic involvement at the college level. Offered in cooperation with the student's major department.

492 PRACTICUM-TEACHING INTERNSHIP (Secondary) 4-6 sem. hrs.

The practicum-teaching internship is designed for a person who is mature and experienced enough to assume major responsibility for a classroom learning situation. Assignments will be supervised in the field by resident teachers and the intern experience will be coordinated by the student's campus adviser. In the practicum which accompanies the internship, consideration will be given to selected procedures and variables in the design and sequencing of instruction and the application of principles from behavioral sciences.

493 PERSPECTIVES OF TEACHER EDUCATION 3 sem. hrs.

For advanced graduate students preparing for positions associated with the preparation of teachers and specialized school personnel. Admission, curricula, instruction, certification, accreditation, evaluation, problems, issues and trends in the selection and preparation of teachers. Prerequisite: Master's degree or permission of instructor.

495 SEMINAR IN CURRICULUM 3 sem. hrs.

Exploration of major developments and experimental programs having an impact upon school curricula. Students will have an opportunity to identify certain curriculum innovations for depth study. Each innovation will be analyzed critically. Research data relevant to the innovation will be examined with problems and means of utilizing the innovation for curriculum improvement considered. Prerequisite: Advanced graduate standing or special permission of the instructor and Education 476.

497 PROFESSIONAL LABORATORY EXPERIENCE 3 sem. hrs.

The role of professional laboratory experiences in teaching and learning. Significant trends, philosophies, and programs of teacher education. Personnel responsible for supervision of pre-service and in-service teachers and for directing observations, participation, and individual studies of pupils and teachers. For experienced teachers, supervisors of instruction, school administrators, and college teachers associated with teacher education programs.

498 INTERNSHIP 3-8 sem. hrs.

Opportunities to work with principals, superintendents, teachers, and lay groups in public school situations. Of special benefit to inexperienced students and for those preparing for administrative work in public schools. Assignments are made by the Dean of the Graduate School on recommendation of the student's academic adviser at least two months prior to beginning internship.

499 INDEPENDENT RESEARCH FOR THE MASTER'S THESIS 1-6 sem. hrs.

A student electing the thesis option must take from four to six hours of 499. A proposal for research must be on file before registration for this course is approved by the student's adviser. While registration beyond six hours may be permitted for the convenience of the student, he may not count more than a total of six hours of 499 among the 32 required for the master's degree.

Educational Administration

Chairman of the Department: Ben C. Hubbard.   Office: 300 North Street

Teaching Staff: D. Bell, M. Chambers, C. Edwards, E. Egelston, L. Garber, G. A. Hickrod, B. Hubbard, J. McGrath, C. Thomas, D. G. Watson.

PROGRAMS OFFERED

Work leading to a master's degree, specialist in education degree, and the Ed.D. and Ph.D. degrees is offered in Educational Administration.

MASTER'S DEGREE PROGRAM

At least 20 semester hours of Education are required including Education 475 and 476, Educational Administration 478, 479, and 481 and Sociology 465. Additional courses are selected following recommendations of the adviser in this curriculum.

Students without teaching experience may be admitted to this program but will be expected to obtain experience in education prior to admission to candidacy for the degree if certification for Administrative positions in Illinois public schools is desired.

University requirements for master's degree programs are listed elsewhere in this catalog.

SPECIALIST AND DOCTORAL PROGRAMS

The College offers work leading to the Specialist in Education degree and the Ed.D. and Ph.D. degrees in Educational Administration. These programs have as their major purpose the preparation of administrators in educational institutions at all levels. In addition, the doctoral program may prepare individuals for research positions in educational administration. University requirements for these degree programs are listed elsewhere in this catalog.

FOREIGN LANGUAGE REQUIREMENTS FOR Ph.D. CANDIDATES

General Graduate School requirements apply. However, when approved by the Chairman of the Department of Educational Administration and Dean of the Graduate School, a student may substitute evidence of proficiency in statistics for one of the two foreign languages specified in the general requirements for the Ph.D. degree. Evidence of having met this statistical proficiency may be shown by:

1. Successful completion of two 400 level courses in statistics and/or psychometrics,

or

2. Passing an examination showing proficiency expected of one having completed two 400 level courses in statistics and/or psychometrics. An examination prepared for this latter option should be the joint responsibility of the Department of Psychology and the Department of Educational Administration.

COURSES

331 INDEPENDENT STUDY IN EDUCATION 1-3 sem. hrs.
(See Education 331.)

430 WORKSHOP IN EDUCATION 2-6 sem. hrs.
(See Education 430.)

431 INDIVIDUALIZED FIELD WORK IN EDUCATION 2 or 3 sem. hrs.
(See Education 431.)

470 SEMINAR IN THE PUBLIC FINANCE OF HIGHER EDUCATION
3 sem. hrs.

Prerequisite: Educational Administration 479, Economics 400, or permission of the instructor.

478 LEGAL BASES OF EDUCATION 3 sem. hrs.

The conceptual and structural design of public education and the American legal system. Includes study of constitutional law, statutory enactments, and judicial decisions, with emphasis upon case law. Authority of the states; local school districts, powers and duties of district officers; legal status of parents and pupils; liability of school districts and officers; use of school property; school support and finance; the school program and Illinois school law.

479 FINANCIAL BASES OF EDUCATION 3 sem. hrs.

Sources of school revenue, analysis of expenditure policies, inter-governmental fiscal relationships, budgeting and salary policy, introduction to the economics of education and other aspects of school finance.

480 SCHOOL PLANT PLANNING 3 sem. hrs.

School sites, buildings, and equipment with emphasis on planning of building programs. Includes visitation of buildings.

481 ADMINISTRATION AND ORGANIZATION OF SCHOOLS 3 sem. hrs.

School administration and organization, showing the relationship of national, state, and local education. Principles of administration and organization relating to the functioning of a school system are explored. Special attention is directed toward selection, retention, improvement of teachers, improvement and development of curriculum, use of records, interpreting the schools to the public, and other problems taken from the necessary experiences of public school administration.

485 THE PRINCIPALSHIP 3 sem. hrs.

Development of knowledge and competencies of the building principal as an instructional leader. Offered as a specialized course for those having a basic preparation in general administration.

494 RESEARCH SEMINAR IN EDUCATION 1 sem. hr.

For advanced graduate students in education who have taken basic courses in research. Research proposals and projects are critically evaluated. A student may enroll in the course as often as approved by his adviser. Prerequisite: Advanced graduate standing.

495 SELECTED STUDIES IN EDUCATIONAL ADMINISTRATION 3 sem. hrs.

The field of study will vary each semester according to the needs and interests of students and the availability of instructors. Provided different material is covered, the course may be taken for credit more than once. Prerequisite: Consent of instructor.

498 INTERNSHIP 3-8 sem. hrs.

Opportunities to work with principals, superintendents, teachers, and lay groups in public school situations. Of special benefit to inexperienced students and for those preparing for administrative work in public schools. Assignments are made by the Dean of the Graduate School on recommendation of the student's academic adviser at least two months prior to beginning internship.

499 INDEPENDENT RESEARCH FOR THE MASTER'S THESIS 1-6 sem. hrs.

A student electing the thesis option must take from four to six hours of 499. A proposal for research must be on file before registration for this course is approved by the student's adviser. While registration beyond six hours may be permitted for the convenience of the student, he may not count more than a total of six hours of 499 among the 32 required for the master's degree.

582 ADMINISTRATION AS A SCIENCE AND AN ART 3 sem. hrs.

Second course in a basic sequence of an administration core; sociological and behavioral implications for organization and administration. Development of understandings, values, concepts through study of theory and its practical application in the educational setting. Decision making; administration and the behavioral sciences, theories of administraton, power and authority, motivation and morale, organization and leadership, and research issues in education. Prerequisites: Educational Administration 481 and advanced graduate standing.

583 EDUCATIONAL LEADERSHIP 3 sem. hrs.

Designed to provide an understanding of the leadership function in formal and informal organizations. Includes study of executive behavior, contributions to administrative theory of non-educational fields; improvement of staff relations; human relations approach to the administrative process; policy development at all levels; evaluation of enterprises and programs; and research issues in education. Required of all doctoral candidates in school administraton. Prerequisites: Educational Administration 481 and 482 and admission to the doctoral program.

584 SUPERINTENDENT AND CENTRAL STAFF 3 sem. hrs.

Development of knowledge, responsibilities, and competencies required of chief administrative officer, and in the case of larger districts, his central staff. Emphasizes district-wide policy making, curriculum development, improvement of instruction, effective leadership of personnel, community relations, and efficient operational procedures. Designed to develop a high degree of understanding and skill in the administration of a school district. Prerequisite: Advanced graduate standing.

586 MANAGEMENT OF EDUCATIONAL FUNDS 3 sem. hrs.

Development of high competence and deeper concepts of school finance, with particular emphasis on the management phase. Includes management of all school funds, program budgeting, financial accounting, financial statements and reports, safeguards, debt service, and management of special problems of finance. Prerequisite: Educational Administration 479 or approval of instructor.

589 FIELD WORK IN EDUCATIONAL ADMINISTRATION 3-4 sem. hrs.

Provides responsibilities and experiences in the study of administrative problems in school-community setting. Students will actually develop for a school system a survey or study of a significant problem. In addition to its clinical aspect, the student will emphasize intellectual and creative exploration of major educational issues, utilizing the total field of education and, where relevant, related disciplines. Prerequisites: Advanced standing and consent of instructor.

590 RESEARCH IN EDUCATION Variable credit

Research relating to research requirements for Specialist, Doctor of Philosophy, and Doctor of Education degrees. Approval of the Head of the Department of the program in which the student is enrolled is required. Maximum of 16 semester hours credit in research may be counted toward residency.

596 SEMINAR IN EDUCATIONAL ADMINISTRATION 3 sem. hrs.

Designed for advanced graduate students in Educational Administration. Content will vary according to the needs of students and the emerging problems that need depth study. May be taken more than once providing the subject matter is not repeated. Prerequisite: Advanced graduate standing.

Elementary Education

Acting Chairman of the Department: George M. Drew.   Office: Moulton Hall 103
Teaching Staff: L. Brubaker, J. Crotts, L. Davies, G. Drew, J. Ewing, W. Frinsko, J. Goeldi, I. Greif, E. Irving, R. Laymon, N. Madore, H. Nance, V. Schnepf, A. Slan, R. Steinkellner.

PROGRAMS OFFERED

Master's degree programs in Elementary Education and related areas of specialization.

ELEMENTARY CURRICULUM

Requirements for the master's degree in Elementary Curriculum are a minimum of 12 semester hours in Education, including Education 403, 475, and 476. Additional courses are selected under advisement from the graduate program adviser.

AREA SPECIALIZATION
Academic Field:
Students may elect to pursue a study concentration within an academic discipline. Advisement appropriate to the area of study will be provided.
Urban Education:
Special program alternatives are available for those students who wish to declare special career interests in urban education.
Preparation to Teach:
Students with an earned degree in a field other than professional education, may pursue a graduate program of studies designed to prepare the student for teaching. The certification requirements will usually be satisfied through this program.

ELEMENTARY READING

The Dean of the College of Education will assign students interested in Elementary School reading to advisement in the department, following their request.

SUPERVISION OF ELEMENTARY SCHOOL INSTRUCTION

The Dean of the College of Education will assign students interested in preparing for positions as elementary supervisors to advisement in the department, following their request.

University requirements for the master's degree are listed on pages 18-22.

COURSES

302 PROSPECTUS IN ELEMENTARY EDUCATION   3 sem. hrs.

Development of elementary education in its proper philosophical and historical context. Study of the learners and the circumstances which conditions his learning environment related to the needed changes in curriculum. Prerequisite: One course in professional education.

304 COLLOQUIUM: MUSIC, ART, AND PHYSICAL EDUCATION IN THE ELEMENTARY SCHOOL   3 sem. hrs.

The objectives and values of art, music and physical education and their role in the elementary school curriculum will be presented. Special emphasis will be given to the elements common to each area of instruction as well as to the role of art, music and physical education in the curriculum.

307 ADVANCED READING METHODS 3 sem. hrs.
Practical problems utilizing group techniques in the teaching of reading in each grade level of the elementary school. Integrates reading with non-reading learning activities. Involves direct experiences with children. Prerequisite: Elementary Education 103.

310 ELEMENTARY SCHOOL CURRICULUM 4 sem. hrs.
Discussion of the relationships between educational philosophy and curriculum organization. Emphasis will center on the development of specific areas of school curriculum. The objectives, content and organization of the language arts, reading, social studies, science and the arts will be studied.

311 TEACHING IN URBAN ELEMENTARY SCHOOLS 3 sem. hrs.
Designed for students preparing to teach in urban elementary schools and for experienced teachers who wish to study these aspects of urban education in depth. Emphasis will be placed on study of processes and effects of urbanization on elementary school children; and on adaptation of curriculum materials, techniques, procedures, and practices for teaching in urban elementary schools. Field trips will be scheduled to urban elementary schools.

331 INDEPENDENT STUDY IN EDUCATION 1-3 sem. hrs.
Intensive, independent study on a problem or topic in education. The number of credit hours received depends upon the nature of the topic or problem studied. A formal written paper is required. Provided different subject matter is covered, the course may be taken more than once, but no more than six semester hours of cumulative credit may be earned. Prerequisite: Permission of the instructor and head of the department.

387 MEASUREMENT AND EVALUATION IN EDUCATION 3 sem. hrs.
Basic principles underlying measurement and evaluation in education. Includes development, use, and improvement of standardized and teacher-made tests and self-rating devices. Stresses interpretation of test data and use of test results. Students may develop measurement and evaluation programs and undertake projects in their major fields. Appropriate for elementary, secondary and college levels.

399 STUDENT TEACHING 1-10 sem. hrs.
(See Professional Laboratory Experiences 399.)

402 RECENT RESEARCH IN READING 3 sem. hrs.
Analysis of recent research in reading at the elementary, secondary, and college levels together with its implications in the areas of modified practices in the teaching of reading, materials of instruction, and teacher preparation.

403 ORGANIZATION AND MANAGEMENT OF CLASSROOM LEARNING 3 sem. hrs.
The role of the classroom teacher in effective learning practices in the changing elementary school. Organizing the school for effective living and learning; effective approaches to learning in the various curriculum areas in order to care for individual differences among children in the classroom.

404 INSTRUCTIONAL PROCEDURES IN ELEMENTARY EDUCATION 3 sem. hrs.
Study of selected instructional procedures employed in elementary education. Planning for instruction, determining of educational goals, nature of substantive content and the uses of staff. Prerequisite: Consent of the instructor.

405 NURSERY-KINDERGARTEN EDUCATION 3 sem. hrs.

Criteria and procedures for developing, organizing and administering early education programs. Intended for persons who plan to be responsible for the establishment and supervision of nursery-kindergarten programs. Prerequisite: Consent of the instructor.

408 PRACTICUM IN READING FOR CLASSROOM TEACHERS 3 sem. hrs.

This course is designed to prepare classroom teachers to help pupils in regular classrooms to overcome their reading problems. Through observation and participation in classrooms, students will become acquainted with ways of diagnosing and correcting reading difficulties. Individual and group conferences with the instructor will be scheduled. Prerequisite: Education 307 or permission of the adviser.

419 SEMINAR IN READING 3 sem. hrs.

The content of the course will depend upon the needs and backgrounds of the students. Group and individual study of current practices, trends, and issues in reading will be employed.

420 SEMINAR IN DIAGNOSIS AND CORRECTION OF READING DISABILITIES 3 sem. hrs.

A seminar designed for depth study in the causes and remediation of reading disabilities. Research findings will be utilized for suggested diagnosis and correction of various types of reading problems. Prerequisite: Education 301 or 401.

430 WORKSHOP IN EDUCATION 2-6 sem. hrs.

For experienced professional workers in the field of education. Emphasis given to serving superintendents, principals, supervisors, and teachers who are presently responsible for some aspect of curriculum study and/or program improvement in their schools. Primary concern with analysis and solution of practical and on-the-job educational problems. Procedure: exact statement of problems for study; critical examination of the literature on research and existing practice in the problem to be followed by reports, discussions, and conclusions. Prerequisite: Teaching experience.

431 INDIVIDUALIZED FIELD WORK IN EDUCATION 2 or 3 sem. hrs.

In order to accommodate the individual needs of graduate students, a variety of direct experiences in working with elementary or high school students, public school curricula and staff, and/or community groups involved in public schools programs are provided. Approval for selecting this course and arranging for individual field work must be made by the department head.

437 ANALYSIS OF TEACHING 3 sem. hrs.

For various school personnel, including prospective college teachers of education who are interested in methodical study of teaching behavior. Major research attempts in assessing teacher effectiveness and problems connected with such efforts. Descriptive studies and conceptual systems of teaching, their nature and possible uses.

476 CURRICULUM THEORY 3 sem. hrs.

The nature of curriculum theory and the sources of knowledge utilized in the formulation of curriculum theory. Critical analysis of major curriculum patterns that have emerged in American education. Approaches to curriculum study, revision, and evaluation.

477 RESEARCH STUDIES IN ELEMENTARY CURRICULUM 4 sem. hrs.

Examination of the professional literature that reports established trends, research efforts, and practice in elementary curriculum. Emphasis on the broad themes which transcend the separate disciplines in elementary education.

496 SEMINAR IN ELEMENTARY EDUCATION 3 sem. hrs.
Prerequisite: Consent of the instructor.

497 INTERNSHIP IN TEACHING: (Elementary) 8 sem. hrs.
Designed for a person who is mature and experienced enough to assume major responsibility for a classroom learning situation. Each assignment will be supervised in the field by a resident teacher. The experience will be coordinated by the student's campus adviser. Prerequisite: Consent of instructor.

498 INTERNSHIP 3-8 sem. hrs.
Opportunities to work with principals, superintendents, teachers and lay groups in public school situations. Of special benefit to inexperienced students and for those preparing for administrative work in public schools. Assignments are made by the Dean of the Graduate School on recommendation of the student's academic adviser at least two months prior to beginning internship.

499 INDEPENDENT RESEARCH FOR THE MASTER'S THESIS 1-6 sem. hrs.
A student electing the thesis option must take from four to six hours of 499. A proposal for research must be on file before registration for this course is approved by the student's adviser. While registration beyond six hours may be permitted for the convenience of the student, he may not count more than a total of six hours of 499 among the 32 required for the master's degree.

Professional Laboratory Experiences

Head of the Department: Cecilia J. Lauby.   Office: Moulton Hall 217

Teaching and Supervisory Staff: J. Clemmons, L. Dieterle, Q. Hrudka, M. Huser, C. Lauby, J. Mees.

COURSES

399 STUDENT TEACHING 1-10 sem. hrs.
Directing the learning of pupils; participating in school and community activities; assuming full responsibility for a group of learners under the supervision of an expert teacher. Assignments are made on the basis of the student's area of specialization. High School student teaching assignments include work in special methods in the subjects taught. Prerequisite: 1. Education 216 for high school student teaching; Elementary Education 204 for junior high school student teaching; one of Elementary Education 202, 203, or 204 for student teaching in the elementary school and special education. 2. Satisfactory preparation in the area of specialization. 3. Approval of the Head of the Department of Professional Laboratory Experiences. 4. One semester of residence, except in Special Education for which eight semester hours of residence work is required. Further information may also be obtained from the office of the Head of the Department of Professional Laboratory Experiences.

431 INDIVIDUALIZED FIELD WORK IN EDUCATION 2-3 sem. hrs.
(See Education 431.)

497 PROFESSIONAL LABORATORY EXPERIENCE 3 sem. hrs.
The role of professional laboratory experiences in teaching and learning. Significant trends, philosophies, and programs of teacher education. Personnel responsible for supervision of pre-service and in-service teachers and for directing observations, participation, and individual studies of pupils and teachers. For experienced teachers, supervisors of instruction, school administrators, and college teachers associated with teacher education programs.

Special Education

Chairman of the Department: Harold R. Phelps.   Office: Fairchild Hall 103
Teaching Staff: R. Anderson, J. Bommarito, G. Fergen, D. Hage, R. Hemenway, H. Little, H. Phelps, S. Price, E. Rex, M. Serra.

PROGRAMS OFFERED

Graduate work for the master's degree is offered in the following areas of specialization: Deaf and Hard of Hearing, The Maladjusted, Mentally Retarded, Visually Impaired, and Physically Handicapped. Program requirements are as follows:

1. At least 12 semester hours in Education and Psychology are required, including Education 475 and Psychology 301.
2. Additional courses are selected following recommendations of the Chairman, Department of Special Education, with reference to areas of specialization.

Students interested in a program of **Clinical Reading** should request the assignment in this department by the Dean of the College of Education. (See requirements on page 54.)

COURSES

301 LABORATORY READING METHODS   3 sem. hrs.

Techniques of diagnosis and instruction for special cases of severe reading disability. Deals with physical, mental, and emotional maladjustments and teaching errors which may become causal factors in reading disabilities. Provides opportunity for preparation of instructional materials and for laboratory work with children having serious reading difficulties. Three double periods per week. Prerequisite: Elementary Education 103.

331 INDEPENDENT STUDY IN EDUCATION   1-3 sem. hrs.

(See Education 331.)

345 SPECIAL CLASSES FOR THE TRAINABLE   3 sem. hrs.

Organization of educational programs for the trainable mentally retarded. Teaching methods, behavior and progress evaluation, reports, and home-school-community relations are considered. Observation and participation with the trainable are required.

346 EDUCATION FOR THE MENTALLY RETARDED   2 sem. hrs.

Study of objectives, curriculum content, units, methods, and organization of work in classes of mentally retarded children. Participation and observation in classes for the educable retarded required.

347 EDUCATION OF THE NEUROLOGICALLY IMPAIRED   2 sem. hrs.

Medical diagnosis, psychological evaluation, anatomy and physiology of the central nervous system, nature and needs of the neurologically impaired child relative to educational adjustments needed and procedures of classroom management of children with severe learning problems and/or perceptual dysfunction. Relationship to other therapies. Observation and planned participation on a limited basis.

348 EDUCATION OF GIFTED CHILDREN   2 sem. hrs.

The meaning of giftedness, characteristics and methods of identification of gifted children, ways of providing for gifted in the school program, and guidance of gifted. For teachers, administrators, and personnel workers.

349 EDUCATION OF PHYSICALLY HANDICAPPED 2 sem. hrs.

Types of educational settings; educational planning; psychological problems; clinical teaching; relationships with the home; vocational planning. For teachers of children with orthopedic handicaps and teachers of children with special health problems. Observation and participation required. Prerequiste: Biological Sciences 381 or equivalent.

350 EDUCATION OF THE PARTIALLY SEEING 2 sem. hrs.

Nature and needs of the partially seeing. Interpretation and evaluation of medical, social, psychological and educational records and report. Types of educational programs. Methods and materials for partially seeing children of school age.

351 EDUCATION OF THE BLIND 3 sem. hrs.

Nature and needs of the blind. Interpretation and evaluation of medical, social, psychological, and educational records and reports. Types of educational programs. Methods and materials for blind children of school age.

352 BRAILLE READING AND WRITING I 2 sem. hrs.

Designed to develop mastery of braille literary code. Use of the braille writer and other devices for writing. Proficiency in production of braille, ink printing and proofreading.

353 EDUCATION OF THE DEAF 2 sem. hrs.

History of education of deaf from social, economic, and political viewpoints. An overview of educational philosophies and methods. Consideration of psychological, social, and learning problems relating to the education of the deaf and hard of hearing. Problems of guidance and vocational placement peculiar to the deaf and hard of hearing.

354 THE TEACHING OF SPEECH TO THE DEAF 4 sem. hrs.

The development of oral communication in hearing children compared to deaf children. Methods of developing speech in the preschool and school age deaf child using the visual, auditory kinesthetic and tactile approaches. Particular emphasis is placed on the importance of auditory training as part of the development of oral communication skills. Includes directed observations and supervised practice in classes for the deaf. Prerequisite: Special Education 353.

355 THE TEACHING OF LANGUAGE TO THE DEAF 4 sem. hrs.

Principles and techniques of teaching language to preschool and school age deaf children. Leading systems of teaching language to the deaf are examined and a thorough study of the Fitzgerald Key. Includes directed observations and supervised professional practice in classes for the deaf. Prerequisite: Special Education 353.

356 BRAILLE READING AND WRITING II 2 sem. hrs.

Designed to develop mastery of the braille mathematics code and the preparation of braille materials. Procedures for the use and teaching of braille. Prerequisite: Special Education 352.

357 PRACTICUM IN CLINICAL TEACHING 3 sem. hrs.

Techniques in diagnosing learning disabilities in reading, arithmetic, spelling and handwriting as well as methods by which corrective measures can be applied. Laboratory experience with emotionally disturbed, socially maladjusted and learning disabled is provided. Laboratory hours arranged. (Enrollment limited.) Prerequisite: Permission of the instructor.

358 EDUCATION OF THE SOCIALLY AND EMOTIONALLY DISTURBED 2 sem. hrs.

Philosophies of teaching, curricular requirements, types of education facilities, teacher qualifications, methods and materials, identification and classification of disturbed children. Theories and methods of behavioral management. Prerequisite: Psychology 347.

359 THE TEACHING OF READING AND ELEMENTARY SCHOOL SUBJECTS TO THE DEAF 4 sem. hrs.

Principles and methods of teaching reading to deaf children at all elementary school levels. Methods of teaching subjects such as arithmetic, social studies, and science, and the use of audio-visual aids in classes for the deaf. Prerequisite: Special Education 353.

399 STUDENT TEACHING 1-10 sem. hrs.
(See Professional Laboratory Experiences 399.)

401 ANALYSIS AND CORRECTION OF READING DISABILITY 3 sem. hrs.

Standardized and informal tests, analysis of test results, and differentiated reading programs based on test findings. Opportunities are provided for administering informal and standardized instruments designed to determine the extent of retardation and the type of reading disability. Practice is given in analyzing test findings and in recommending psychological and teaching procedures that will provide for the specific needs of subjects with reading difficulties. Prerequisites: Education 103 and 301 or teaching experience.

420 SEMINAR IN DIAGNOSIS AND CORRECTION OF READING DISABILITIES 3 sem. hrs.

A seminar designed for depth study in the causes and remediations of reading disabilities. Research findings will be utilized for suggested diagnosis and correction of various types of reading problems. Prerequisite: Education 301 or 401.

430 WORKSHOP IN EDUCATION 2-6 sem. hrs.
(See Education 430.)

431 INDIVIDUALIZED FIELD WORK IN EDUCATION 2 or 3 sem. hrs.
(See Education 431.)

445 CURRICULUM DEVELOPMENT FOR THE MENTALLY RETARDED 3 sem. hrs.

Designed to aid students in the development of curriculum and methods suited to their particular problems with the mentally retarded. For principals, supervisors, and teachers now engaged in the field, or those having a background in psychology and mental retardation contemplating the field. Attention is given to organization and curriculum at elementary and secondary levels. Methods and materials adapted to age groupings; pupil guidance and evaluation; study of job outlets and work try-outs or other subjects of student's choice.

446 SEMINAR IN SPECIAL EDUCATION AND REHABILITATION 2 sem. hrs.

Advanced study for graduate students interested in exploring various problems in the areas of special education and rehabilitation. Opportunities will be given to develop program models or research designs relating to the education and training of the handicapped. A student may repeat the seminar if different material is covered. Prerequisite: Permission of instructor.

447 COORDINATING EDUCATIONAL PROGRAMS FOR EXCEPTIONAL CHILDREN 2 sem. hrs.

Principles and problems involved in the administration of educational programs for exceptional children.

448 INSTRUCTIONAL PROCEDURES FOR EMOTIONALLY DISTURBED PUPILS   3 sem. hrs.

Organizing and administering laboratory procedures for maladjusted and educationally retarded pupils. Emphasis on reading abilities. Selection and use of learning materials. Research pertaining to personality factors as related to school success. Supervised laboratory work with children. Prerequisites or concurrent registration: Education 103 and 301.

498   INTERNSHIP   3-8 sem. hrs.
(See Education 498.)

499   INDEPENDENT RESEARCH FOR THE MASTER'S THESIS   1-6 sem. hrs.

A student electing the thesis option must take from four to six hours of 499. A proposal for research must be on file before registration for this course is approved by the student's adviser. While registration beyond six hours may be permitted for the convenience of the student, he may not count more than a total of six hours of 499 among the 32 required for the master's degree.

English

Head of the Department: Henry H. Adams.   Office: Stevenson Hall 409-D

Director of Graduate Studies: Pasquale DiPasquale, Jr. Office: Stevenson Hall 409-B

Teaching Staff: H. Adams, R. Allen, R. Bellas, F. Bishop, G. Canning, Jr., N. Crowell, C. Cox, P. DiPasquale, Jr., P. Drawver, R. Duncan, D. Edwards, D. Ericksen, H. Fielding, V. Gimmestad, J. Heissler, Jr., R. Henline, J. Hill, V. Hutton, M. Jochums, S. Kagle, F. Kroeger, W. Linneman, W. Morgan, T. Ranta, C. Spencer, C. Suits, R. Sutherland, R. Tarr, D. Vetter, R. White, W. Woodson.

The Department of English offers work leading to the master's degree in two areas: the Liberal Arts and Sciences area, and the teaching area.

In the Liberal Arts and Sciences area, the student must, except by special arrangement with the Head of the Department of English, complete all thirty-two hours of classwork in English. He may not apply courses that are peculiar to institutes and similar programs or the following courses toward the degree: 370, 372, 375, 390, 395, 490, 491, 492, 493. He may work towards a Master of Arts degree or a Master of Science degree by fulfilling the Special Degree requirements specified in this catalog.

In the teaching area, the student may elect to fulfill the requirements of either the College Teaching Program or the Secondary Teaching Program. He must complete twenty-six hours in English and six hours in education or psychology as specified in the Program which he chooses. He may work toward a Master of Arts degree, a Master of Science degree, or a Master of Science in Education degree by meeting the Special Degree requirements specified in this catalog.

The following comments are applicable to both areas. French and German are the preferable languages for the student in English who wishes to take, or to proceed beyond, a Master of Arts degree. The candidate for the master's degree must show credit for English 310 and 382 at the undergraduate or graduate level and for English 397, the latter of which should be taken early in the graduate program. A student may choose one of two methods of completing his work toward the master's degree: he may complete thirty-two hours of course work and undergo an oral comprehensive examination; or he may complete twenty-eight hours of course work and write a thesis followed by an oral examination.

A student should normally elect courses which would provide concentration in the literature areas. A student in the Secondary Teaching Program may choose to concentrate in children's literature or professional studies, but he must take at least six hours in literatures of England or America.

A student may take a course designated "Studies" more than once provided the course does not duplicate subject matter previously covered.

An M.A. candidate may offer no more than six hours of course work from Related Courses.

Before enrolling for a 300-level course, the masters student should have had either a survey in English or American literature (whichever is applicable), a 200-level course in the period or genre, or permission from the Director of Graduate Studies in English. The courses at this level stress depth studies of authors, periods, and genres, with emphasis on the literary texts.

Before enrolling for a 400-level course, the student should have had English 397 and a 200 or 300-level course (or equivalent) in the period, author, or genre covered by the 400-level course. Lacking these, he must have the written approval of his adviser and the Director of Graduate Studies. Courses at the 400-level stress critical and scholarly analyses of periods, authors, texts, and genres; and in these analyses, both the content and form of scholarly articles and monographs are utilized in producing original contributions to knowledge in term papers of article length.

Masters candidates must have at least four courses at the 400-level.

Before enrolling in a 500-level seminar, the student should have acquired substantial familiarity with the literature of the period or area of specialization to which the seminar is devoted. Successful performance in a 400-level course in the area of specialization will satisfy this requirement. The seminars stress intensive study and original research which may lead to choosing a topic and writing a dissertation in the area covered by the seminar. Masters candidates may enroll in 500-level courses only with written permission of the Director of Graduate Studies in English and the Head of the Department.

COURSES

310 HISTORY AND DEVELOPMENT OF THE ENGLISH LANGUAGE
3 sem. hrs.

Historical approach to the development of the English language, to help student and prospective teacher discover reasons behind the meanings, spelling, syntax, and usage of contemporary English.

311 OLD ENGLISH 3 sem. hrs.

The elements of Old English grammar, with selected readings.

312 ADVANCED OLD ENGLISH: BEOWULF AND OTHER POEMS 3 sem. hrs.

Beowulf and other Anglo-Saxon poetry in Old English with discussion of forms, types, and characteristics. Prerequisite: English 311.

313 MIDDLE ENGLISH LANGUAGE AND LITERATURE 3 sem. hrs.

Introduction to Middle English language and literature (1100-1500) with selected readings in the five major dialects of Middle English. Chaucer not included.

317 PHILOSOPHICAL AND CRITICAL PROSE OF THE VICTORIAN PERIOD
3 sem. hrs.

Chief prose writers of the century and their contributions to the thought of the present time.

320 CHAUCER 3 sem. hrs.

A literary and linguistic study of the major writings of Chaucer, chiefly *The Canterbury Tales*. Readings in Middle English.

324 MILTON 3 sem. hrs.

Chief prose writings and poems of John Milton. Chief attention to *Paradise Lost*. Includes John Bunyan.

325 ENGLISH DRAMA BEFORE 1642 3 sem. hrs.

English Drama from its beginnings in the Medieval Church to the closing of the theatres with special emphasis upon the plays of Marlowe and Johnson.

327 RESTORATION AND EIGHTEENTH CENTURY ENGLISH DRAMA 3 sem. hrs.

English Drama from the Restoration in 1660 through Sheridan.

328 MODERN BRITISH AND AMERICAN DRAMA 3 sem. hrs.

Readings in twentieth-century British and American Plays and related critical documents.

332 SELECTED FIGURES IN AMERICAN LITERATURE 3 sem. hrs.

Concentrated coverage of one or more important literary figures. Prerequisite: English 130.

341 INTRODUCTION TO DESCRIPTIVE LINGUISTICS 3 sem. hrs.

Aims and methods of linguistic science. Nature and functions of language; phonemics, morphemics, syntactic structures, synchronic dialectology. Some attention to non-Indo-European language systems and the relationship of language to culture.

342 INTRODUCTION TO HISTORICAL LINGUISTICS 3 sem. hrs.

Writing systems, reconstruction of extinct languages, historical comparative linguistics concentrating on the Indo-European family. Causes and effects of linguistic change: phonological, grammatical, lexical, and semantic with attention to languages in contact and the formation and divergence of dialects. Prerequisite: English 341.

382 LITERARY CRITICISM 3 sem. hrs.

Survey of critical and esthetic theory designed to aid the student in evaluating ancient and modern literature.

386 THE EIGHTEENTH-CENTURY ENGLISH NOVEL 3 sem. hrs.

The English novel from its English origin through the eighteenth century. Prerequisite: English 110.

387 THE NINETEENTH-CENTURY ENGLISH NOVEL 3 sem. hrs.

The English novel from Mathew Lewis through Thomas Hardy.

388 THE TWENTIETH-CENTURY ENGLISH NOVEL 3 sem. hrs.

The twentieth-century English novel from Arnold Bennett through Lawrence Durrell.

397 RESEARCH SEMINAR 2 sem. hrs.

Introduction to bibliography, methods of scholarly research and the critical evaluation of research in the field.

413 STUDIES IN MEDIEVAL ENGLISH LITERATURE (excluding Chaucer) 3 sem. hrs.

Advanced study of selected linguistic, textual, or literary topics in Middle English (1100-1500). Prerequisite: English 313, 320 or equivalent.

414 STUDIES IN SIXTEENTH CENTURY ENGLISH LITERATURE 3 sem. hrs.

A study of one or several important authors of the period, such as More, Sidney, and Spenser, or of a particular literary movement or genre.

415 STUDIES IN SEVENTEENTH CENTURY ENGLISH LITERATURE 3 sem. hrs.

An intensive study of the poetry and prose of selected seventeenth century writers exclusive of Milton.

416 STUDIES IN EIGHTEENTH CENTURY ENGLISH LITERATURE 3 sem. hrs.

A critical study of one or more important authors of the period, such as Dryden, Pope, Swift, and Johnson, or of a particular genre.

417 STUDIES IN THE LITERATURE OF THE ROMANTIC PERIOD 3 sem. hrs.

A study of selected authors, such as Blake, Wordsworth, Coleridge, Byron, Shelley, and Keats, with some attention to minor writers.

418 STUDIES IN VICTORIAN LITERATURE 3 sem. hrs.

A critical study of one or several important authors in the period, such as Browning, Tennyson, and Arnold, or of a particular literary movement or genre.

419 STUDIES IN CONTEMPORARY ENGLISH LITERATURE 3 sem. hrs.

Study and research in the works of Conrad, Joyce, Lawrence, Greene, Thomas, and other major recent writers.

420 STUDIES IN CHAUCER 3 sem. hrs.

Study and research in the life and works of Geoffrey Chaucer.

422 STUDIES IN SHAKESPEARE 3 sem. hrs.

An approach to Shakespeare through sources, textual problems, criticism, and modern scholarship.

424 STUDIES IN MILTON 3 sem. hrs.

Study and research in the life and works of John Milton.

428 STUDIES IN DRAMA 3 sem. hrs.

A study of a major genre such as verse tragedy in British and American dramatic literature. Prerequisites: A course in Shakespeare and another 200 or 300 level course in drama.

431 STUDIES IN EARLY AMERICAN LITERATURE 3 sem. hrs.

Intensive study of one or more literary figures or movements in the period from 1607 to 1830.

432 STUDIES IN AMERICAN LITERATURE 1830-1914 3 sem. hrs.

Intensive study of critical and scholarly problems in authors such as Emerson, Hawthorne, and Melville.

434 STUDIES IN CONTEMPORARY AMERICAN LITERATURE 3 sem. hrs.

Wide reading in the works of Faulkner, T. S. Eliot, and other recent American authors.

440 STUDIES IN ENGLISH LINGUISTICS 3 sem. hrs.

Study and research in various aspects of the English language. Prerequisites: English 310, 341, 342, and consent of the instructor.

450 STUDIES IN ANCIENT LITERATURE 3 sem. hrs.

Selected readings from antiquity, both from the Eastern and Western worlds. Prerequisite: English 150 or consent of the head of the department.

452 STUDIES IN THE RENAISSANCE 3 sem. hrs.

Consideration of the Renaissance and its major authors.

453 STUDIES IN THE ENLIGHTENMENT 3 sem. hrs.

Consideration of The Enlightenment, chiefly in France from 1650 to 1750.

454 STUDIES IN EUROPEAN ROMANTICISM 3 sem. hrs.

Consideration of the Romantic movement and its major authors.

456 STUDIES IN MODERN WORLD LITERATURE 3 sem. hrs.

A study in depth of the fiction and drama after World War I from all parts of the world other than the United States.

482 STUDIES IN LITERARY CRITICISM 3 sem. hrs.

Individual studies in literary criticism treating poetics, aesthetics, themes, or movements (naturalism, neo-classicism, realism, romanticism, etc.). Prerequisite: English 382 or equivalent graduate level course in literary criticism.

483 STUDIES IN RHETORIC AND ENGLISH PROSE STYLE 3 sem. hrs.

Studies in the historical development and peculiar characteristics of English prose style and the influence of rhetorical theory at various stages of its development. Prerequisites: English 310 and 397.

486 STUDIES IN THE ENGLISH NOVEL 3 sem. hrs.

A study of the English novel in relation to a theme, to historical development, or to one or more aspects of the novel. Prerequisite: A 200 or 300 level course in the English novel.

487 STUDIES IN THE AMERICAN NOVEL 3 sem. hrs.

The novel in the United States with emphasis on the nineteenth and twentieth centuries.

493 TOPICS IN ENGLISH 1-3 sem. hrs.

An intensive course covering one or more aspects of English. A student may enroll in this course for credit more than once, provided the subject matter covered is not duplicated.

496 STUDIES IN BIBLIOGRAPHY 2 sem. hrs.

A study of bookmaking with emphasis on the gathering of bibliographical evidence, of the relation of manuscript copy to the printed text, and of the techniques and problems of editing. Prerequisite: English 397.

498 INDEPENDENT READING 1-3 sem. hrs.

Available only by permission of the head of the department to those students who would profit more from directed reading than from an existing course.

499 INDEPENDENT RESEARCH FOR THE MASTER'S THESIS 1-6 sem. hrs.

A student electing the thesis option must take from four to six hours of 499. A proposal for research must be on file before registration for this course is approved by the student's adviser. While registration beyond six hours may be permitted for the convenience of the student, he may not count more than a total of six hours of 499 among the 32 required for the master's degree.

SEMINARS FOR ADVANCED GRADUATE STUDENTS

The seminars for advanced graduate students involve intensive study and original research in the period, topic, genre or other special category indicated. A formal research paper, possibly leading to a dissertation, is required.

513 SEMINAR IN ENGLISH LITERATURE TO 1500 5 sem. hrs.

Specialized study of selected topics in Old or Middle English literature, with emphasis on a research paper suitable for expansion into a dissertation. Prerequisites: Reading knowledge of Old or Middle English and consent of the instructor.

514 SEMINAR IN THE ENGLISH RENAISSANCE 1500-1660 5 sem. hrs.

Specialized study of selected topics in the Renaissance with emphasis on research leading to the dissertation. Prerequisite: At least one graduate course in the Renaissance.

516 SEMINAR IN EIGHTEENTH CENTURY ENGLISH LITERATURE 1660-1785 5 sem. hrs.

Specialized study of selected topics in eighteenth-century English literature with emphasis on research leading to the dissertation. Prerequisite: At least one graduate course in eighteenth-century English literature.

517 SEMINAR IN NINETEENTH CENTURY ENGLISH LITERATURE 1785-1900 5 sem. hrs.

Seminar in selected Romantic or Victorian writers, in genres, or in the history of ideas. Presentation and discussion of projects in areas of specialization. Prerequisites: Two graduate courses in Romantic or Victorian literature or equivalent.

518 SEMINAR IN TWENTIETH CENTURY ENGLISH LITERATURE 5 sem. hrs.

Students pursue original research on a twentieth century British literary figure or topic. Prerequisite: At least one graduate course in twentieth century British literature.

531 SEMINAR IN AMERICAN LITERATURE TO 1890 5 sem. hrs.

Students will do intensive study and original research as preparation for writing a dissertation in one of these areas: Colonial literature, Romanticism, Transcendentalism, or Realism. Prerequisite: English 431 or 432, or equivalent.

533 SEMINAR IN AMERICAN LITERATURE SINCE 1890 5 sem. hrs.

Students will do intensive study and original research as preparation for writing a dissertation in one of the areas of twentieth century American literature, such as Literary Naturalism. Prerequisite: English 434, or equivalent.

540 SEMINAR IN LANGUAGE 5 sem. hrs.

Students will utilize the disciplines and materials of lower-level courses in language by doing a piece of independent research and will defend the paper in the seminar. Prerequisites: English 310, 341, 342 (or equivalents) and consent of the instructor.

580 SEMINAR IN SPECIAL AREAS 5 sem. hrs.

The material covered will vary with the specialist interests of the various instructors who offer it. Some possible areas are: critical theory, genre study, interdisciplinary study (e.g., psychology and literature, music and literature, literature and myth, etc.), linguistic analysis of literary works, computer analysis of literary works, folklore, comparative philology, etc. Prerequisite: Consent of instructor. Particular 300 or 400 level courses may be required.

599 DISSERTATION RESEARCH Variable credit

The student may register for this course after his dissertation topic has been approved.

RELATED COURSES

306 REGIONAL AND AREA STUDIES 1-9 sem. hrs.

An intensive study of particular lands, environments, cultures, literatures, and peoples. May be given in cooperation with other departments, on or off campus. The areas to be studied, participating departments, and credit hours available in the several departments will be announced each time the course is offered.

368 PLAYWRITING 3 sem. hrs.

Playwriting techniques of selected masters of dramaturgy, with practical application of the techniques in the writing of original plays. Both literary and professional aspects of writing for the theatre are considered. When possible, opportunity will be provided for the laboratory production of original scripts of quality in University theatre-workshop projects.

370 STUDIES IN THE HISTORY OF LITERATURE FOR YOUNG PEOPLE 3 sem. hrs.

Advanced critical, chronological study of literature for children and young people to 1900.

372 STUDIES IN CONTEMPORARY LITERATURE FOR YOUNG PEOPLE 3 sem. hrs.

Advanced study in contemporary literature for children and young people.

375 STUDIES IN LITERATURE FOR ADOLESCENTS 3 sem. hrs.

Advanced study of literature for grades seven through twelve.

395 PROBLEMS IN THE TEACHING OF ENGLISH 2 sem. hrs.

Critical examination of current practice and research in the teaching of language, literature, and composition in the junior high school and the senior high school in order to aid the teacher in meeting individual problems. Prerequisite: Experience in teaching (student teaching accepted) or 296 or 297.

399 MULTI-DISCIPLINARY SEMINAR 3 sem. hrs.

Intensive study in selected topics of a multi-disciplinary nature to be offered cooperatively by two or more departments.

491 INTERNSHIP-SEMINAR IN COLLEGE TEACHING OF ENGLISH 3 sem. hrs.

Credit for the course is given in Education (see Education 491).

492 RECENT RESEARCH IN THE ENGLISH LANGUAGE ARTS 3 sem. hrs.

Advanced study of significant research in the language arts for the elementary and junior high levels with emphasis on empirical research by members of the class. Some previous work in statistics recommended.

Foreign Language

Head of the Department: Thomas E. Comfort.   Office: Stevenson Hall 425

Teaching Staff: A. Billingsley, T. Comfort, A. G. Ferguson, W. Freese, W. Fuehrer, V. Gaigalas, B. Kuhn, J. Laurenti, H. Manahan, J. Martin, D. Parent, K. Parker, R. Perry, J. Rodriguez, K. Rothmann, P. Tarrant, H. Zimmermann.

The Department of Foreign Languages reserves the right to examine transfer students as to their ability to carry courses on the 300 level.

The department offers work leading to the following degrees: M.A., M.S. in Ed. The master's degree program is flexible, permitting specialization in either French, Latin, or Spanish. Courses are approved by major adviser and Head of the Department of Foreign Languages. A thesis may be required at the discretion of the head of the department.

GENERAL COURSES

300 RESEARCH IN FOREIGN LANGUAGES 1-3 sem. hrs.

Supervised work in a foreign language, in comparative language studies, or in educational materials for a foreign language laboratory. Assignments will depend on the preparation and interest of the student. By arrangement with the Head of the Department of Foreign Languages.

491 INTERNSHIP-SEMINAR IN COLLEGE TEACHING IN THE FOREIGN LANGUAGES 1-3 sem. hrs.

Credit for this course is given in Education (see Education 491).

497 RESEARCH SEMINAR 1-6 sem. hrs.

Introduction to bibliography, methods of scholarly research and the critical evaluation of research in the field. Must be taken by first year graduate students unless the department requires Education 475. May be repeated by more advanced students who desire direction and constructive criticism as they pursue research problems.

499 INDEPENDENT RESEARCH FOR THE MASTER'S THESIS 1-6 sem. hrs.

A student electing the thesis option must take from four to six hours of 499. A proposal for research must be on file before registration for this course is approved by the student's adviser. While registration beyond six hours may be permitted for the convenience of the student, he may not count more than a total of six hours of 499 among the 32 required for the master's degree.

FRENCH

301 FRENCH ROMANTICISM 3 sem. hrs.

Reading of poetry, novels, plays, criticism, stories, and history. Prerequisites: French 221, 222.

302 FRENCH CLASSICISM 3 sem. hrs.

Reading of plays by Corneille, Racine, and Moliere, and of selections from other seventeenth century writers. Prerequisites: French 221, 222.

309 FRENCH PHONETICS 2 sem. hrs.

A scientific approach to French pronunciation. Correct formation of French sounds; practical application of the theory of phonetics to teaching. Practice in the diction of ordinary conversation as well as the more formal diction of public reading and speaking. Prerequisites: Two courses in French literature.

316 FRENCH LITERATURE OF THE SIXTEENTH CENTURY 3 sem. hrs.

An analysis of the Renaissance as it expressed itself in the leading writers of France in the 16th century. Prerequisites: Two courses in French literature.

318 MOLIERE 3 sem. hrs.

Major comedies of Moliere, together with some of the farces and comedies.

322 LE MOYEN AGE 3 sem. hrs.

A study of Medieval French literature in modern French translation.

332 FRENCH LYRIC POETRY 2 sem. hrs.

Reading of French lyrics from the 16th century to the present; study of the schools of poetry; explication de texte; oral reading. Prerequisites: Two courses in French literature.

385 SELECTED STUDIES IN FRENCH LITERATURE 3 sem. hrs.

Intensive study of a genre, group of authors or a single major writer in French Literature. The field of study will vary each semester according to the interests and needs of students and the availability of instructors. Provided different material is covered, the course may be taken for credit more than once.

401 TWENTIETH CENTURY AUTHORS 1900-1945   3 sem. hrs.
Trends in contemporary prose, with readings from the novel and the drama.

402 STYLISTICS   3 sem. hrs.
Intensive, advanced grammar and composition, including analysis of style.

403 TWENTIETH CENTURY AUTHORS SINCE 1945   3 sem. hrs.
A study in depth of the fiction, drama, and poetry in French literature since World War II.

404 BALZAC   3 sem. hrs.
Balzac's work with emphasis on his novels as a mirror of his time, and their influence on the development of the novel as a literary form.

416 MONTAIGNE   3 sem. hrs.
A detailed study of the life and works of Montaigne.

418 LA FONTAINE   3 sem. hrs.
A detailed study of the life and works of La Fontaine.

420 THE AGE OF ENLIGHTENMENT   3 sem. hrs.
Intensive and critical study in French of the major authors and works of the eighteenth century.

421 HISTORY OF FRENCH LANGUAGE   3 sem. hrs.
Evolution of the language from its origins to the present day.

430 REALISM AND NATURALISM   3 sem. hrs.
A detailed analysis of French literature of the late nineteenth century, including the works of Flaubert, Zola, and Baudelaire.

431 LE SYMBOLISME ET LE PARNASSE   3 sem. hrs.
A detailed study of French poetry in the late nineteenth century.

GERMAN

302 and 303 GOETHE AND SCHILLER   Each 3 sem. hrs.
Classic German literature with emphasis on dramas of Goethe and Schiller. Lectures, collateral reading, and reports. Prerequisites: Two courses in German beyond 116.

309 GERMAN PHONETICS   2 sem. hrs.
A scientific approach to German pronunciation; correct formation of German sounds; practical application of the theory of phonetics to its teaching. Prerequisites: Two courses in German literature.

313 ADVANCED GERMAN COMPOSITION AND CONVERSATION   2 sem. hrs.
Free discussion of topics of contemporary interest; assignment of oral and written themes based on class discussions. Prerequisite: German 213 or equivalent.

318 GOETHE'S FAUST   3 sem. hrs.
A critical study of Parts I and II of *Faust* as literature and as an expression of Goethe's philosophy. Lectures, assigned readings, and reports. Prerequisites: Two courses in German beyond 116.

332 GERMAN LYRIC POETRY   2 sem. hrs.
Reading and interpretation of German lyric poetry from 800 A.D. to the present.

385 SELECTED STUDIES IN GERMAN LITERATURE 3 sem. hrs.

Intensive study of a genre, group of authors or a single major writer in German Literature. The field of study will vary each semester according to the interests and needs of students and the availability of instructors. Provided different material is covered, the course may be taken for credit more than once.

LATIN

315 HORACE: ODES AND EPODES 3 sem. hrs.

Translation, interpretation, and metrical reading of Horace's lyric poetry. Critical study of the characteristic features of his style. Life in the Augustan Age and Horace's philosophy.

316 ROMAN SATIRE 3 sem. hrs.

The history and development of satire as a literary genre; reading of representative selections from Ennius, Lucilius, Horace, Persius, and Juvenal; a consideration of their influence upon later literature.

318 TACITUS 2 sem. hrs.

Agricola and *Germania*. An introduction to the prose of the Silver period.

319 SELECTIONS FROM THE LETTERS OF CICERO 2 sem. hrs.

Translation of some of the most interesting and important letters of Cicero as a commentary upon the manners, history, and politics of the period of the Republic.

320 SELECTIONS FROM THE LETTERS OF PLINY 2 sem. hrs.

Readings from the correspondence of Pliny selected for their importance as a commentary on Roman life and manners during the period of the Empire. Study of the letters both as human documents and as literary compositions.

385 SELECTED STUDIES IN LATIN LITERATURE 3 sem. hrs.

Intensive study of a genre, group of authors or a single major writer in Latin Literature. The field of study will vary each semester according to the interests and needs of students and the availability of instructors. Provided different material is covered, the course may be taken for credit more than once.

401 SUETONIUS' LIVES OF THE CAESARS 2 sem. hrs.

Translation of the biographies of some of the most important of the Caesars and a study of the place of the Caesars in history. Designed to give the teacher of Latin a good historical background.

402 LUCRETIUS 3 sem. hrs.

Reading of selected portions of the *De Rerum Natura*. Study of ancient philosophy with special emphasis on Stoicism and Epicureanism.

403 THE ANNALS OF TACITUS 3 sem. hrs.

Translation of selections from the *Annals* covering the events of the early Empire. Critical study of Tacitus as an historian.

404-405 HISTORY OF LATIN LITERATURE Each 3 sem. hrs.

Development of Latin literature from its beginning to the close of the Republic. Works of the writers of the Empire period. Translation of representative selections.

406 THE ELEGIAC POETS 2 sem. hrs.

Readings from the Roman elegiac poets; the influence of these poets upon English and American literature.

407 CICERO'S ORATIONS 3 sem. hrs.

Translation and interpretation of representative works drawn from the forensic orations of Cicero, with particular attention to the details of the life of Cicero and the history and politics of the last century of the Roman Republic.

410 ADVANCED LATIN PROSE COMPOSITION 3 sem. hrs.

Application of the major principles of Latin grammar and syntax in writing connected discourse based on different Latin authors as a means of developing facility in the use of Latin forms and constructions.

415 VERGIL'S GEORGICS AND ECLOGUES 2 sem. hrs.

Reading of the Georgics and Eclogues of Vergil; the style of Latin pastoral and didactic poetry.

421 HISTORY OF THE LATIN LANGUAGE 2 sem. hrs.

Development of the Latin language with attention directed to the grammatical forms and syntactical usage in selected writings of the early, classical, and postclassical authors. Some treatment of the relation of the various Indo-European languages to each other, the place of Latin and English among these languages, and the history of Latin elements in English.

424 PROBLEMS IN THE TEACHING OF LATIN 2 sem. hrs.

Aims, subject matter, and methods of the teaching of Latin in the light of new emphasis in the high school curriculum. Critical examination of current high school texts, preparation of syllabi and tests, and a study of audio-visual materials available for Latin classes.

SPANISH

304. LA CIVILIZACIÓN MEXICANA (Spanish) 2 sem. hrs.

A study of the formation of the Mexican nationality of today, as the fusion of Hispanic and Indian cultures. A consideration of the development of attitudes, traditions, and way of life of the Mexican people.

309 SPANISH PHONETICS 2 sem. hrs.

An analysis of the speech sounds of Spanish; a consideration of the difficulties an English speaker encounters in learning and using correct Spanish pronunciation, stress, and intonation; exercises aimed at improvement of pronunciation and intonation.

310 SINTAXIS ESPAÑOLA 2 sem. hrs.

A descriptive study of modern Spanish with frequent reference to psychological and historical forces that have influenced its present form.

320 PROBLEMS IN THE TEACHING OF SPANISH 2 sem. hrs.

Re-evaluation of traditional methods of teaching Spanish. Examination and evaluation of modern techniques. Problems related to the teaching of Spanish in general. Problems related to specific methods and techniques.

331 SPANISH AMERICAN LITERATURE 3 sem. hrs.

History of Spanish American literature from the colonial period to the late 19th century. A consideration of the development of literary forms and traditions. Prerequisite: Spanish 116 or consent of the instructor.

332 SPANISH AMERICAN LITERATURE 3 sem. hrs.

History of Spanish American literature from late 19th century to present day. A continuation of Spanish 331. Prerequisite: Spanish 116 or consent of the instructor.

335 MEXICAN LITERATURE (Spanish) 2 sem. hrs.

An intensive survey of Mexican literature and its cultural background from the period of the conquistadors to the present.

372 SPANISH DRAMA OF THE SIGLO DE ORO 3 sem. hrs.

Class and collateral reading of selected plays from the great dramatists of Spain's Golden Age. Prerequisites: Two courses in Spanish literature.

385 SELECTED STUDIES IN SPANISH LITERATURE 3 sem. hrs.

Intensive study of a genre, group of authors or a single major writer in Spanish Literature. The field of study will vary each semester according to the interests and needs of students and the availability of instructors. Provided different material is covered, the course may be taken for credit more than once.

411 SPANISH-AMERICAN NOVEL 3 sem. hrs.

The Spanish-American Novel of the nineteenth and twentieth centuries with emphasis on the most characteristic author of each period and each genre.

421 HISTORY OF THE SPANISH LANGUAGE 3 sem. hrs.

History of the Spanish language with attention to both external and internal aspects of its development.

423 INTRODUCTION TO ROMANCE LINGUISTICS 3 sem. hrs.

The historical and phonological development of the major Romance languages.

435 LEADERS IN SPANISH-AMERICAN THOUGHT 3 sem. hrs.

The writers of prose—exclusive of fiction—who have shaped or influenced thought and action in Spanish America during the past two centuries, from the beginning of the movement for independence to the present day.

463 SEMINAR IN SPANISH LITERATURE BEFORE 1500 3 sem. hrs.

Intensive and critical study of a major work of the period. The work studied will be varied in successive semesters.

464 SEMINAR IN GOLDEN AGE PROSE 3 sem. hrs.

A study of the important works of the Renaissance and Baroque periods: the novel in its various forms, the short story, religious literature, moral and historical writings.

466 THE PICARESQUE NOVEL 3 sem. hrs.

A study of the Picaresque Novel and its influence on modern world literature. Emphasis on *Lazarillo de Tormes, Guzmán de Alfarache, La vida de Marcos de Obregón, La vida del Buscón, Vida y hecho de Estebanillo González.*

467 SEMINAR IN GOLDEN AGE POETRY 3 sem. hrs.

Intensive and critical study of Spanish poetry from Garcilaso to Quevedo, with particular attention to Italian influences, to mysticism, to the aesthetics of the Renaissance and Baroque periods, and to the traditional forms.

468 LOPE DE VEGA AND HIS PREDECESSORS 3 sem. hrs.

A study of the creation of national theatre by Lope de Vega and his predecessors, with attention to the development of preceding forms of religious and secular drama, Italian influences, and the crystallization of the spirit of the Spanish Counter-Reformation. Prerequisite: Spanish Drama of the Siglo de Oro 372.

469 THE THEATRE OF CALDERON AND HIS CONTEMPORARIES 3 sem. hrs.

Emphasis will be placed both on Calderon's late dramas and upon a critical analysis of the drama of his contemporaries. Questions to be considered: national characteristics, intellectual and religious implication, the role of the individual, problems of style and ideological interpretation. Prerequisite: Spanish Drama of the Siglo de Oro 372.

470 DON QUIXOTE 3 sem. hrs.
Reading of the Quixote with special attention to problems of interpretation and literary criticism.

484 SEMINAR IN CONTEMPORARY SPANISH LITERATURE 3 sem. hrs.
A study of the twentieth century novel, essay, poetry, or drama. The genre will be varied in successive semesters.

485 SELECTED STUDIES IN LINGUISTICS 3 sem. hrs.
Intensive study of a linguistic problem, work, technique, or language. The field of study will vary according to the interests and needs of the students. The course may be repeated for credit provided that different areas are explored.

French

(See Foreign Languages)

Geography

Head of the Department: John Trotter.   Office: Schroeder Hall 125
Teaching Staff: P. Brand, W. Calef, R. Hart, P. Mattingly, E. J. Miller, J. Patterson, E. Schmidt, T. Searight, J. Trotter, D. Wheeler.

The department offers work leading to the following degrees: M.A., M.S., M.S. in Ed. University requirements for master's degrees are described elsewhere in this catalog.

COURSES

300 CARTOGRAPHY AND GRAPHICS 3 sem. hrs.
Graphic representation of statistical data, including compilation and preparation of various types of maps and graphs. Map projections, scales, symbolisms, dot maps, and their use.

305 AERIAL PHOTOGRAPH INTERPRETATION 3 sem. hrs.
An introduction to the basic principles of photogrammetry and the techniques and applications of aerial photograph interpretation, emphasizing the functional relationships of features located upon the earth's surface.

306 REGIONAL AND AREA STUDIES 1-9 sem. hrs.
An intensive study of particular lands, environments, cultures, and peoples. May be given in cooperation with other departments, on or off the campus. The areas to be studied, participating departments, and credit hours available in the several departments, will be announced each time the course is offered.

308 QUANTITATIVE METHODS IN GEOGRAPHY 3 sem. hrs.
Use and interpretation of basic statistical techniques in geographical problems. Measures of central tendency and dispersion, frequency curves, sampling, sample analysis, and correlation are applied to the spatial aspects of phenomena.

310 TECHNIQUES OF FIELD WORK 3 sem. hrs.

Techniques of mapping and interpretation of the phenomena of the natural and cultural landscapes. Most of the time in the field is spent in doing original study and mapping.

315 METHODS AND CONCEPTS IN AMERICAN GEOGRAPHY 2 sem. hrs.

A survey of selected professional publications designed to acquaint the student with the development of basic concepts and methods in American geography. Enables the student to evaluate geographic viewpoints and approaches in research and teaching.

320 RURAL LAND USE AND AGRICULTURAL GEOGRAPHY 3 sem. hrs.

Principles of agricultural geography, and related land use; types of agriculture and production units, agricultural regions, and distributional patterns of chief crops and livestock. Includes study of factors and decisions influencing the location of agricultural activities. Prerequisite: Economic Geography 130 or consent of instructor.

325 WORLD POPULATION AND RESOURCES 3 sem. hrs.

Population growth and resource distribution and their impact on national policy, levels of living, education, and food supply.

330 GEOGRAPHY OF TRANSPORTATION 3 sem. hrs.

The study of the spatial aspects of transportation systems: land, air, and water; the agents of transportation, and the effects of transportation on regional and economic development. Transportation realms and regions of the world. Prerequisite: Economic Geography 130 or consent of the instructor.

335 INDUSTRIAL GEOGRAPHY 3 sem. hrs.

Distribution and locational factors influencing distribution of American industries. Relationship of American industries to world industrial patterns.

340 CLIMATES OF THE CONTINENTS 2 sem. hrs.

Climates of the various continents and associated controls. Analysis of classifications of climate and problems of climatic classifications.

345 PROBLEMS IN CONSERVATION 3 sem. hrs.

Investigations of specific problems in conservation of soils, water, forests, wildlife, minerals, and recreational land. These problems are explored in their complex national, regional, and local contexts.

365 GEOGRAPHIC MATERIALS IN EDUCATION 3 sem. hrs.

The role of maps, globes, and other aids in teaching geography. Practical experience in selection and organization of geographic materials under laboratory situations.

380 GEOMORPHOLOGY 3 sem. hrs.

Detailed study of the origin, classification, description, and interpretation of land forms. Prerequisite: Physical Geology 175.

400 ADVANCED CARTOGRAPHY 3 sem. hrs.

Techniques of cartographic presentation. Compilation and construction of maps and diagrams for research and teaching. Prerequisites: Cartography and Graphics 300.

405 GEOGRAPHY IN EDUCATION 2 sem. hrs.

Historical development of the science and teaching of geography. Modern geography and its contribution to general education. Evaluation of current teaching materials.

410 GEOGRAPHY OF DISCOVERY AND EXPLORATION 2 sem. hrs.

Contributions made by discovery and exploration to the geographical knowledge of the world from ancient to early modern times.

412 CULTURAL GEOGRAPHY 3 sem. hrs.

The forms and processes of man's occupance and use of his habitat within cultural regions, which may be areally defined and studied through time. Examples from North America and Western Europe are presented in depth, along with an examination of cultural origins, cultural dispersals and cultural landscapes.

415 ADVANCED URBAN GEOGRAPHY 3 sem. hrs.

Detailed analysis of the spatial aspects of urban developments. Focus on urban morphology, and external relationships.

420 PHYSIOGRAPHY OF NORTH AMERICA 3 sem. hrs.

Physiographic regions of North America. Emphasis placed upon the development of surface features of each area as a background for present geographic patterns of that region. One two-day field trip is required.

425 GLACIOLOGY AND PLEISTOCENE HISTORY 3 sem. hrs.

The formation, movement, work, and landforms resulting from glaciers. Analysis of the effects of the Pleistocene Epoch on climates, vegetation, weathering, soils, and landscape development. Prerequisite: Physical Geology 175.

430 GEOGRAPHY OF LATIN AMERICA 3 sem. hrs.

Intensive study of selected areas with emphasis upon settlement patterns, resources and interregional relations.

435 GEOGRAPHY OF WESTERN EUROPE 3 sem. hrs.

A regional and economic development of the British Isles and continental Europe. Intensive investigations of resource, industrial, agricultural, and population patterns of Europe. Illustrated local units of occupance.

440 MEDITERRANEAN LANDS 3 sem. hrs.

Regional survey of the physical, cultural, and economic aspects of southern Europe, the Levant, and North Africa.

445 GEOGRAPHY OF THE MIDDLE EAST 3 sem. hrs.

Survey of the lands and peoples of southern and southwestern Asia. Resource and population patterns of regional and political units.

450 GEOGRAPHY OF THE FAR EAST 3 sem. hrs.

Lands and peoples of eastern Asia, with emphasis on China and Japan. International, national, and regional characteristics and problems.

470 SEMINAR IN REGIONAL GEOGRAPHY 3 sem. hrs.

Prerequisite: Advanced standing in geography or consent of instructor.

471 SEMINAR IN ECONOMIC-RESOURCE GEOGRAPHY 3 sem. hrs.

Prerequisites: Economic Geography 130 and/or Conservation of Natural Resources 205, or consent of instructor.

472 SEMINAR IN PHYSICAL GEOGRAPHY

Prerequisite: Consent of instructor.

473 SEMINAR IN HUMAN GEOGRAPHY

Prerequisite: Consent of instructor.

491 INTERNSHIP-SEMINAR IN COLLEGE TEACHING IN GEOGRAPHY
3 sem. hrs.
Credit for this course is given in Education (see Education 491).

497 RESEARCH SEMINAR 1-6 sem. hrs.
Introduction to bibliography, methods of scholarly research and the critical evaluation of research in the field. Must be taken by first year graduate students unless the department requires Education 475. May be repeated by more advanced students who desire direction and constructive criticism as they pursue research problems.

499 INDEPENDENT RESEARCH FOR THE MASTER'S THESIS 1-6 sem. hrs.
A student electing the thesis option must take from four to six hours of 499. A proposal for research must be on file before registration for this course is approved by the student's adviser. While registration beyond six hours may be permitted for the convenience of the student, he may not count more than a total of six hours of 499 among the 32 required for the master's degree.

DIRECTED STUDIES IN GEOGRAPHY

Individual reading or research on specialized aspects of geography under the direction and guidance of an instructor. For advanced graduate students only.

500 DIRECTED STUDIES IN REGIONAL GEOGRAPHY 3 sem. hrs.
501 DIRECTED STUDIES IN ECONOMIC-RESOURCE GEOGRAPHY 3 sem. hrs.
502 DIRECTED STUDIES IN PHYSICAL GEOGRAPHY 3 sem. hrs.
503 DIRECTED STUDIES IN HUMAN GEOGRAPHY 3 sem. hrs.

590 RESEARCH IN GEOGRAPHY Variable credit
Research and data collection for the dissertation required for the Ph.D. Prerequisite: Approval of the head of the department.

AUXILIARY GEOLOGY COURSES

(Not applicable to a graduate degree program in geography)

375 ECONOMIC GEOLOGY 3 sem. hrs.
Earth materials of economic importance. Characteristics and uses of common metallic and nonmetallic minerals and rocks. Prerequisite: Geography 175.

385 INVERTEBRATE PALEONTOLOGY 4 sem. hrs.
Concepts of evolution, taxonomy, and paleontological species; invertebrate phyla, with emphasis on groups with paleocologic and stratigraphic significance. Three hours of lecture, three hours of laboratory. Prerequisites: Historical Geology 180 or Life of the Geologic Past 275 and Biological Sciences 191.

390 OPTICAL MINEROLOGY 5 sem. hrs.
A study of the optical properties of rock forming minerals including an introduction to the techniques employed in the use of the petrographic microscope. Lecture and laboratory.

395 GENERAL PETROGRAPHY 3 sem. hrs.
Representatives of the major rock groups will be studied in thin section employing the use of the petrographic microscope. Lecture and laboratory.

German

(See Foreign Languages)

Health and Physical Education

Head of the Department (Men): Arley F. Gillett.   Office: Horton Field House 203-A

Teaching Staff: B. Bass, L. Bitcon, J. Collie, L.D. Cruse, P. Dohrmann, A. Gillett, E. Hill, R. Koehler, R. Liverman, B. O'Connor, W. Truex, M. Weisbecker.

Chairman of the Department (Women): Phebe M. Scott.
Office: McCormick Gymnasium 101

Teaching Staff: F. Clark, V. Crafts, B. Frey, M. Gray, B. Hall, E. C. Imel, M. Jones, E. Kelly, B. Keough, G. L. Mabry, P. Scott, G. Smith, D. Workman.

The Department offers work leading to the following degrees: M.A., M.S., M.S. in Ed.

Students working on a master's degree must complete at least 18 hours in Health and Physical Education excluding thesis credit. Programs must also include from this department 442 and 497. Students pursuing the non-thesis comprehensive examination option must include in their programs at least two semester hours of credit from 449. Students who desire a concentration in dance will complete 460, 469, and 497; 10 more semester hours in dance or other physical education courses for a total of 18 semester hours; and write a thesis which may be a creative project or a statistical study.

University requirements for master's degrees are listed elsewhere in this catalog.

COURSES

304 TEACHING OF SPORTS   2 sem. hrs.

Assessment of content, teacher behavior and situational conditions necessary for optimal learning in human movement; analysis of sports and development of meaningful instructional approaches; application of recent research and psychological and sociological principles.

321 THE ELEMENTARY SCHOOL PHYSICAL EDUCATION PROGRAM 2 sem. hrs.

Principles and purposes of physical education in elementary schools. Current trends in program planning, recent research, methods of evaluation, school-community cooperation. Prerequisite: Health and Physical Education 221, 222 or 223.

340 HISTORY OF PHYSICAL EDUCATION   2 sem. hrs.

The relationship, from ancient to modern times, between physical education and factors in society: economic, political, social, educational, and religious.

341 ORGANIZATION AND ADMINISTRATION OF HEALTH AND PHYSICAL EDUCATION   3 sem. hrs.

Factors essential to the administration and program development of health education and physical education in elementary and secondary schools.

347 TESTS AND MEASUREMENTS IN PHYSICAL EDUCATION   3 sem. hrs.

Analysis of motor performance, using objective tests, subjective ratings, and achievement tests. Construction and evaluation of knowledge tests. Use of basic statistical concepts for interpreting test scores.

349 APPLIED MOTOR LEARNING   3 sem. hrs.

Presents research and theory of learning, performance, and related factors as applied to gross motor skills. Intended for teachers, coaches, and those concerned with human performance in motor activity.

360 THE TEACHING OF DANCE 2 sem. hrs.

Teaching methods in modern, folk, square, round, and social dance; selection, progression, and grade placement of dance materials in the secondary school and college curriculum; practice in perfecting dance techniques; evaluation of dance skills and knowledges. Prerequisite: Health and Physical Education 160.

361 HISTORY OF DANCE I 2 sem. hrs.

The history and development of dance as a social and cultural medium from primitive times through the nineteenth century.

362 PRINCIPLES OF PERFORMANCE 3 sem. hrs.

Principles governing public performance in physical education; dance, swimming, gymnastics, and other physical education activities. A survey of costuming, lighting, accompaniment, and related problems in production.

363 HISTORY OF DANCE II 2 sem. hrs.

Dance trends in the twentieth century; their relationships to older cultures and forms of dance and to social patterns of the present; approaches, styles, and contributions of leading dance personalities of the twentieth century. Prerequisite: Health and Physical Education 361.

364 MUSICAL ANALYSIS FOR DANCE ACCOMPANIMENT 2 sem. hrs.

Basic principles of accompanying modern dance; selection of appropriate music, both live and recorded, from traditional and current repertories, for use with folk, social, and theatre forms of dance; brief history of music and music for dance.

365 TEACHING OF THE FOLK FORMS OF DANCE 2 sem. hrs.

Methods of teaching the folk and social forms of dance in the secondary school, college, and recreational situation; appraisal of the patterned dances in the traditional and current repertory; sources of curricular materials from dance books, magazines, workshops, clinics, festivals, conventions, institutes, and summer schools and camps; advanced techniques in folk, round, square, and social dance; basic skills in tap dance. Prerequisite: Health and Physical Education 360.

367 PROBLEMS IN DANCE 2 sem. hrs.

Current problems in the teaching of dance on all levels, in the administration of dance curricula, in the organization and supervision of dance clubs and extra-curricular activities.

368 PRACTICUM IN COMPOSITION 2 sem. hrs.

Progressive experiences in individual and group composition: in design, rhythm, and dynamics; compositional group works based upon extensive investigation into the subject matter to be communicated. Prerequisite: Previous experience in modern dance.

369 DANCE FOR CHILDREN 2 sem. hrs.

Methods and materials in traditional and creative activities; movement explorations for stunts, tumbling, and games; interrelationships of dance with art, music, drama, science, and other elementary school activities. Prerequisite: Health and Physical Education 162 or 222.

372 CAMP EXPERIENCE WITH PHYSICALLY HANDICAPPED 3 sem. hrs.

Actual experience as a counselor in a summer camp for physically handicapped children. Conferences and discussions on planning the child's day; general organization of activities, camp equipment, and program. A student may enroll for credit a second time. Prerequisite: Approval of the Head of the Department of Special Education and head of the Department of Health and Physical Education for men or women.

373 WORKSHOP IN RECREATION AND CAMPING 3 sem. hrs.

Preparation of materials for use in recreation and camping situations; sources for obtaining materials and information; cooperative work among various departments and organizations. Includes crafts, music, story telling and dramatics.

383 BODY MECHANICS AND CORRECTIVE PROCEDURES 2 sem. hrs.

Methods, materials, and activities appropriate for the body mechanics and adapted physical education program in elementary and secondary schools. Prerequisite: Health and Physical Education 282.

384 ATHLETIC INJURIES 2 sem. hrs.

Designed to familiarize the coach with symptoms of common athletic injuries, their immediate treatment and care. Prerequisite: Health and Physical Education 182.

385 PHYSICAL DEFECTS—SURVEY AND REHABILITATION 3 sem. hrs.

Physical defects of handicapped children and procedures used in their rehabilitation. For those preparing to teach special classes of physically handicapped children. Includes special services, equipment, and procedures used in school programs. Lecture and laboratory. Also offered as Biological Sciences 385. Prerequisite: Health and Physical Education 282.

386 PHYSICAL EDUCATION AND RECREATION FOR HANDICAPPED CHILDREN 2 sem. hrs.

Materials and methods involved in planning recreational programs for handicapped children and adolescents. Designed primarily for teachers of exceptional children and physical education. Prerequisite: Health and Physical Education 383 or Psychology 346 and 2-3 hrs. from Health and Physical Education 221, 222, 223, 224, or 321.

403 PROBLEMS IN ADMINISTRATION OF SPORTS 3 sem. hrs.

Critical analysis of the current problems that confront the director of physical education in the organization and administration of sports activities with special reference to national, state, and local control.

424 SUPERVISION OF PHYSICAL EDUCATION 2 sem. hrs.

Techniques of supervision of physical education in elementary and secondary schools; in-service training of the classroom and physical education teacher; relationships with teachers, administrators, and community.

442 PHILOSOPHY OF PHYSICAL EDUCATION 3 sem. hrs.

An examination of the philosophical bases of physical education in historical perspective and in the American culture with implications for purposes, programs, and methodology.

443 PROBLEMS IN HEALTH, PHYSICAL EDUCATION, AND RECREATION 2 sem. hrs.

Consideration of current problems in these fields as they affect the teacher of physical education; guidance in individual and group solution of selected professional problems.

447 EVALUATION IN PHYSICAL EDUCATION 3 sem. hrs.

Methods for testing and evaluating in the school situation, interpreting data, and understanding statistics in research. Prerequisite: Health and Physical Education 347 or equivalent.

448 CURRENT RESEARCH IN HPER 2 sem. hrs.

Review and critical analysis of selected research studies. Prerequisite: Introduction to Research 497.

449 SELECTED STUDIES IN HPER 1-6 sem. hrs.

Students will undertake independent problems or projects and may meet on occasion as a group or independently under the direction of the instructor.

460 SEMINAR IN DANCE 2 sem. hrs.

Student participation in lectures, reports, demonstrations, and discussions to gain fluency in oral and written presentation while criticizing or defending concepts related to dance education; critical evaluation of pertinent research and thesis plans; reaction to points of view expressed by occasional guest lectures.

466 SELECTED STUDIES IN DANCE 1-6 sem. hrs.

Studies in depth within any area of dance education, including both folk forms and theatre forms, approved by the instructor and the head of the department. A student may enroll more than once if there is no duplication of content, and the total does not exceed 6 semester hours.

469 MOVEMENT PHENOMENOLOGY AND PERCEPTION 3 sem. hrs.

The phenomenon of human movement; perceptual movement relationships and communication; theories of motion and muscular movement, movement behavior. Prerequisite: Health and Physical Education 282.

472 CAMPING ADMINISTRATION 2 sem. hrs.

Functions and principles of camp administration in organizational and private camps.

475 ORGANIZATION AND ADMINISTRATION OF RECREATION 3 sem. hrs.

Factors concerning the organization and administration of a recreation program; course designed to meet the needs of the administrators of town, community, or school recreational programs.

481 APPLIED PHYSIOLOGY 2 sem. hrs.

Application of human physiology to the teaching of physical education; the effects of exercise on the heart, lungs, circulation, and respiration; discussion of current studies pertinent to tests of physical efficiency.

482 MECHANICAL ANALYSIS OF MOVEMENT 2 sem. hrs.

Principles of physics applied to body movement; analysis of body positions and modes of locomotion; muscular and mechanical analysis of selected movement skills.

483 ADVANCED CORRECTIVE PROCEDURES 2 sem. hrs.

Selected screening and evaluative techniques; applications of recent advances in exercise physiology: individualization of health exercise, and rest programs; administration of school and college adapted and corrective program; school-community liaison. Prerequisite: Health and Physical Education 383.

491 INTERNSHIP-SEMINAR IN COLLEGE TRAINING IN HEALTH AND PHYSICAL EDUCATION 3 sem. hrs.

Credit in this course is given in Education (see Education 491).

497 INTRODUCTION TO RESEARCH 3 sem. hrs.

Introduction to research methodology, including use of the library, problem selection, differences in research techniques, and application of statistical models to research designs.

499 INDEPENDENT RESEARCH FOR THE MASTER'S THESIS 1-6 sem. hrs.

A student electing the thesis option must take from four to six hours of 499. A proposal for research must be on file before registration for this course is approved by the student's adviser. While registration beyond six hours may be permitted for the convenience of the student, he may not count more than a total of six hours of 499 among the 32 required for the master's degree.

History

Chairman of the Department: Roger J. Champagne.   Office: Schroeder Hall 334

Teaching Staff: H. Cavanagh, R. Champagne, J. Grabill, M. P. Holsinger, G. Homan, F. Kohlmeyer, M. Plummer, E. Reitan, T. Sands, E. Schapsmeier, K. Sessions, L. M. Simms, Jr., L. Tasher, L. Walker.

The department offers work leading to the following degrees: M.A., M.S., M.S. in Ed. University requirements for these degrees are listed elsewhere in this catalog. Departmental requirements are as follows:

MASTER'S DEGREE IN HISTORY

Courses are taken in history and such related fields as the student's adviser recommends. Each student must earn at least five graduate hours of course work in an historical field other than his major historical field (for example, U.S. History, European History, or some other history field). A thesis is required.

MASTER'S DEGREE IN THE SOCIAL SCIENCES

A program offered jointly by the departments of economics, history, political science and sociology-anthropology and permitting an interdisciplinary approach. The program is described under Social Sciences.

COURSES

301 SELECTED STUDIES IN EUROPEAN HISTORY   3 sem. hrs.

The field of study will vary each semester according to the interests and needs of the students and the availability of instructors. Provided different material is covered, the course may be taken for credit more than once.

302 SELECTED STUDIES IN AMERICAN HISTORY   3 sem. hrs.

The field of study will vary each semester according to the interests and needs of the students and the availability of instructors. Provided different material is covered, the course may be taken for credit more than once.

303 SELECTED STUDIES IN THE HISTORY OF ASIA   2 sem. hrs.

The field of study will vary each semester according to the interests and needs of students and the availability of instructors. Provided different material is covered, the course may be taken for credit more than once.

304 SELECTED STUDIES IN LATIN AMERICAN HISTORY   3 sem. hrs.

The field of study will vary every semester according to the interests and the needs of the students and the availability of instructors. Provided different material is covered, the course may be taken for credit more than once.

306 REGIONAL AND AREA STUDIES   1 to 9 sem. hrs.

An intensive study of particular lands, environments, cultures, and peoples. May be given in cooperation with other departments, on or off campus. The areas to be studied, participating departments, and credit hours available in the several departments, will be announced each time the course is offered.

310 SEVENTEENTH CENTURY AMERICA 3 sem. hrs.

Establishment and development of the American Colonies, from Jamestown to the end of the 17th Century. Special emphasis is given to Puritan New England. Prerequisite: History 231.

311 AGE OF THE AMERICAN REVOLUTION 3 sem. hrs.

The emergence of the United States as an independent nation, from 1763 to the Constitutional Convention of 1787. Prerequisite: History 234.

313 THE AGE OF JACKSON 3 sem. hrs.

A survey of the awakening of American nationalism as typified by the economic, political, and social and cultural changes of the Jacksonian Period. Prerequisite: History 233.

317 THE UNITED STATES AND THE TWENTIETH CENTURY I 3 sem. hrs.

The history of the United States from the turn of the century to 1932. Subjects to be examined are Populism, Imperialism, Progressivism, World War I, Era of Normalcy, and the Great Depression.

318 THE UNITED STATES AND THE TWENTIETH CENTURY II 3 sem. hrs.

The history of the United States from 1933 to the present. Subjects to be examined are New Deal, Isolationism, World War II, Cold War, Fair Deal, and problems confronting our contemporary society.

320 LINCOLN: THE MAN AND HIS TIMES 2 sem. hrs.

Emphasis on the use of biography and collections of Lincoln materials, both private and public. Attention directed especially toward the work of Lincoln in Illinois, his leadership during the Civil War, and his relationships with men and events of his time.

321 HISTORY OF AMERICAN DIPLOMACY TO 1898 3 sem. hrs.

The history of the diplomatic activities of the American government from the Revolution to 1898.

322 HISTORY OF AMERICAN DIPLOMACY SINCE 1898 3 sem. hrs.

The history of the diplomatic activities of the American government since 1898 to the present.

323 AMERICAN CULTURAL AND INTELLECTUAL HISTORY I 3 sem. hrs.

American progress in the fine arts, philosophy, literature and science from Puritan times to 1860.

324 AMERICAN CULTURAL AND INTELLECTUAL HISTORY II 3 sem. hrs.

The impact of naturalism, industrialization, secularization, and urbanization upon American culture since 1860.

325 CONSTITUTIONAL HISTORY OF THE UNITED STATES TO 1865
3 sem. hrs.

The history of American constitutional development from European backgrounds to Reconstruction.

326 CONSTITUTIONAL HISTORY OF THE UNITED STATES SINCE 1865
3 sem. hrs.

The history of American Constitutional development from Reconstruction to the present.

330 THE ANTE-BELLUM SOUTH 3 sem. hrs.

Characteristics of and institutions of the South from colonial times to the Civil War. Emphasis on physical, social, economic, and ideological factors.

331 HISTORY OF THE MISSISSIPPI VALLEY 3 sem. hrs.

Study in regionalism. Emphasis on the frontier, population movements, natural resources, and unique economic, political and social development.

340 EUROPEAN ECONOMIC HISTORY 3 sem. hrs.

Evaluation of Capitalism, corporations, business cycles, trade, imperialism, industry, labor movements, land tenure and other economic aspects of Western civilization viewed sequentially from ancient times to the present; comparative analysis of the dynamic process of growth as related to the specific sectors in various countries. Prerequisite: Economics 171.

341 EUROPEAN INTELLECTUAL HISTORY TO 1600 3 sem. hrs.

The study of the ideas of the ancient world, Middle Ages, Renaissance Reformation, examined in a social, political and economic context.

342 EUROPEAN INTELLECTUAL HISTORY SINCE 1600 3 sem. hrs.

A study of the ideas of the scientific revolution, enlightenment, nineteenth century, and twentieth century, examined in a social, political, and economic context.

344 EUROPE IN THE 19TH CENTURY: 1815-1914 3 sem. hrs.

Liberalism, nationalism, democracy, militarism, imperialism, and the forces that led to World War I.

347 CONTEMPORARY WORLD HISTORY 3 sem. hrs.

An investigation of the forces of change in the contemporary world. The causes and nature of W.W. I, W.W. II, and the Cold War; Communism, Fascism; impact of industrialization, science, and liberalism; emergence of new nations in Asia and Africa.

352 THE HELLENISTIC WORLD 3 sem. hrs.

A comprehensive study of the world bequeathed by Alexander the Great from his death in 323 B.C. to the founding of the Roman Empire in 30 B.C.

354 ECONOMIC AND SOCIAL HISTORY OF THE MIDDLE AGES 3 sem. hrs.

Medieval agriculture, trade, industry, and towns.

355 INTELLECTUAL AND CULTURAL HISTORY OF MIDDLE AGES 3 sem. hrs.

A study of the intellectual, spiritual, and cultural developments of medieval civilization from late Roman times until the Renaissance. Special attention is focused on the medieval Latin Christian world, primarily, and in the Islamic and Byzantine worlds, secondly.

360 TUDOR-STUART ENGLAND, 1485-1689 3 sem. hrs.

General survey of English history from the beginning of the Tudor dynasty to the Revolution of 1688-89; emphasis is placed on constitutional development, the Church, and overseas expansion.

362 MODERN BRITAIN, 1815 TO THE PRESENT 3 sem. hrs.

A general survey of British history in the nineteenth and twentieth centuries.

363 MODERN FRANCE 3 sem. hrs.

A survey of the major political, economic, and cultural developments in France from 1815 to the present, with special emphasis on France's position in world affairs.

364 MODERN GERMANY, 1848 TO THE PRESENT 3 sem. hrs.
An analysis of the importance of social, political, and economic factors during the Empire, the Weimar Republic, and the National Socialist Era; and a survey of the background of German unification, and of the period following 1945 in East and West Germany.

366 SOVIET RUSSIA, 1917 TO THE PRESENT 3 sem. hrs.
An evaluation of the origins and rise of Bolshevik power, concentrating on those aspects of economic, cultural, and social developments that transformed the USSR into a great power.

380 HISTORY OF THE MIDDLE EAST I 3 sem. hrs.
A political, cultural, social and economic survey of the Middle East from Muhammed to the Ottoman Empire, with emphasis on the origins, development and achievements of the Islamic Age.

381 HISTORY OF THE MIDDLE EAST II 3 sem. hrs.
A political, cultural, social and economic survey of the Middle East from the Ottoman Empire to the present, with emphasis on the decay of Islamic civilization and the rise of nationalism in the modern Middle East.

401 SEMINAR IN EUROPEAN HISTORY 3 sem. hrs.
Emphasizes methods and materials of research, and the writing of research papers. General area of study investigated in the seminar will vary each semester according to the special competence of the instructor and the research materials available. Provided different material is studied, the course may be taken for credit more than once.

402 SEMINAR IN AMERICAN HISTORY 3 sem. hrs.

411 SEMINAR: EIGHTEENTH CENTURY AMERICA 3 sem. hrs.

413 SEMINAR: THE COMING OF THE CIVIL WAR 3 sem. hrs.

414 SEMINAR: CIVIL WAR AND RECONSTRUCTION 3 sem. hrs.

417 SEMINAR: TWENTIETH CENTURY AMERICA 3 sem. hrs.

421 SEMINAR: MAKERS OF AMERICAN HISTORY 3 sem. hrs.

422 HISTORY OF AMERICAN AGRICULTURE 3 sem. hrs.
American agriculture from colonial times to the present. Emphasis on changing farm patterns, efforts to solve production problems, farm organizations and governmental policies.

423 SEMINAR: AMERICAN ECONOMIC HISTORY 3 sem. hrs.

424 SEMINAR IN AMERICAN CULTURAL AND INTELLECTUAL HISTORY 3 sem. hrs.

426 SEMINAR IN AMERICAN CONSTITUTIONAL HISTORY 1607-1865 3 sem. hrs.

431 SEMINAR: THE OLD NORTHWEST, 1840-1880 3 sem. hrs.

432 RESEARCH PROBLEMS IN LOCAL HISTORY 3 sem. hrs.
Intensive study of a problem connected with the political, cultural, and social development of Illinois. For advanced students.

443 READINGS IN HISTORY   1-3 sem. hrs.

For the student in residence who, for approved reasons, cannot fit a specific course into his graduate program. The consent of the student's academic adviser is required.

444 SEMINAR: EIGHTEENTH CENTURY BRITAIN   3 sem. hrs.

463 SEMINAR IN MODERN FRANCE   3 sem. hrs.

491 INTERNSHIP-SEMINAR IN COLLEGE TEACHING IN HISTORY
3 sem. hrs.

Credit for the course is given in Education (see Education 491).

497 RESEARCH SEMINAR   1-6 sem. hrs.

Introduction to bibliography, methods of scholarly research and the critical evaluation of research in the field. Must be taken by first year graduate students unless the department requires Education 475. May be repeated by more advanced students who desire direction and constructive criticism as they pursue special research problems.

499 INDEPENDENT RESEARCH FOR THE MASTER'S THESIS   1-6 sem. hrs.

A student electing the thesis option must take from four to six hours of 499. A proposal for research must be on file before registration for this course is approved by the student's adviser. While registration beyond six hours may be permitted for the convenience of the student, he may not count more than a total of six hours of 499 among the 32 required for the master's degree.

Home Economics

Acting Chairman of the Department: Blossom Johnson.   Office: Turner Hall 134

Teaching Staff: J. James, B. Johnson, J. Karch.

The department offers work leading to the following degrees: M.A., M.S., M.S. in Ed. University requirements for the master's degree are listed elsewhere in this catalog.

COURSES

301 EVALUATION IN HOME ECONOMICS   2 sem. hrs.

Examination of various concepts of evaluation and basic principles involved. Study of methods and techniques. Opportunity to work on individual problems.

304 CURRICULUM DEVELOPMENT IN HOME ECONOMICS   3 sem. hrs.

Principles of curriculum development as applied to home economics. Attention given to organization, methods, materials, and evaluation in relation to types of program and age level. Opportunity to work on individual or group problems.

313 FOOD CUSTOMS AROUND THE WORLD   2 sem. hrs.

An appreciation course considering the food customs of other nations and how they have influenced American meal patterns. Includes laboratory preparation.

316 FOOD INVESTIGATION   3 sem. hrs.

An experimental approach to principles underlying food preparation. Prerequisite: Home Economics 111 or 113.

320 DEMONSTRATION TECHNIQUES 2 sem. hrs.

Development of techniques and standards for demonstrations in the various areas of home economics. Individual and team demonstrations. Prerequisite: Home Economics 113.

322 PROBLEMS IN CLOTHING 3 sem. hrs.

Individual investigation and reports of problems in the field of clothing. Prerequisite: Home Economics 124 or consent of the instructor.

323 ADVANCED TEXTILES 2 sem. hrs.

Survey of recent developments in the textile field, particularly the man-made fibers and their products. Attention is given to the textile market situation's significance to the consumers. Prerequisite: Home Economics 120.

324 ADVANCED COSTUME DESIGN AND DRAPING 3 sem. hrs.

Theory of design development through the application of the draping technique. Garment designs are created and interpreted by draping on a dress form. Dress form may be constructed as a part of the course. Prerequisite: Home Economics 124 or consent of the instructor.

401 SUPERVISION OF STUDENT TEACHING IN HOME ECONOMICS 3 sem. hrs.

Critical survey of the objectives of the student teaching program; responsibilities of the supervising teacher, and techniques of supervision. Practical experience in the preparation of supervisory materials.

402 SEMINAR IN HOME ECONOMICS 2 sem. hrs.

Critical investigation of recent literature in the field of home economics and evaluation of pertinent research studies.

406 HOUSEHOLD EQUIPMENT 2 sem. hrs.

Equipment for the modern home and home economics laboratory. Group and individual experiences with various types of labor-saving equipment.

408 FAMILY AND CHILD DEVELOPMENT 3 sem. hrs.

Fundamental and current problems regarding the child and the family. Students will obtain practice in problem solving and committee projects.

409 RECENT TRENDS IN HOME ECONOMICS 2 sem. hrs.

Developments in the field as reflected in more recent practices, survey of methods and materials being used, and review of current professional literature.

410 FAMILY HOUSING PROBLEMS 3 sem. hrs.

Current trends and problems in housing with emphasis on family living as related to aesthetic, social, economic, and managerial aspects.

412 ADVANCED HOME MANAGEMENT 3 sem. hrs.

Planning, directing, and coordinating material and human resources in the home. Experiences are provided which enable students to know and use principles basic to modern household processes. Prerequisite: Home Economics 236.

414 SPECIAL PROBLEMS: CLOTHING 3 sem. hrs.

Individual advanced work on specific problems. May include work on several different problems or a more intensive study in one special phase of clothing.

416 ADVANCED PROBLEMS IN FOOD INVESTIGATION 3 sem. hrs.

Experimental study of foods and food preparation. Opportunity for individual and small group investigations.

418 SELECTION OF PROCESSED FOODS 2 sem. hrs.

Appraisal of processed foods to determine practical utilization of various types. Reports and discussion will be supplemented by field trips and comparative studies in the laboratory. Prerequisite: Home Economics 113.

420 ADVANCED NUTRITION 3 sem. hrs.

Current nutrition research as applied to improved dietary planning. Prerequisites: Home Economics 106, 113; Physical Sciences 110.

422 HISTORY OF COSTUME 3 sem. hrs.

The development of costume through the ages as an expression of social, economic, and cultural life of the time.

424 SELECTED PROBLEMS IN HOME ECONOMICS 1-6 sem. hrs.

May be chosen by the student for investigation in any of the areas of home economics. Approval by the instructor and the head of the department is required. A student may enroll in the course more than once if there is no duplication of material.

426 ADVANCED TAILORING 3 sem. hrs.

Various tailoring techniques. Students tailor garments selected to provide a variety of experiences using those techniques that insure a well-made professional product.

491 INTERNSHIP-SEMINAR IN COLLEGE TEACHING IN HOME ECONOMICS 3 sem. hrs.

Credit for this course is given in Education (see Education 491).

499 INDEPENDENT RESEARCH FOR THE MASTER'S THESIS 1-6 sem. hrs.

A student electing the thesis option must take from four to six hours of 499. A proposal for research must be on file before registration for this course is approved by the student's adviser. While registration beyond six hours may be permitted for the convenience of the student, he may not count more than a total of six hours of 499 among the 32 required for the master's degree.

Industrial Technology

Chairman of the Department: Joe E. Talkington   Office: Turner Hall 136

Teaching Staff: W. Ashbrook, C. Bell, R. Blomgren, J. Johnston, F. Kagy, F. Kenel, C. Porter, J. Talkington, E. Wiseman, W. Zook.

The department offers work leading to the following degrees: M.A., M.S., M.S. in Ed. University requirements for master's degrees are listed elsewhere in this catalog.

COURSES

300 CONTEMPORARY INDUSTRIAL EDUCATION 2 sem. hrs.

Prominent leaders and analysis of trends in industrial education.

301 INDUSTRIAL ARTS IN THE ELEMENTARY SCHOOL 2 sem. hrs.

Educational principles underlying industrial arts and their application in the elementary activity program.

302 EVALUATION TECHNIQUES IN THE PRACTICAL ARTS AND OCCUPATIONAL EDUCATION 3 sem. hrs.

Historical background of measurement; examination of objectives and methods; evaluation of student abilities and growth; evaluation of facilities and equipment.

303 PRINCIPLES OF GENERAL SHOP ORGANIZATION 2 sem. hrs.
Organizing and teaching procedures in the multiple-activity shop.

304 OCCUPATIONAL AND JOB ANALYSIS 3 sem. hrs.
Techniques and procedures for analyzing occupations and jobs for instructional purposes.

305 IMPROVEMENT OF INSTRUCTION IN THE PRACTICAL ARTS AND OCCUPATIONAL EDUCATION 3 sem. hrs.
Objectives, content, and techniques for improving teaching.

306 PART-TIME COOPERATIVE EDUCATION 3 sem. hrs.
Designed to acquaint the prospective coordinator with the nature and procedures involved in organizing and operating effective programs in this phase of vocational education.

331 MACHINE SHOP TECHNOLOGY III 4 sem. hrs.
Advanced machine shop technology and practice, including problems in machine design and construction through the use of various steels and castings. Includes set-up computations, project designs and development, technical reports, production setups on the turret lathe, and numerical control machine programing. Prerequisite: Industrial Technology 231, or consent of instructor.

346 INDUSTRIAL ELECTRONICS 3 sem. hrs. (Formerly 246)
Types, operation, and characteristics of selected, special purpose electron tubes and semiconductors and their associated circuits in non-communication applications. Laboratory practice in assembly, testing, and analysis of representative industrial electronic circuits. Prerequisite: Industrial Technology 242, or 244.

361 MOTOR VEHICLE DIAGNOSIS 3 sem. hrs.
Motor vehicle systems diagnosis. Laboratory experiences accent electrical and fuel systems testing with some consideration of mechanical systems testing. Prerequisite: Industrial Technology 261 or 262.

371 ALCOHOL AND ACCIDENT PHENOMENON 3 sem. hrs.
An extensive investigation of the effects of alcohol and its relationship to accident causation and occurrence. The psychological, physiological, and pharmacological actions of alcohol will be treated in the view of medical, sociological, religious, and economical aspects of society.

373 AGRICULTURAL ACCIDENT PREVENTION 3 sem. hrs.
The study of accident prevention and the need for such training in Agriculture; major areas of emphasis to include theories of accident causation and prevention applicable to agricultural accidents.

374 METHODS AND MATERIALS OF TEACHING DRIVER EDUCATION 3 sem. hrs.
Materials and measures appropriate for driver education. Development of teaching units, student evaluation procedures peculiar to driver education. Laboratory experience includes programing and teaching beginning drivers in traffic simulators, behind-the-wheel, on the street, and in the classroom. Prerequisite: Industrial Technology 375 or 377, or consent of the instructor.

375 TRAFFIC ENFORCEMENT 2 sem. hrs.
An intensive survey of the courts, the Division of Motor Vehicle Administration and Enforcement, dealing with the organization and administration of these divisions and specialized areas of accident investigation, court functions and procedures, qualifications and standards for court personnel, driver licensing, safety and financial re-

sponsibility laws, and driver improvement. Prerequisite: Industrial Technology 172 or concurrent enrollment.

376 PROBLEMS AND RESEARCH IN DRIVER EDUCATION   3 sem. hrs.

Overview of problems confronting persons in this field and major research findings applicable to this area. Emphasis is given to gaining a better understanding of research data planning for greater utilization of research findings in both school and community traffic safety endeavors. Prerequisite: Industrial Technology 273 or concurrent enrollment.

377 TRAFFIC ENGINEERING   2 sem. hrs.

An investigation of the traffic engineering function relating to the cost of financing road systems. Acquisition of right-of-way, highway geometric design, collection, analysis, and interpretation of accident records, and other data needed to bring about the modification of existing physical features necessary to reduce accidents, to alleviate congestion within an area, and to plan for future needs within a community. Prerequisite: Industrial Technology 172 or concurrent enrollment.

378 DISASTER PREPAREDNESS   3 sem. hrs.

A course to prepare individuals to organize, direct and coordinate disaster services in schools, industry and local government. In addition, students will receive training in shelter management and radiological monitoring that meets the guidelines established by the office of Civil Defense/Office of the Secretary of the Army.

386 TECHNICAL COMPUTER PROGRAMING   3 sem. hrs. (Formerly 306)

A study of digital computer systems, the programing of digital computers, and the use of a computer to solve problems related to applied science and technology (Laboratory arranged).

401 FOUNDATIONS OF INDUSTRIAL EDUCATION   3 sem. hrs.

Underlying movements and philosophies which have influenced the development of industrial education.

402 ORGANIZATION AND ADMINISTRATION OF THE PRACTICAL ARTS AND OCCUPATIONAL EDUCATION   3 sem. hrs.

Consideration of the problems confronting the teacher and administrator and the basis for their solution.

403 SEMINAR IN INDUSTRIAL TECHNOLOGY   2 sem. hrs.

Consideration of problems in industrial technology and accident prevention which are of greatest concern to the group and to the individual student. May be repeated for credit up to six hours.

404 SPECIAL PROJECTS IN INDUSTRIAL TECHNOLOGY   1-3 sem. hrs.

Individual investigation of one or more selected areas of industrial technology or accident prevention. Some laboratory work may be done. Provided different subject matter is covered, the course may be taken more than once, but no more than six semester hours of cumulative credit may be earned. Prerequisite: Filing a plan of study with adviser and consent of the department chairman during the session prior to enrollment.

405 PHILOSOPHY OF THE PRACTICAL ARTS AND OCCUPATIONAL EDUCATION   3 sem. hrs.

Philosophy and principles upon which the practical arts and occupational education are based. Intended to serve administrators and teachers, especially teachers of the practical arts and occupational subjects.

470 CONCEPTUAL MODELS OF ACCIDENT PREVENTION 4 sem. hrs.

Approaches employed in the study of accident causation and prevention. Special emphasis on human factors, man-machine relations, and those factors which influence or impair machine-human functions that result in systems failure.

490 EXTERNSHIP: INDUSTRIAL TECHNOLOGY/ACCIDENT PREVENTION 3-8 sem. hrs.

Work with business and industrial firms, or governmental agencies in administrative positions. Primary experiences to be at mid-management level in dealing with problems of production, technical sales and services, personnel, systems and program planning. Experiences determined on the basis of student needs to be confirmed two (2) months prior to assignment by the department head with a copy filed in the office of the Dean of the Graduate School.

491 INTERNSHIP-SEMINAR IN COLLEGE TEACHING IN INDUSTRIAL EDUCATION 3 sem. hrs.

Credit for the course is given in Education (see Education 491).

499 INDEPENDENT RESEARCH FOR THE MASTER'S THESIS 1-6 sem. hrs.

A student electing the thesis option must take from four to six hours of 499. A proposal for research must be on file before registration for this course is approved by the student's adviser. While registration beyond six hours may be permitted for the convenience of the student, he may not count more than a total of six hours of 499 among the 32 required for the master's degree.

Latin

(See Foreign Languages)

Mathematics

Head of the Department: Clyde T. McCormick.   Office: Stevenson Hall 313

Teaching Staff: K. Berk, D. Bey, F. Brown, L. Brown, R. Crumley, L. Eggan, D. F. Fox, K. Ha, A. Insel, T. Laetsch, C. McCormick, P. O'Daffer, A. Otto, K. Retzer, H. Schmidt, Jr., C. Vanden Eynden.

The Department of Mathematics offers graduate work leading to the degrees of Master of Science and Master of Arts. Each student must meet the general University requirements for the degree he seeks, and he must meet the following departmental requirements: (1) Of the 32 semester hours required for the degree, at least 24 must be in approved courses in mathematics, and at least 12 of these in 400 level courses. The remaining 8 hours may be taken in mathematics or, with the approval of the Head of the Mathematics Department, students may elect 8 hours in an outside minor. (2) Two basic year sequences chosen from 312-313, 315-316, 347-348, 350-351 are required. Students are expected to meet at least half of this requirement on the undergraduate level. (3) All candidates for the degree of Master of Science or Master of Arts in Mathematics must pass a comprehensive examination over at least three areas in mathematics which are included on the current list approved by the Head of the Department, and in one other area, which may be within the department or in a minor field. A thesis is optional.

Students wishing to meet requirements for the secondary or college teaching programs should plan their programs accordingly with their advisers.

The Master of Science in Education degree may be elected by students meeting the undergraduate and graduate requirements listed on pages 18, 19.

COURSES

301 MATHEMATICAL TOPICS FOR ELEMENTARY TEACHERS 3 sem. hrs.

Significant problems, points of view, and trends in the teaching of arithmetic. Investigation of research related to organization, content, and techniques in this field. May not be used to satisfy the requirements for a major, comprehensive major, minor, or a graduate degree in mathematics. Prerequisite: Mathematics 201 or consent of instructor.

302 MATHEMATICAL TOPICS FOR JUNIOR HIGH TEACHERS 2 sem. hrs.

Significant problems, points of view, and trends in the teaching of junior high school mathematics. Discussion of the implication of logic and foundations of mathematics for the teaching of selected topics in junior high school mathematics. May not be used to satisfy the requirements for a major, comprehensive major, minor, or a graduate degree in mathematics. Prerequisite: Mathematics 201 or 202 or teaching experience.

306 SET THEORY 3 sem. hrs.

Elementary logic; set algebra; relations and functions; axioms for set theory; equivalence; ordinals and cardinals. Prerequisite: Mathematics 116 or 175.

308 MATRIX THEORY 2 sem. hrs.

Computational theory of matrices; matrix operations; inversion; solution to linear systems; eigenvalues and eigenvectors. Prerequisite: Mathematics 116 or 175.

310 NUMBER THEORY 3 sem. hrs.

Development of the number system; repeating decimals; congruences; Diophantine equations; continued fractions; nonlinear congruences; quadratic residues. Prerequisite: Mathematics 116 or 175.

312 HIGHER GEOMETRY I 3 sem. hrs.

Geometric transformations; groups of transformations; invariants; transformations on the Euclidean plane, including motions, similarities, affine transformations and projections. Prerequisite: Mathematics 116 or 136.

313 HIGHER GEOMETRY II 3 sem. hrs.

Topological transformations on the Euclidean plane; the projective plane; synthetic and analytic projective geometry; projective conics. Prerequisite: Mathematics 312.

315 INTRODUCTION TO ABSTRACT ALGEBRA I 3 sem. hrs.

Sets and mappings; groups; homomorphisms; quotient groups; the Sylow theorems; rings and ideals; fields; Euclidean rings. Prerequisite: Mathematics 116 or 175.

316 INTRODUCTION TO ABSTRACT ALGEBRA II 3 sem. hrs.

Polynomials; vector spaces; extension fields; the beginnings of Galois theory; matrices; the theorems of Wedderburn or Frobenius. Prerequisite: Mathematics 315.

317 LINEAR ALGEBRA 3 sem. hrs.

Vector spaces, linear transformations, dual space, inner product spaces, eigenvalues and eigenvectors, rational and Jordan canonical forms, self-adjoint, unitary and normal operators, quadratic and bilinear forms. Prerequisite: Mathematics 175 or 251 or consent of the Head of the Department.

320 HISTORY OF MATHEMATICS 2 sem. hrs.

Development of mathematics in the area of number, form, directness, continuity and application. Some emphasis on recent developments in mathematics. Prerequisite: Mathematics 116 or 136.

323 MATHEMATICS FOR THE SECONDARY SCHOOL 3 sem. hrs.

Current issues in the teaching and learning of mathematics. Problems and points of view in the selection and placement of topics of secondary mathematics. Use of language and symbolism. Analysis of experimental programs, recent trends, and practices in the classroom. Prerequisite: Mathematics 116, 136, or 302.

325 FINITE MATHEMATICAL STRUCTURES 2 sem. hrs.

Methods of proof; finite algebra; partition and counting; stochastic processes; matrix algebra; theory of games and linear programming; application to behavioral science problems. Prerequisite: Mathematics 116 or 175.

335 ADVANCED CALCULUS I 3 sem. hrs.

Differential calculus of functions of several variables; vector differential calculus; integral calculus of functions of several variables; vector integral calculus; infinite series. Prerequisite: Mathematics 116 or 176.

336 ADVANCED CALCULUS II 3 sem. hrs.

Applications of differential calculus; Taylor's series of several variables; transformation of coordinates, maxima and minima. Integral calculus of functions of several variables; line integrals, surface integrals, change of variables of integrals. Vector fields; differential operations, divergence theorem; Green's and Stokes' theorem. Prerequisite: Mathematics 335.

340 DIFFERENTIAL EQUATIONS I 3 sem. hrs.

First order ordinary differential equations; linear differential equations; existence theorems and numerical methods of solution. Use of analog computers. Prerequisite: Mathematics 116 or 176.

341 DIFFERENTIAL EQUATIONS II 3 sem. hrs.

Theory of linear equations, proof of basic existence and uniqueness theorem, dependence of solutions on initial conditions, Sturm theory, Sturm-Liouville problems, orthogonality, Fourier series, non-linear equations. Prerequisite: Mathematics 340.

345 VECTOR ANALYSIS 2 sem. hrs.

The dot and cross product; vector differentiation; gradiant, divergence, and curl; vector integration; the divergence theorem, Stokes' theorem, and related integral theorems; curvilinear coordinates. Prerequisite: Mathematics 116 or 176.

347 INTRODUCTION TO REAL ANALYSIS I 3 sem. hrs.

Sequences and series of real numbers; continuity; metric space topology; the Riemann Integral; the fundamental theorems of calculus. Prerequisite: Mathematics 116 or 176.

348 INTRODUCTION TO REAL ANALYSIS II 3 sem. hrs.

The elementary functions; sequences and series of functions; the Lebesgue Integral. Fourier Series. Prerequisite: Mathematics 347.

349 COMPLEX ANALYSIS I 3 sem. hrs.

Fundamentals of analytic function theory: the complex number plane; differentiability and analyticity; Cauchy's theorem and its implications; sequence and series including Taylor series and Laurent series. Prerequisite: Mathematics 335 or 347.

350 MATHEMATICAL STATISTICS I 3 sem. hrs.

Sample spaces and random variables; frequency functions; linear functions of random variables; nature of statistical functions; moment generating function and application to standard frequency functions. Prerequisite: Mathematics 116 or 136.

351 MATHEMATICAL STATISTICS II 3 sem. hrs.

Correlation and regression equations; development of Chi-square; student's t and F distributions; likelihood ratio tests; analysis of variance and nonparametric methods. Prerequisite: Mathematics 350.

365 MATHEMATICAL LOGIC 3 sem. hrs.

Propositional calculus; independence; many-valued logics; interpretations; satisfiability and truth; first-order theories; consistency and completeness theorems. Prerequisite: Mathematics 116 or 175.

366 BOOLEAN ALGEBRA AND LOGICAL DESIGN 3 sem. hrs.

Switching circuits; Boolean algebra as a model for propositional calculus; use of diagrams as an aid to logical design; logical design of digital computers; experience with logical programming. Prerequisite: Mathematics 116 or 175.

368 PRINCIPLES OF DIGITAL COMPUTERS 3 sem. hrs.

Fundamental concepts of assembly languages; experience in writing assembler programs and subprograms and running them on the IBM 360. Prerequisite: Mathematics 116; knowledge of programming in a compiler language.

370 NUMERICAL ANALYSIS 3 sem. hrs.

Interpolation and approximation; error analysis; integration; techniques for solving differential equations; Newton's method; matrix manipulation. Prerequisites: Mathematics 116 or 176, and knowledge of FORTRAN programing, Mathematics 251 or 308 recommended.

375 INTRODUCTION TO TOPOLOGY 3 sem. hrs.

Topology of metric spaces, introduction to general topological spaces, and other topics. Prerequisite: Mathematics 116 or 176.

390 INDEPENDENT STUDY 1 to 3 sem. hrs.

Intensive work in a special area of mathematics based on the student's written outline or prospectus. Each individual project is to culminate in a comprehensive written report and/or examination. Open only to students who have demonstrated ability to profit from independent study. A maximum of six hours of credit in independent study may be applied toward graduation. Prerequisite: Permission of the instructor and head of the department.

407 ABSTRACT ALGEBRA I 3 sem. hrs.

Group theory, Galois theory, rings, ideals, modules, chain and structure theorems. Prerequisite: Mathematics 316 or consent of instructor.

408 ABSTRACT ALGEBRA II 3 sem. hrs.

Field and ring theory, the basics of representation theory and homological algebra. Prerequisite: Mathematics 407 or consent of instructor.

410 NUMBER THEORY 3 sem. hrs.

A continuation of Mathematics 310. Additional topics including Pell's equation, continued fractions. Diophantine approximation. Prerequisite: Mathematics 310.

412 PROJECTIVE GEOMETRY 3 sem. hrs.

Emphasis on fundamentals common to all geometry. Topics include a study of invariance under a variety of transformations giving rise to projective, affine and metric geometries. Use is made of homogeneous point and line coordinates in n—dimensional space. Prerequisite: Mathematics 313.

415 THEORY OF GROUPS 3 sem. hrs.

Semigroups and groups; homomorphisms; products; finite abelian groups; Sylow's theorems; solvable groups; nilpotent groups; Prerequisite: Mathematics 408 or consent of instructor.

416 THEORY OF RINGS 3 sem. hrs.

Rings: Ideals and Homomorphisms; subdirect sums; rings of linear transformations; the density theorem; the Jacobson radical. Prerequisite: Mathematics 408 or consent of instructor.

421 TOPICS IN ALGEBRA FOR TEACHERS 3 sem. hrs.

Problems in the teaching of secondary school algebra. Investigation of reports, research, and recent trends in this area. Opportunity for study of particular problems of individual interest. Prerequisite: Mathematics 175, 251, or 315.

422 TOPICS IN GEOMETRY FOR TEACHERS 3 sem. hrs.

Problems in the teaching of secondary school geometry. Investigation of reports, research, and recent trends in this area. Special emphasis is given to the objectives and content of secondary school geometry. Opportunity for the study of particular problems of individual interest. Prerequisite: Mathematics 211 or 312.

440 DIFFERENTIAL EQUATIONS III 3 sem. hrs.

Theory of linear and nonlinear systems; Picard Lindeloff and Peano existence theorems, extension of solutions, oscillation and comparison theorems; asymptotic behavior. Prerequisite: Mathematics 341 or consent of instructor.

441 DIFFERENTIAL EQUATIONS IV 3 sem. hrs.

Stability, Lyapunov functions, perturbation theory. Poincare-Bendixson theory, periodic solutions. Prerequisite: Mathematics 440.

445 DIFFERENTIAL GEOMETRY 3 sem. hrs.

The theories of curves and surfaces in three-dimensional Euclidean space; local intrinsic and non-intrinsic properties of a surface; differential geometry in the large; differential geometry of n— dimensional space; tensor analysis; Riemannian geometry. Prerequisite: Consent of instructor.

446 FUNCTIONAL ANALYSIS 3 sem. hrs.

Normed and Banach spaces along with metric spaces; inner product spaces and Hilbert spaces; spectral theory. Prerequisites: A course in linear algebra and Mathematics 348.

447 REAL ANALYSIS I 3 sem. hrs.

A review of the Riemann-Stieltjes integral and the Lebesgue integral for bounded functions; the general Lebesgue integral; functions of bounded variation and absolute continuity; introduction to general measure and integration theory. Prerequisite: Mathematics 348.

448 REAL ANALYSIS II 3 sem. hrs.

A continuation of Mathematics 447. Lp spaces; general measure and integration theory. Prerequisite: Mathematics 447.

449 COMPLEX ANALYSIS II 3 sem. hrs.

Application of the elementary theory is made to the study of conformal mappings, Riemann surfaces, meromorphic functions, infinite products of holomorphic functions, and the integration of differential forms. Prerequisite: Mathematics 349.

450 FINITE SAMPLING I 3 sem. hrs.

Application and theory of sampling. Mathematical sampling: simple, stratified, and cluster. Evaluating sampling plans with respect to precision and cost. Prerequisite: Mathematics 350.

451 FINITE SAMPLING II 3 sem. hrs.

Analysis of sampling designs from numerous fields of application. Use of basic sampling theorems in the development of efficient statistical models. Prerequisite: Mathematics 450.

452 THEORY OF STATISTICS 3 sem. hrs.

Order statistics, limiting distributions, sufficient statistics in the theory of estimation noncentral distributions, likelihood ratio tests, distribution of certain quadratic forms in the analysis of variance. Prerequisite: Mathematics 351.

453 LINEAR STATISTICAL MODELS 3 sem. hrs.

Multivariate normal distribution; distribution of quadratic forms; the general linear hypothesis of full rank, regression models, analysis of variance models, and associated problems in statistical inference. Prerequisite: Mathematics 351; Mathematics 452 or consent of instructor.

455 STOCHASTIC PROCESSES 3 sem. hrs.

Sequences of events governed by probabilistic laws having applications in physics, engineering, biology, medicine, psychology, oceanography, and economics. Basic models include the Wiener and Poisson processes, renewal counting processes, Markov chains, random walks, and birth and death processes. Prerequisite: Mathematics 351.

458 THE DESIGN OF EXPERIMENTS 3 sem. hrs.

The practical application of general theorems to the problems of testing hypotheses in major fields of knowledge. The logic of planned experimentation, choice of statistical technique and analysis of data. Prerequisite: Mathematics 351.

470 GENERAL TOPOLOGY I 3 sem. hrs.

Topological spaces; uniform spaces; product and quotient spaces; separation properties and connected spaces; compact spaces. Prerequisite: Mathematics 347 or 375.

471 GENERAL TOPOLOGY II 3 sem. hrs.

A continuation of Mathematics 470. Metrizability conditions, continuity; the theory of convergence using both filters and nets; completions and compactifications. Prerequisite: Mathematics 470.

476 TOPOLOGICAL DYNAMICS 3 sem. hrs.

Dynamical systems, limit points, stability, recurrent and almost periodic motions, asymptotic trajectories. Prerequisite: Mathematics 440 or 470 or consent of instructor.

480 FOUNDATIONS OF MATHEMATICS 3 sem. hrs.

The linear continuum and the real number system; groups and their significance for the foundations; the reduction of mathematics to a logical form; the Frege-Russell thesis; calculus of propositions; intuitionism and formalism. Prerequisite: Mathematics 365 or consent of instructor.

490 SEMINAR IN MATHEMATICS 1 to 4 sem. hrs.

Topics in theoretical and applied mathematics discussed by staff and visiting lecturers; individual study and student papers. The student may enroll in the seminar for credit more than once if the subject matter is not duplicated and the total credit earned does not exceed eight semester hours. Prerequisite: Consent of instructor.

491 INTERNSHIP-SEMINAR IN COLLEGE TEACHING IN MATHEMATICS 3 sem. hrs.

Credit for the course is given in Education (see Education 491). Prerequisite: Mathematics 312, 315, 347; or consent of instructor.

499 INDEPENDENT RESEARCH FOR THE MASTER'S THESIS 1-6 sem. hrs.

A student electing the thesis option must take from four to six hours of 499. A proposal for research must be on file before registration for this course is approved by the student's adviser. While registration beyond six hours may be permitted for the convenience of the student, he may not count more than a total of six hours of 499 among the 32 required for the master's degree.

Microbiology

(See Biological Sciences)

Music

Chairman of the Department: Joseph M. Wilson.   Office: Centennial Building, East 155-B

Teaching Staff: D. Armstrong, L. Farlee, J. Ferrell, W. Kim, R. Oppelt, H. Peithman, A. Peters, D. Poultney, J. Rehm, J. Roderick, H. Rye, R. Smith, I. Spector, J. Wilson, L. Young.

The department offers work leading to the following degrees: M.A., M.M.E., M.M., and M.S. All students seeking an advanced degree in music must take placement examinations in the areas of theory, history and literature, and piano. Departmental requirements will be determined in part by the results of the placement tests, and students should check with their departmental adviser to develop their individual programs of study. Students must also have taken the music sections of the Graduate Placement Examination prior to their acceptance as candidates for the degree.

All graduate students in music will take a minimum of six semester hours as a core requirement. (Core requirements vary with respect to the specific degrees.) In addition, all graduate students will select an area of concentration consisting of a minimum of twelve semester hours. The following concentrations are available: Musicology, Theory and Composition, Performance, Music Education, and Sacred Music.

Any student wishing to take graduate applied music must audition in his specific performance area.

Thesis options include: thesis, recital, composition, comprehensive examination.

For more information regarding core requirements, concentrations, and specific degree requirements, the student should see his graduate adviser.

COURSES

301 FORM AND ANALYSIS IN MUSIC 3 sem. hrs.

Structure of classical music ranging from simpler compositions as found in piano works to more elaborate material as found in major sonatas and symphonies.

303 MODAL COUNTERPOINT 3 sem. hrs.

Study of the C clefs and church modes; practical experience through writing specie counterpoint in two and three parts; combined counterpoint in three parts; combined counterpoint in triple time, writing without cantus firmus; four-part writing. Prerequisite: successful completion of Music 104, or consent of instructor.

304 TWENTIETH CENTURY THEORY 3 sem. hrs.

Study of idiomatic intervals and scale materials; construction of chords in seconds, thirds, and fourths; added note chords, polychords; compound and mirror harmony; harmonic direction; timing and dynamics, embellishment and transformation, key centers, harmonic synthesis. Prerequisite: Music 104 or consent of instructor.

305 COMPOSITION AND FORM 3 sem. hrs.

Free composition in larger forms with opportunities for performance of original works for voices, instrumental combinations, or full orchestra.

309 ADVANCED ORCHESTRATION 3 sem. hrs.

Review of instruments: ranges, timbres, technical difficulties and limitations. Arranging for combinations of instruments, full band and orchestra. Study of problems contained in standard repertory. Special attention to problems of school band and orchestra scoring. Prerequisite: Music 209 or consent of instructor.

330 PEDAGOGY AND LITERATURE (brass, woodwind, percussion, voice, strings, piano, organ). 2 sem. hrs.

Current methods of teaching, both class and individual instruction, with emphasis on technique and a comparison of the strengths and weaknesses of various teaching procedures. Survey of important literature and composers for each medium. May be repeated for credit when subject matter varies. More than one area may be taken concurrently if subject matter varies.

351 THE OPERA 2 sem. hrs.

Historical development of the opera with emphasis on stylistic elements and trends of various periods. Study of the plots and music through recordings, piano scores, full scores, as well as live performances.

353 HYMNOLOGY 3 sem. hrs.

A study of Christian hymns from early Greek and Roman times; covers the historical periods of development including outstanding hymn writers and composers. Hymns are analyzed and studied with emphasis on their appropriate place in the church year. Various denominational hymnals are examined and evaluated.

354 SACRED MUSIC REPERTOIRE 2 sem. hrs.

Reading and evaluating choral literature of all periods covering motets, anthems, plainchant, and response for both adult and children's choir. Attention is given to organ music, instrumental music, and cantata and oratorio.

357 MUSIC BIBLIOGRAPHY 2 sem. hrs.

Introduction to methods of research. Critical examination of dictionaries, encyclopedias, catalogs and other aids to research.

358 NOTATION 2 sem. hrs.

Black notation in Medieval music: square, pre-Franconian. Tablatures and white notation in Renaissance solo and ensemble music.

361 INSTRUMENTAL TECHNIQUES 3 sem. hrs.

Problems and procedures in developing instrumental classes and organizations.

363 CHORAL TECHNIQUES 2 sem. hrs.

Clinical aspects of the chorus rehearsal, contemporary choral practices, repertorie and source material, interpretation and program building. Prerequisite: Course in conducting or practical experience.

366 TONAL MEASUREMENT 3 sem. hrs.

Physical measurement of musical tone in relation to the problems in the classroom, the rehearsal, and the performance.

371 MUSIC FOR THE EXCEPTIONAL CHILD 3 sem. hrs.

Trends in musical education for exceptional children. Techniques and materials for a functional program of singing, playing, listening, and creative activities based upon needs of the exceptional child.

377 MUSIC EDUCATION IN THE ELEMENTARY GRADES 3 sem. hrs.

An advanced course dealing with the purposes, content, materials and teaching procedures in general music classes in elementary schools and including supervisory practices, in-service workshops and curriculum planning. Designed to meet the needs of music resource persons in elementary education, elementary classroom teachers, music teachers, and music supervisors. Students must have had a prior course comparable in content to Music 277 or Music 262.

384 OPERA PRODUCTION 3 sem. hrs.

Operas and operettas including the problems of presenting high school and college productions. Members of the class participate in the production of an opera or operetta. Prerequisite: Approval of the head of the department.

402 FORM AND ANALYSIS IN MUSIC 3 sem. hrs.

Continuation of Music 301 with emphasis on harmonic structure.

404 CHROMATIC HARMONY 3 sem. hrs.

Practical experience in writing polyphonically and homophonically using various kinds of embellishments and chromatically altered tones. A major creative project is required. This may be in the form of an original composition, arrangement, or transcription.

431 APPLIED MUSIC—BRASS 1 or 2 sem. hrs.

Individual instruction on trumpet, cornet, French horn, trombone, baritone, and tuba. This course may be repeated for credit.

432 APPLIED MUSIC HARPSICHORD 1 or 2 sem. hrs.

Individual instruction on harpsichord.

433 APPLIED MUSIC—ORGAN 1 or 2 sem. hrs.

Individual instruction on organ. This course may be repeated for credit.

434 APPLIED PERCUSSION 1 or 2 sem. hrs.

Individual instruction on percussion instruments.

435 APPLIED MUSIC—PIANO 1 or 2 sem. hrs.

Individual instruction on piano. This course may be repeated for credit.

436 APPLIED MUSIC—STRINGS 1 or 2 sem. hrs.

Individual instruction in violin, viola, cello, stringed bass. This course may be repeated for credit.

437 APPLIED MUSIC—VOICE 1 or 2 sem. hrs.

Individual instruction in voice. This course may be repeated for credit.

438 APPLIED MUSIC—WOODWINDS 1 or 2 sem. hrs.

Individual instruction in flute, clarinet, oboe, bassoon, and saxophone. This course may be repeated for credit.

452 THE SYMPHONY 3 sem. hrs.

Survey of the symphony orchestra and symphonic literature from early eighteenth century to the present day. Study through recordings, orchestral scores, and piano scores.

453 SEMINAR IN MUSICOLOGY 3 sem. hrs.

Prerequisite: Music 357 or consent of instructor.

454 HISTORY OF MUSICAL INSTRUMENTS 2 sem. hrs.

Evolution of musical instruments from the origins to the present, with particular regard to music and general culture. The development of primitive, Oriental, and western instruments.

455 MUSIC IN AMERICA 3 sem. hrs.

Indigenous and borrowed influences in American music from the time of the early settlements through periods of expansion to present day activities. A background of American musical style and culture and an understanding of present trends will be developed.

456 STUDIES IN SACRED MUSIC 3 sem. hrs.

Guided discussion and observation or practice in the field of sacred music with an emphasis on current trends. Attention is given to projects in research.

460 PSYCHOLOGY OF MUSIC EDUCATION 3 sem. hrs.

Study of the psychology of music and the psychology of learning in relation to practical applications in music education.

461 SEMINAR IN MUSIC EDUCATION 3 sem. hrs.

Study of aesthetic theory and educational theory in relation to current and persistent issues in music education.

462 TESTS AND MEASUREMENTS IN MUSIC 3 sem. hrs.

Bases upon which aptitude and achievement in music have been and may be measured.

463 EXPERIMENTAL STUDIES 3 sem. hrs.

Experimental method as applied to problems of music learning, including a survey of research of music education and related areas. An individual experimental term project will be required.

464 TEACHING OF THEORY 2 sem. hrs.

Analysis of current practices in the teaching of theory; techniques of teaching theory during the regular rehearsal of performing groups, and an analysis of source material. Project: the development of a practical course in theory as it relates to the student's own teaching situation. Prerequisite: teaching experience or advanced standing in theory.

465 SENSORY INTEGRATION IN MUSIC LEARNING 2 sem. hrs.

Practical considerations necessary for the operation and use in the classroom of audio-visual aids to music learning.

468 CONDUCTING 2 sem. hrs.

Critical examination of scores with reference to tempo, phrasing, nuance, balance, timbre, and baton techniques involved. For experienced teachers.

491 INTERNSHIP-SEMINAR IN COLLEGE TEACHING IN MUSIC 3 sem. hrs.

Credit for the course is given in Education (see Education 491).

497 RESEARCH SEMINAR 3 sem. hrs.
Introduction to bibliography, methods of scholarly research and critical evaluation of research. Must be taken by first year graduate students in the secondary curriculum unless the department requires Education 475.

499 INDEPENDENT RESEARCH FOR THE MASTER'S THESIS 1-6 sem. hrs.
A student electing the thesis option must take from four to six hours of 499. A proposal for research must be on file before registration for this course is approved by the student's adviser. While registration beyond six hours may be permitted for the convenience of the student, he may not count more than a total of six hours of 499 among the 32 required for the master's degree.

Physical Education

(See Health and Physical Education)

Physics

Head of the Department: Harold J. Born.   Office: Science Building 128

Teaching Staff: H. Born, J. Crew, C. Frahm, K. Jesse, M. Luther, T. Pratt, J. Schroeer, R. Young.

MASTER'S DEGREE IN PHYSICS

The department offers work in physics leading to the following degrees: M.S., M.S. in Ed. University requirements for master's degrees are described elsewhere in this catalog.

MASTER'S DEGREE IN PHYSICAL SCIENCES

The department offers work jointly with the Department of Chemistry leading to the following degrees: M.S., M.S. in Ed. These are flexible programs, permitting a combination of the two fields. University requirements for the master's degrees are listed elsewhere in this catalog.

COURSES

300 BASIC CONCEPTS OF PHYSICS 3 sem. hrs.
Modern aspects of mechanics, heat, light, sound, electricity, and atomic physics. Designed for teachers of elementary and junior high school science with limited background in the area of physics. Not open to students who have had one semester of college laboratory physics within the past ten years, or with first or second fields in chemistry, physics, and the physical sciences. Prerequisite: Physics 100, 101, or 205, or two years of teaching experience.

301 PROBLEMS IN THE TEACHING OF HIGH SCHOOL PHYSICAL SCIENCES
 3 sem. hrs.
(Offered jointly with the Department of Chemistry)
A study of modern methods and problems confronting the teachers of Physical Science. Involves a careful study of CBA, Chem Study, PSSC, and regular high school chemistry and physics. Brief overview of the K-12 physical science program will be undertaken. For teaching majors only. Prerequisites: Ten semester hours each of physics and chemistry.

302 MUNICIPAL AND INDUSTRIAL SCIENCE 3 sem. hrs.
(Offered jointly with the Department of Chemistry)
Specific aspects of community and industrial problems. Includes trips to industries and research laboratories. Lectures and discussion periods involving related chemical and physical principles are coordinated with the field trip program. Gives a background in applied science as an enrichment for classroom teaching. Prerequisites: Twenty-two hours of physical sciences including one year of general chemistry, one year of general physics, and two 200- or 300-level courses in chemistry or physics.

305 GENERAL SCIENCE 3 sem. hrs.
(Offered jointly with the Department of Chemistry)
Objectives of general science. Selection of subject matter, tests, texts, workbooks, equipment, and supplies will be considered. For teachers qualified to teach general science in the elementary, junior high, and senior high schools.

320 MECHANICS 3 sem. hrs.
A continuation of Mechanics 220 with emphasis on accelerated coordinate systems, Lagrange's equations, rigid body motion on three dimensions, Hamilton's equations, and theory of small vibrations. Prerequisites: Physics 220 and Mathematics 340.

340 ELECTRICITY AND MAGNETISM 3 sem. hrs.
Maxwell's equations and boundary value problems, alternating currents, electronics, radiation and propagation of electromagnetic waves. Prerequisites: Physics 220, 240, and Mathematics 340.

352 MODERN PHYSICS 3 sem. hrs.
The photon, electromagnetic radiation, neutrons and nuclear forces, radio activity and its detection, nuclear reactions, elementary particles, and high energy physics. Prerequisites: Physics 252, Mathematics 340.

384 INTRODUCTION TO QUANTUM MECHANICS 3 sem. hrs.
Mathematical formulation of quantum theory and application to simple systems. Prerequisites: Physics 252 and Mathematics 340.

387 METHODS OF MATHEMATICAL PHYSICS 3 sem. hrs.
An introduction to the mathematical methods needed in advanced physics. Topics included are vector calculus, linear vector spaces, matrix algebra, and tensor analysis; orthogonal polynomials; Fourier analysis. Applications to relativity and classical physics. Prerequisites: Physics 280 and 282, or consent of instructor.

420 ADVANCED MECHANICS 3 sem. hrs.
Reference frames and their transformations; dynamics of particles and system of particles; dynamics of rigid rotators; Hamilton's principle; Lagrange's equations; introductory elasticity and fluid dynamics. Prerequisite: Physics 320.

440 ADVANCED ELECTRICITY AND MAGNETISM 3 sem. hrs.
Maxwell's equations; scalar, vector potentials; dielectrics and conductors; Maxwell's theory of the electromagnetic field. Prerequisite: Physics 340.

456 NUCLEAR PHYSICS 3 sem. hrs.
Properties of nuclei, radioactivity, nuclear interactions, nuclear models, conservation laws and symmetry principles, and elementary particles. Prerequisite: Physics 352 or 384.

460 INTRODUCTION TO SOLID STATE PHYSICS 3 sem. hrs.
Description and classification of crystals, with an explanation of their elastic, electric and magnetic, electronic and optical properties. Prerequisite: Twelve semester hours of physics numbered 200 or higher.

470 GRADUATE LABORATORY 1-3 sem. hrs.

Techniques and experiments in areas of modern physical research. May be repeated for a total of three semester hours of credit, but no more than two semester hours may be earned per registration. Prerequisite: Physics 270 or consent of instructor.

484 ADVANCED QUANTUM MECHANICS 3 sem. hrs.

A review of the revisions of classical physics made necessary by experimental evidence. Mathematical formulation of quantum mechanics and applications to the hydrogen atom and simple systems. Scattering theory. Various approximation methods including perturbation theory. Prerequisite: Physics 384.

486 THEORETICAL PHYSICS 3 sem. hrs.

Selected topics in the mathematical techniques needed for graduate physics and applications of these techniques to mechanics, electricity and magnetism, and relativity. Prerequisites: Physics 220, 240 and Mathematics 335 or consent of instructor.

491 INTERNSHIP-SEMINAR IN COLLEGE TEACHING IN PHYSICS 3 sem. hr.

Credit for the course is given in Education (see Education 491).

499 INDEPENDENT RESEARCH FOR THE MASTER'S THESIS 1-6 sem. hrs.

A student electing the thesis option must take from four to six hours of 499. A proposal for research must be on file before registration for this course is approved by the student's adviser. While registration beyond six hours may be permitted for the convenience of the student, he may not count more than a total of six hours of 499 among the 32 required for the master's degree.

Political Science

Acting Chairman of the Department: Hibbert R. Roberts.   Office: Schroeder Hall 306

Teaching Staff: A. Ebel, J. Honan, W. Kohn, F. Roberts, H. Roberts, J. Verner, H. Zeidenstein.

MASTER'S DEGREE IN POLITICAL SCIENCE

The department offers work leading to the following degrees: M.A., M.S., M.S. in Ed. Students may take either a comprehensive program, which requires courses in five sub-fields, or a thesis program which requires courses in at least three sub-fields. Detailed information about program requirements should be obtained from the department's graduate adviser.

MASTER'S DEGREE IN SOCIAL SCIENCES

The department offers work jointly with the departments of economics, history, and sociology-anthropology, leading to the following degrees; M.A., M.S., M.S. in Ed. The program is described under Social Sciences.

COURSES

306 REGIONAL AND AREA STUDIES 1-9 sem. hrs.

An intensive study of particular lands, environments, cultures, and people. May be given in cooperation with other departments, on or off campus. The areas to be studied, participating departments, and credit hours available in the several departments, will be announced each time the course is offered.

312 PUBLIC OPINION AND PROPAGANDA 3 sem. hrs.

Basic implications, modern techniques, and current machinery of communication. Control exercised by the folkways, government, business, religion, motion pictures, radio, and education. Special attention is focused on those phases of the material which are related to the work of the school. May be considered political science as well as sociology.

313 COLLECTIVE DECISION-MAKING 3 sem. hrs.

A game theoretical analysis of coalition formation and decision-making in n-person groups. The context will be legislative bodies, but the essential notions apply to international relations, labor negotiations, oligopoly, and complex organizations.

315 AMERICAN CONSTITUTIONAL LAW 3 sem. hrs.

Analysis and discussion of leading cases interpreting the United States Constitution with consideration given to the political and economic conditions underlying the decisions. Prerequisite: Political Science 105.

330 PROBLEMS OF PUBLIC ADMINISTRATION 3 sem. hrs.

Consideration of issues and problems of current interest in the field of public administration. Extensive use is made of actual case studies in administration. This course is intended to provide work for undergraduates and also to serve as an introduction to the field for graduate students without previous training in public administration.

331 PUBLIC PERSONNEL ADMINISTRATION 3 sem. hrs.

A detailed examination of the personnel process in modern government: values and personnel administration; the merit system; personnel procedures, such as recruitment, classification, pay, promotion, collective negotiation, employee protection; organization of the personnel agency; human relations in public administration.

341 BRITISH GOVERNMENT 3 sem. hrs.

Intensive study of the structure and function of the government of Britain and its political processes.

342 SOVIET GOVERNMENT AND POLITICS 3 sem. hrs.

Study of the government of the Soviet Union, the theory and practice of Communism, and its impact on the modern world.

343 LATIN AMERICAN POLITICS 3 sem. hrs.

An introduction to the politics and government of Latin America with an emphasis on political-socio-economic developments and special problems associated with developments; analysis of political institutions using selected republics as primary examples.

363 AMERICAN POLITICAL THOUGHT 2 sem. hrs.

A survey of major political thinkers and statesmen who have contributed to the development of American political thought and institutions from the colonial period to the present.

380 POLITICAL DEVELOPMENT AND NATION-BUILDING 3 sem. hrs.

A comparative analysis of traditional and modern political systems featuring efforts to explain and describe the processes of change.

392 POLITICAL SYSTEMS: THEORY AND PRACTICE 2-3 sem. hrs.

The origin, theory, and practice of constitutional democracies and of totalitarian regimes. The democratic challenge to dictatorships. The autocratic challenge to constitutionalism. Provided different material is covered, the course may be taken for credit more than once.

397 INTRODUCTION TO RESEARCH 3 sem. hrs.

An introduction to the epistemological, methodological, statistical, and empirical problems of research in political science. Emphasis is placed on the empirical behavioral methods of analyzing political-social phenomena.

411 SELECTED STUDIES IN AMERICAN GOVERNMENT 3 sem. hrs.

National, state, and local governments. Will vary from one semester to another according to the interests and needs of students and availability of instructors. Provided different material is covered, the course may be taken for credit more than once.

414 SEMINAR IN THE AMERICAN PRESIDENCY 3 sem. hrs.

Prerequisite: Political Science 397 or 497 or comparable course in empirical research in the social sciences.

421 SEMINAR IN STATE AND LOCAL POLITICS 3 sem. hrs.

422 URBAN PROBLEMS 3 sem. hrs.

The politics of urban problems. Analysis of these problems, evaluation of policies currently being implemented and various solutions which have been proposed.

431 SEMINAR IN PUBLIC ADMINISTRATION 3 sem. hrs.

Advanced study for graduate students interested in special research projects in the field of public administration. Provided different material is covered, the course may be taken for credit more than once. Admission to seminar by consent of the instructor.

441 SELECTED STUDIES IN FOREIGN GOVERNMENTS AND INTERNATIONAL ORGANIZATIONS 3 sem. hrs.

Intensive study of particular national or international systems and structures. The general field covered in this course will vary according to the interests and needs of the students and the availability of instructors. Provided different material is covered, the course may be taken for credit more than once.

461 POLITICAL THOUGHT 3 sem. hrs.

Intensive study of some of the most important authors of political ideas—Plato, Aristotle, Machiavelli, Hobbes, Locke, Montesquieu, Rousseau, Jefferson, Marx, Mill. Their impact on our modern world.

490 READINGS IN POLITICAL SCIENCE 1-3 sem. hrs.

A course for the graduate student who would benefit more from a specialized independent type of study adapted to his background and needs. To be taken by permission of the head of the department and the instructor involved.

491 INTERNSHIP-SEMINAR IN COLLEGE TEACHING IN POLITICAL SCIENCE 3 sem. hrs.

Credit for the course is given in Education (see Education 491).

497 RESEARCH SEMINAR 1-6 sem. hrs.

Introduction to bibliography, methods of scholarly research and the critical evaluation of research in the field. Must be taken by first year graduate students unless the department requires Education 475. May be repeated by more advanced students who desire direction and constructive criticism as they pursue special research problems.

499 INDEPENDENT RESEARCH FOR THE MASTER'S THESIS 1-6 sem. hrs.

A student electing the thesis option must take from four to six hours of 499. A proposal for research must be on file before registration for this course is approved by the student's adviser. While registration beyond six hours may be permitted for the convenience of the student, he may not count more than a total of six hours of 499 among the 32 required for the master's degree.

Psychology

Chairman of the Department: Walter H. Friedhoff.   Office: 225 N. University

Teaching Staff: C. Berger, R. E. Brown, V. Cashen, P. Chesebro, H. Clark, R. Crist, E. Fitzpatrick, W. Friedhoff, W. Gnagey, A. Grupe, R. Hogan, F. Holmes, S. Hutter, I. Jacks, J. Johnson, J. Kirchner, K. Leicht, E. Lemke, M. Lewis, D. Livers, Jr., S. Marzolf, G. McCoy, Jr., R. Meyering, S. Murrell, G. Ramseyer, R. Rumery, H. Tiedeman, W. Vernon, M. Williams.

The department offers the M.A., M.S., and M.S. in Ed. degrees in School Psychology and the M.A. and M.S. in Psychology. Requirements for the master's program are as follows:

PSYCHOLOGY

The following courses are required for a master's degree in Psychology: Psychology 361, 363, 418, 440, 334. Additional courses are selected on the basis of recommendations of the student's adviser. Students majoring in Psychology may select particular sequences of courses leading to an area of concentration if they desire. Course offerings allow for concentration in General-Experimental (Human Learning), Measurement in the Behavioral Sciences, Counseling (Especially for those students interested in working in junior and senior colleges), and Student Personnel Work in higher education. University requirements for the master's degree are listed elsewhere in this catalog.

SCHOOL PSYCHOLOGY

The following courses are required for the master's degree in School Psychology: 334, 347, 361, 363, 418, 420, 421, 432, 433, 436, and 440. (The State of Illinois requires that students wishing to be certified as school psychologists complete the following requirements: 56 semester hours of psychology at the undergraduate and graduate level, a masters degree in psychology or educational psychology and a one year internship.) Depending on the student's background, other courses may be required for the masters degree.

COURSES

301 DEVELOPMENTAL PSYCHOLOGY I 3 sem. hrs.

Study of available research on the motor, mental, and emotional development; growth of understanding; personality of children during pre-adolescence. Prerequisite: Psychology 111.

302 DEVELOPMENTAL PSYCHOLOGY II 3 sem. hrs.

Study of the available research on the motor, mental and emotional development and personality of the adolescent. Prerequisite: Psychology 111.

320 HISTORY AND SYSTEMS OF PSYCHOLOGY 3 sem. hrs.

A survey of the historical antecedents of modern psychology, beginning with Aristotle. Examination of modern psychology from a systemic point of view. Prerequisite: Twelve semester hours of psychology.

330 EXPERIMENTAL PSYCHOLOGY I 3 sem. hrs.

Simple experiments in the psychological laboratory to give appreciation of the problems of control in the scientific study of behavior. Two lectures and one laboratory period per week plus additional laboratory assignments. Prerequisite: Psychology 111.

331 EXPERIMENTAL PSYCHOLOGY II 3 sem. hrs.

Lectures, demonstrations and laboratory experiments dealing with methodology, results, and interpretation of human and animal behaviors with emphasis on sensory processes, perception, and learning. Prerequisite: Psychology 340 or concurrent registration.

333 EXPERIMENTAL ANALYSIS OF BEHAVIOR 3 sem. hrs.

A survey of factors influencing various behavior patterns, emphasizing the literature of laboratory experimentation with both human and animal subjects. Prerequisite: Psychology 111.

334 PSYCHOLOGICAL MEASUREMENT 3 sem. hrs.

Selection, interpretation and evaluation of psychological tests, with emphasis on theory at a beginning level. Selection and evaluation criteria and methods of scoring are considered with respect to use of tests as indicators of psychological constructs and/or use in specific decision situations. Meets the requirements for psychological testing for students in special education. Prerequisite: Psychology 111.

340 STATISTICS I 3 sem. hrs.

Basic statistics used in education and the behavioral sciences. Intensive study of frequency distributions, measures of central tendency and dispersion, and standard scores. Sampling error theory, simple hypothesis testing, correlation techniques, and regression analysis are also covered. The emphasis is on application and interpretation. Prerequisite: Psychology 111 or Sociology 106.

346 PSYCHOLOGY OF EXCEPTIONAL CHILDREN 2 sem. hrs.

The study of children who deviate markedly above or below the norms of their groups in reference to one or several intellectual, emotional, physical, or social attributes, or any combination of these, so as to create a special problem in regard to their education, development, or behavior. Emphasis is placed on the implications for educational and treatment programs. Prerequisites: Psychology 232 and 331.

347 BEHAVIOR DISORDERS IN CHILDREN 3 sem. hrs.

Medical, psychological, sociological aspects of behavioral disorders of children. Prerequisite: Psychology 115 or Education 102.

348 MENTAL RETARDATION 3 sem. hrs.

Medical, psychological and sociological characteristics and behavior of the mentally retarded. Methods of classification, causes, and rehabilitative aspects. Prerequisite: Psychology 115 or Education 102.

350 PSYCHOPATHOLOGY 3 sem. hrs.

Psychological aspects of the behavior disorders, including study of the neuroses, psychoses, character disorders, mental deficiencies, and other psychopathological conditions. Prerequisite: Twelve semester hours of Psychology.

360 LEARNING 3 sem. hrs.

Experimental data bearing on the problem of human learning; learning theory; learning data and theory in relation to the problems of the teacher. Prerequisite: Psychology 111.

361 PERCEPTION 3 sem. hrs.

Cognitive processes and their relationship to other processes. The relationship of sensation, attention, and memory to perception and the factors which influence perception. Prerequisite: Nine semester hours of Psychology.

362 COMPARATIVE PSYCHOLOGY 3 sem. hrs.

The study, analysis, and investigation of the relationships among different species with regard to their behavior, emotions, and mental processes. Prerequisite: Nine semester hours of Psychology.

363 PHYSIOLOGICAL PSYCHOLOGY 3 sem. hrs.

Physiological and biochemical factors which underlie the behavior of organisms and the mechanisms which mediate between the impinging of stimuli upon the organism and the effect of the organism upon the environment. Prerequisite: Nine semester hours of Psychology.

364 MOTIVATION 3 sem. hrs.

Experimental study of drives, social motives, theories of motivation, practical applications. Prerequisite: Nine semester hours of Psychology.

416 ADVANCED EDUCATIONAL PSYCHOLOGY 3 sem. hrs.

A consideration of topics such as learning, retention and forgetting, transfer of training, reading, individual differences, intelligence, language, social class influences on education and mental hygiene in the classroom. Emphasis is placed on the application of psychology to education. Prerequisite: Psychology 115 or Education 102.

418 THEORIES OF LEARNING 3 sem. hrs.

A consideration of the major contemporary learning theories and their relationship to experimental data. Prerequisite: Psychology 330 or 360.

420 THEORIES OF PERSONALITY 3 sem. hrs.

Analysis of major theoretical formulations concerning personality with emphasis upon their current status and evidential bases.

421 BEHAVIOR MODIFICATION 3 sem. hrs.

Techniques for changing behavior through manipulation of environment. General principles of conditioning plus their application to patterns of problem behavior. Prerequisite: Graduate standing in Psychology.

422 PRACTICUM: BEHAVIOR MODIFICATION 3 sem. hrs.

Use of conditioning techniques under controlled conditions with students personally disturbed by minor behavior problems. Emphasis will also be given to establishing methods for assessing the effectiveness of the techniques employed. Prerequisite: Psychology 421.

432 PSYCHODIAGNOSTICS I 3 sem. hrs.

Training in individual mental testing with emphasis on the Binet and the Wechsler. Prerequisite: Psychology 350 or concurrent registration.

433 PSYCHODIAGNOSTICS II 3 sem. hrs.

Theory of projective methods and development of competence in the use of selected procedures. Prerequisite: Psychology 432.

434 PSYCHODIAGNOSTICS III 3 sem. hrs.

Multi-dimensional approaches to personality assessment, with emphasis on the Rorschach test. Prerequisite: Psychology 433.

435 DIAGNOSTIC PROCEDURES 3 sem. hrs.

The use of interviews, observations and various evaluative devices for diagnostic purposes. Emphasis is on the development of hypotheses. Interest is in the use of the evaluative techniques rather than the instruments themselves. Prerequisite: Graduate standing in Psychology.

436 PRACTICUM I 4 sem. hrs.

Clinical practice in the University Psychological Services and other selected agencies. Provides training in diagnosis and treatment. Fifteen hours per week. School Psychology Practicum: Prerequisites: Psychology 432 and 433 (Concurrent registration in Psychology 433 may be permitted) and consent of instructor. Clinical and Counseling Practicum: Prerequisites: Psychology 432 and 464 and consent of instructor.

437 GROUP PSYCHOTHERAPY AND COUNSELING 3 sem. hrs.

Theory and research in group dynamics, techniques of group therapy and group counseling, and methods of evaluating groups, as well as direct experiences as group members and group leaders. Prerequisites: Education 464 and consent of instructor.

438 TECHNIQUES OF OBJECTIVE PSYCHOLOGICAL ASSESSMENT 3 sem. hrs.

Clinical application of representative techniques of objective measurement in the areas of personality, interests, academic achievement, vocational and scholastic aptitude, and social attitudes. Selection, integration, and interpretation of test batteries. Practice in administration, scoring, and reporting of results will be afforded. Prerequisites: Psychology 334, and permission of instructor.

440 STATISTICS II 3 sem. hrs.

The logic of statistical inference. An examination of the statistical techniques most commonly employed in research in education and the behavioral sciences. Topics included are interval estimation, the t and f tests, *chi-square*, one factor analysis of variance, multiple regression, and non-parametric statistics. The emphasis is on application and interpretation. Prerequisite: Psychology 340.

441 EXPERIMENTAL DESIGN 3 sem. hrs.

The statistical principles of experimental design. Selection, analysis, and interpretation of the most widely employed designs are emphasized. Designs included are the simple randomized, factorial, repeated measures, randomized blocks, latin square, and analysis of covariance. Topics such as multiple comparisons, power, and trend analysis are also covered. Prerequisite: Psychology 440.

443 PSYCHOMETRICS II-CORRELATIONAL ANALYSIS 3 sem. hrs.

Theory and practice of the psychometric treatment of behavioral data. Particular attention is given to multiple predictors and criteria. Selection of these variables is approached through discussion of various data reduction models. Topics to be covered include: test theory, multiple, partial, and canonical correlation factor and component analysis. Prerequisites: Psychology 334 and 340.

444 PSYCHOMETRICS III-SCALING 3 sem. hrs.

Theory and methods of constructing scales to represent behavioral variable. Psychological scales, attitude and opinion scales and mental tests are considered within a theoretical framework for the classification of data and data collection methods. Prerequisite: Psychology 340.

450 INDEPENDENT STUDY 1-6 sem. hrs.

Independent study or investigation of topics of special interest to the individual student. Prerequisites: Formulation of a study or research plan with a faculty supervisor and the approval of the department head.

452 DIFFERENTIAL PSYCHOLOGY 3 sem. hrs.

Differences and variations in psychological characteristics among individuals and groups. Effects of various factors in creating individual or group differences. Prerequisite: Psychology 334.

464 THEORIES AND TECHNIQUES OF COUNSELING 3 sem. hrs.

Goals, methods and procedures as seen from a number of differing theoretical positions. Emphasis on interpersonal dimensions of counseling interviews. Case material illustrating applications in a variety of counseling situations—schools, community, college and university, focusing on problems of personal-social, educational, and vocational adjustment.

465 VOCATIONAL COUNSELING 2 sem. hrs.

Acquiring and using occupational and educational information. Consideration of job requirements and training opportunities; developing occupational units; nature of vocational development.

480 SEMINAR IN PSYCHOLOGY 2-3 sem. hrs.

Prerequisite: Permission of the instructor.

481 COMMUNITY MENTAL HEALTH 3 sem. hrs.

The study of social systems as they affect individual mental health. Conceptual models, typical programs, methods of analyzing communities, and methods for designing community mental health programs. Prerequisite: Psychology 350.

491 INTERNSHIP-SEMINAR IN COLLEGE TEACHING OF PSYCHOLOGY
3 sem. hrs.

Credit for this course is given in Education (see Education 491).

499 INDEPENDENT RESEARCH FOR THE MASTER'S THESIS 1-6 sem. hrs.

A student electing the thesis option must take from four to six hours of 499. A proposal for research must be on file before registration for this course is approved by the student's adviser. While registration beyond six hours may be permitted for the convenience of the student, he may not count more than a total of six hours of 499 among the 32 required for the master's degree.

Social Sciences

Adviser: Benjamin J. Keeley.   Office: Schroeder Hall 420

MASTER'S DEGREE IN THE SOCIAL SCIENCES

This program is offered jointly with the Departments of Economics, History, Political Science, and Sociology-Anthropology, leading to the following degrees: M.A., M.S., M.S. in Ed. This interdisciplinary program *requires* a minimum of 32 semester hours of course work with at least 14 hours and a thesis in one of the four social science departments. In addition, a minimum of 8 semester hours of course work must be taken in one of the other four departments. Course work, however, may be taken in all four. University requirements for a master's degree are listed elsewhere in this catalog. For the courses offered for this degree see the departments of Economics, History, Political Science, and Sociology-Anthropology.

Sociology-Anthropology

Chairman of the Department: Shailer Thomas.   Office: Schroeder Hall 363

Teaching Staff: P. Baker, D. Eaton, S. Grupp, L. Huang, E. Jelks, B. Keeley, M. Moran, V. Pohlmann, M. Pratt, R. Schmitt, S. Thomas, R. Walsh.

MASTER'S DEGREE IN SOCIOLOGY

The department offers work leading to the following degrees in sociology: M.A., M.S., M.S. in Ed. The 32 hours of graduate work includes five hours of Thesis. Specific course requirements are Sociology 466 (Seminar in Sociological Theory), Sociology 497 (Seminar in Sociological Research), and three hours of Statistics at either the 300 or 400 level. University requirements for the master's degree are listed elsewhere in this catalog.

MASTER'S DEGREE IN SOCIAL SCIENCES

The department offers work jointly with the departments of economics, history, and political science, leading to the following degrees: M.A., M.S., M.S. in Ed. The program is described above.

COURSES IN ANTHROPOLOGY

306 REGIONAL AND AREA STUDIES   1-9 sem. hrs.

An intensive study of particular lands, environments, cultures, and peoples. May be given in cooperation with other departments, on or off campus. The areas to be studied, participating departments, and credit hours available in the several departments, will be announced each time the course is offered.

382 THE AMERICAN INDIAN   3 sem. hrs.

Analysis of the social, economic, religious, and artistic developments of various representative American Indian societies. Environmental and historical factors shaping these ways of life; particular attention to Indians as they are today—their reservation cultures, the federal policies toward them, and their future prospects. Prerequisite: Anthropology 281 or permission of instructor.

383 SELECTED STUDIES IN THE CULTURES OF AREAS   3 sem. hrs.

Concentrated study of cultural patterns of selected areas. Introduction to the physical characteristics and history of the aboriginal peoples and study of their social, political, and intellectual life. An analysis of the dynamics of culture change together with the human problems resulting from these changes. Prerequisite: Anthropology 281.

384 SELECTED STUDIES IN ANTHROPOLOGY   3 sem. hrs.

The field of study will vary each semester according to the needs and interests of the students and the availability of instructors. Provided different material is covered, the course may be taken for credit more than once. Prerequisite: Permission of instructor.

COURSES IN SOCIOLOGY

312 PUBLIC OPINION AND PROPAGANDA   3 sem. hrs.

The study of public opinion as a part of the communication process. The formation, properties, and distribution of public opinion. Includes attitude formation, psychological processes, opinion change, mass media, measurement. Attention given to the relation of public opinion to the political decision-making process. May be considered as political science or sociology. Prerequisite: Sociology 106 or Political Science 105.

323 CHILD WELFARE SERVICES   3 sem. hrs.

Examination of policies, personnel, facilities, and practices for the care of dependent, neglected, delinquent, physically-handicapped, and mentally-retarded children. Consideration given to adoptive procedures, foster-home placements, probation, parole, and vocational placements. Prerequisite: Introduction to Social Work 221 or Special Education major.

332 SMALL GROUPS   3 sem. hrs.

Study of the structure and functioning of small human groups. Special attention to conditions affecting interaction in small groups, the small group as an ongoing social system, and products of interaction in a small group. Limited research project. Prerequisite: Sociology 131 or other introductory course in Social Psychology.

340 STATISTICS I   3 sem. hrs.

Basic statistics used in education and the behavioral sciences. Intensive study of frequency distributions, measures of central tendency and dispersion, and standard scores. Sampling error theory, simple hypothesis testing, correlation techniques, and regression analysis are also covered. The emphasis is on application and interpretation. Prerequisite: Sociology 106 or Psychology 111.

365 JUVENILE DELINQUENCY   3 sem. hrs.

Delinquency as a social and legal problem; theories of delinquency, causation; the juvenile court; prevention and treatment. Prerequisite: Sociology 263.

366 CONTEMPORARY SOCIAL MOVEMENTS   2 sem. hrs.

Analysis of social unrest as indicative of social disorganization; patterns of collective behavior; structure and functions of social movements. An examination of various types of social movements—religious, political, revolutionary, youth, agrarian, and reform. Analysis of morale, strategy, types of leaders, and control mechanisms. Prerequisite: Sociology 106.

367 CRIMINOLOGY   3 sem. hrs.

Criminological theory and practice. Crime as a social and legal problem. Problems in the administration of justice. Prerequisite: Sociology 263.

369 SELECTED STUDIES IN SOCIOLOGY   3 sem. hrs.

The field of study will vary each semester according to the needs and interests of students and the availability of instructors. Provided different material is covered, the course may be taken for credit more than once. Prerequisite: Consent of the instructor.

370 HISTORY OF SOCIOLOGICAL THOUGHT   3 sem. hrs.

Analysis and appraisal of classical works in sociology from Comte to the early twentieth century. Such men as Weber, Durkheim and Marx will be discussed. Prerequisite: Sociology 106.

371 INTRODUCTION TO SOCIOLOGICAL RESEARCH   3 sem. hrs.

A one-semester introduction to sociological research focusing on the convergence of theory and research in sociology; the design of inquiry conceptualization and measurement of social variable, collection of data, analysis and interpretation of data. Emphasis is upon the survey design. Individual and collective research projects form a part of the course. Prerequisite: Sociology 106 or Political Science 105.

410 SOCIOLOGY OF URBAN AREAS   3 sem. hrs.

Analysis of current theory and research in urban sociology; application to current issues in urban areas.

431 ADVANCED SOCIAL PSYCHOLOGY 3 sem. hrs.

Intensive study of a major sub-area of social psychology. Socialization, social role theory, self theory, collective behavior, attitude formation and measurement.

440 STATISTICS II 3 sem. hrs.

The logic of statistical inference. An examination of the statistical techniques most commonly employed in research in education and the behavioral sciences. Topics included are interval estimation, the t and f tests, *chi-square*, one factor analysis of variance, multiple regression, and non-parametric statistics. The emphasis is on application and interpretation. Prerequisite: Sociology 340.

441 EXPERIMENTAL DESIGN 3 sem. hrs.

The statistical principles of experimental design. Selection, analysis, and interpretation of the most widely employed designs are emphasized. Designs included are simple randomized, factorial, repeated measures, randomized blocks, latin square, and analysis of covariance. Topics such as multiple comparisons, power, and trend analysis are also covered. Prerequisite: Sociology 440.

461 READINGS IN SOCIOLOGY AND ANTHROPOLOGY 1-3 sem. hrs.

A course for the graduate student who would benefit more from a specialized independent type of study adapted to his background and needs. To be taken by permission of the head of the department and the instructor involved.

465 SOCIOLOGY OF FORMAL ORGANIZATIONS 3 sem. hrs.

Analysis of the theory of social groups with special emphasis on formal, complex, and bureaucratic organizations; emergence of informal patterns.

466 SOCIOLOGICAL THEORY 3 sem. hrs.

An analysis of recent theoretical developments in sociology. Attention will focus on a variety of social theories found useful in explaining social phenomena.

467 SOCIOLOGY OF LAW 3 sem. hrs.

Law as a socio-legal institution. Theory of law, functions of law, law as a control measure. Prerequisite: Sociology 367.

469 SEMINAR IN SOCIOLOGY 3 sem. hrs.

Advanced study for graduate students interested in developing theoretical models or in special research topics in sociology. Provided different material is covered, the course may be taken for credit more than once.

491 INTERNSHIP-SEMINAR IN COLLEGE TEACHING IN SOCIOLOGY-ANTHROPOLOGY 3 sem. hrs.

Credit for the course is given in Education (see Education 491).

497 RESEARCH SEMINAR 1-6 sem. hrs.

Introduction to bibliography, methods of scholarly research and the critical evaluation of research in the field. Must be taken by first year graduate students unless the department requires Education 475. May be repeated by more advanced students who desire direction and constructive criticism as they pursue special research problems.

499 INDEPENDENT RESEARCH FOR THE MASTER'S THESIS 1-6 sem. hrs.

A student electing the thesis option must take from four to six hours of 499. A proposal for research must be on file before registration for this course is approved by the student's adviser. While registration beyond six hours may be permitted for the convenience of the student, he may not count more than a total of six hours of 499 among the 32 required for the master's degree.

Spanish

(See Foreign Languages)

Special Education

(See Education)

Speech

Acting Chairman of the Department: Martin A. Young   Office: Centennial Building, East 286

Teaching Staff: E. Andreasen, G. B. Barber, R. Brake, B. Cronin, G. Cronkhite, D. Eckelmann, R. Foreman, R. Hauseman, W. Hodgson, C. Howard, B. Hutchinson, T. Jackson, J. Kirk, R. Lane, J. McCroskey, C. Pritner, S. Rives, J. Scharfenberg, R. Smith, G. Soderberg, G. Taylor, S. Vargo, C. White, M. Young.

The department offers work leading to the following degrees: M.A., M.S., M.S. in Ed. Students may plan programs with an emphasis in drama, in rhetoric and public address, in audiology, or in speech pathology.

The candidate for the master's degree in audiology or speech pathology must meet the academic requirements for the American Speech and Hearing Association for clinical competency. If he also desires certification for the public schools in Illinois, he must also meet these requirements.

University requirements for the above degrees are listed elsewhere in this catalog.

COURSES

300 HISTORY OF THE MOTION PICTURE   3 sem. hrs.

The development and appreciation of the motion picture from its beginning to the present, with emphasis upon social backgrounds and cultural-artistic values. Laboratory: screening of significant films from various periods and countries.

301 RHETORIC AND WESTERN MAN I   3 sem. hrs.

Investigation of selected historical issues as treated rhetorically by the Greeks and Romans, British, Americans, and other western peoples. Appraisal of public speeches and other rhetorical discourse and the historical conditions which gave rise to them. Oratory of wartime, the struggle for freedom, imperialism, progressivism, and socialism.

302 RHETORIC AND WESTERN MAN II   3 sem. hrs.

Investigation of selected historical issues as treated rhetorically by the Greeks and Romans, British, Americans, and other western peoples. Appraisal of public speeches and other rhetorical discourse and the historical conditions which gave rise to them. Evolution of the welfare state, foreign policy during the cold war, reform movements, higher education and social change, religious controversy.

303 CONTROVERSY AND CONTEMPORARY SOCIETY   3 sem. hrs.

A study of contemporary public speaking on current, significant, controversial issues.

304 FREEDOM OF SPEECH 3 sem. hrs.

Consideration of the nature of and limitations upon freedom of expression with attention to the problems of civil disorder, national survival, and censorship. Application of concept of free speech to current campus and community issues.

311 PHONETICS 3 sem. hrs.

Sound system of American speech and its standard and sub-standard variations. Practice in transcribing and reading phonetic symbols.

316 INTRODUCTION TO ORGANIC DISORDERS OF SPEECH 3 sem. hrs.

Speech disorders related to structural, neurological, and endocrine pathologies. Emphasis on diagnostic and remedial procedures. Approximately 20 hours of clinical participation required. Prerequisite: Speech 212 or 215.

317 SPEECH CLINIC 1-6 sem. hrs.

Diagnostic tests and methods of speech correction applied to those enrolled in the Speech and Hearing Clinic. Students enrolling in this course should have the permission of the instructor. Prerequisite: Speech 212 or 215.

318 ORGANIZATION OF THE SCHOOL SPEECH CORRECTION PROGRAM 3 sem. hrs.

Professional attitudes, ethics, and organizations. History and development of the program in the schools. Procedures for setting up and maintaining the program. Evaluation and therapy techniques and material applicable to the school setting. Relationship to school and community agencies. Prerequisite: Consent of instructor.

319 STUTTERING I 3 sem. hrs.

Introductory course in stuttering, including the nature and history of the disorder, current theories as to etiology, basic therapeutic techniques, and observations of therapy. Clinical procedures in speech stressed. Prerequisite: Speech 212 or 215 or consent of the instructor.

320 SPEECH AND LANGUAGE DEVELOPMENT 3 sem. hrs.

A comprehensive study of the acquisition of speech and language by the child with major emphasis on the first six years.

321 SPEECH COMPOSITION 3 sem. hrs.

Theory and practice in demonstrative, deliberative, and forensic address through a study of theories of style and historically significant models.

322 PROSEMINAR IN COMMUNICATION RESEARCH 3 sem. hrs.

An introduction to theory and empirical research in communication. Includes units on empirical research; methods in communication; an overview and analysis of the process of communication in general; theory and research in language behavior; the analysis of individual units of communication; and theory and research dealing with the special considerations imposed by group size, group complexity, and the available media.

323 THEORY AND RESEARCH IN SMALL GROUP PROCESSES 3 sem. hrs.

A survey of theoretical and experimental literature dealing with small group discussion processes as a means of decision-making in a free society.

324 THEORY AND RESEARCH IN PERSUASION 3 sem. hrs.

A survey of theoretical and experimental literature dealing with the question of how an individual's attitudes, beliefs, and social behavior may be affected by communication.

330 ADVANCED STAGE LIGHTING 3 sem. hrs.

The study of lighting design for complex proscenium and non-proscenium production with attention to system design. Prerequisites: Speech 135 and 136 and consent of the instructor.

333 MODERN DRAMA 3 sem. hrs.

Trends in dramatic literature and theatrical production from Ibsen to the present day. Reading reports and discussions of the plays of the leading dramatists of Europe, Great Britain, and America.

334 HISTORY AND STYLES OF STAGE COSTUMING 3 sem. hrs.

Concentrated history of costumes from the ancient Egyptian period to the present time. Emphasis on the costume's reflection of cultural and social milieu. Consideration of the costume's practical application to the stage. Laboratory to be arranged with the instructor. Prerequisite: Speech 134.

335 HISTORY OF THE THEATRE 3 sem. hrs.

Background for the study and production of plays including the reading of great plays of different historical periods, a study of the manner in which they were produced, and their relation to the cultural life of the time.

336 PROBLEMS IN ACTING 3 sem. hrs.

Introduction to and practice in the various advanced styles of acting prevalent in the more important periods of theatrical history and native to specific forms of comic and serious drama. Laboratory to be arranged with instructor. Course may be repeated for credit. Up to six hours credit may be applied toward a master's degree. Prerequisite: Speech 132.

337 PROBLEMS IN DIRECTING 3 sem. hrs.

Theories and techniques of directing plays of differing forms, styles and historical periods. Concentration on various aesthetic principles involved in directing. Laboratory to be arranged with instructor. Course may be repeated for credit. Up to six hours credit may be applied toward a master's degree. Prerequisites: Speech 237 and consent of instructor.

340 ADVANCED DESIGN 3 sem. hrs.

Intensive work in the areas of design and rendering for the stage, with emphasis upon new materials and techniques. Prerequisite: Speech 231.

341 ORAL INTERPRETATION OF LITERATURE II 3 sem. hrs.

The oral study of selected types of literature with emphasis upon drama and poetry; projects in organizing materials; presentation of individual and multiple reading projects. Prerequisite: Speech 141.

345 DEVELOPMENT OF MODERN THEATRE 3 sem. hrs.

Developments in stagecraft, directing, acting, and theatrical theory from the late nineteenth century to the present. Prerequisites: None except those for a 300 level course.

350 BASIC AUDIOLOGY 3 sem. hrs.

Methods of screening hearing; basic equipment and methods for the measurement of various aspects of the hearing function; causes of hearing loss; interpretation of test results. Not open to students who have taken former courses Speech 350, Audiometry and Hearing Aid Selection, or Speech 356, Conservation of Hearing.

351 SPEECH READING AND AUDITORY TRAINING 3 sem. hrs.

Principles and practices of speech reading and auditory training. Survey of traditional methods. Communication disorders arising from hearing impairment; the visual and auditory speech stimuli. The operation and use of hearing aids and auditory training equipment. Five hours of participation outside of class time required. Prerequisites: Speech 215 and 311.

352 PROFESSIONAL PRACTICE IN SPEECH READING AND AUDITORY TRAINING 1-3 sem. hrs.

Practice in providing speech reading training and auditory training for children and adults in group and individual situations. Consideration of instructional materials, equipment, and special problems of habilitation and rehabilitation for the hearing impaired. Prerequisite: Speech 351.

358 PRACTICUM IN BASIC AUDIOLOGY 1-3 sem. hrs.

Supervised clinical practice in basic procedures used in audiology. For each semester hour of credit, at least 45 clock hours of practice will be required. Prerequisite: Consent of instructor.

360 MASS COMMUNICATION IN SOCIETY 3 sem. hrs.

A study of the mass media of communication—an explanation of the several media (press, radio, television, films) emphasizing their aesthetic and communicative possibilities, social responsibilities, structure, problems of regulation and management, and educational-entertainment-commercial content.

361 THE REGULATION OF BROADCASTING 3 sem. hrs.

A study of Federal and State legislation concerning communications media in relation to the codes of practice of broadcasters with emphasis on the rights, privileges and responsibilities—ethical as well as legal—of the radio-tv industry. Prerequisite: Consent of the instructor.

362 INSTRUCTIONAL TELEVISION 3 sem. hrs.

Television as a medium of instruction: history, forms, techniques, utilization, evaluation, function in education. Prerequisite: Consent of instructor.

365 FILM THEORY AND CRITICISM 3 sem. hrs.

Comparative studies of theories relating to the art of film making; the nature of the medium; its narrative, dramatic, aesthetic and social characteristics; consideration of writings of critics, theorists, and directors. Prerequisites: Speech 300 and consent of instructor.

368 PLAYWRITING 3 sem. hrs.

Playwriting techniques of selected masters of dramaturgy, with practical application of the techniques in the writing of original plays. Both literary and professional aspects of writing for the theater will be considered. When possible, opportunity will be provided for the laboratory production of original scripts of quality in University theater-workshop projects.

370 PSYCHOLOGY OF LANGUAGE 3 sem. hrs.

A survey of theories and experimental research relating to the development and functions of language within the individual, including contributions from the fields of speech, psychology, linguistics, and communication.

371 SPEECH SCIENCE 3 sem. hrs.

Principles of physics involved in the production and reception of spoken language.

372 ANATOMY AND PHYSIOLOGY OF THE SPEECH AND HEARING MECHANISM 3 sem. hrs.

A study of the mechanism used in producing and receiving speech; the function of a normal mechanism and the effect that deviations from this may have on the end product. Prerequisite: Biological Sciences 181.

380 DIRECTED PROJECT 1-3 sem. hrs.
Individually supervised study for the advanced student who wishes to undertake a production product or to pursue a research problem. Prerequisite: Consent of instructor and area chairman. May be repeated for credit when projects vary.

381 PROBLEMS IN THE TEACHING OF SPEECH 2 sem. hrs.
Present trends in the teaching of speech and evaluation of current teaching materials.

414 VOICE AND ARTICULATION DISORDERS 3 sem. hrs.
Recent developments and research related to organic and functional disorders of voice and articulation. Prerequisites: Speech 215, Speech 311, and Speech 372 or equivalent.

415 SEMINAR IN LANGUAGE DISORDERS 2 sem. hrs.
Prerequisite: Speech 212 or 215.

417 CLINICAL PRACTICE IN SPEECH CORRECTION 1 to 6 sem. hrs.
Supervised work with speech disorders of various types. Prerequisites: Speech 212 or 215, study of phonetics and clinical services, previous clinical experience, and consent of Director of Clinic.

418 STUTTERING 3 sem. hrs.
Study of the research relating to stuttering and of methods of examination, diagnosis, and remedial procedures. Prerequisite: Speech 319.

419 APHASIA 3 sem. hrs.
This course is designed to provide the student with a knowledge of the past and current research and theory on the etiologies, diagnoses of, and therapies for aphasia in children and adults. Emphasis is on diagnostic and remedial procedures.

421 SELECTED STUDIES IN RHETORIC AND PUBLIC ADDRESS 1-3 sem. hrs.
The field of study will vary each semester according to interests and needs of students. Units include: Medieval and Renaissance rhetorical theory, British and American rhetorical theory, British public address, contemporary public address, and special problems in rhetoric and the history and criticism of public address. Provided different material is covered, the course may be taken for credit more than once.

423 THE PROCESS OF COMMUNICATION 3 sem. hrs.
A study of the process of communication as it occurs between two individuals, in small groups, in organizations, and in mass societies. The study will cover theoretical and research literature from the fields of speech, psychology, sociology, and communication.

424 SEMINAR IN PERSUASION 3 sem. hrs.
A study of special topics in persuasion. May be repeated if different material is covered. Prerequisite: Speech 324 or consent of the instructor.

425 SEMINAR IN ARGUMENTATION AND FORENSICS 2 sem. hrs.
Advanced study in argumentation and debate theory with attention to the problems of directing a forensics program.

426 CLASSICAL RHETORIC 3 sem. hrs.
Ancient rhetoricians from Corax to Quintillian, with special emphasis upon the works of Aristotle and Cicero.

427 RHETORICAL CRITICISM 3 sem. hrs.

Critical consideration of rhetorical and psychological principles involved in meeting speech situations.

431 THEATRES AND AUDITORIUMS: PLANNING AND DESIGN 3 sem. hrs.

Technical problems in stage and auditorium design and planning with special emphasis on stage, lighting, and sound equipment and control. Laboratory to be arranged with the instructor. Prerequisite: Speech 231.

435 THE BRITISH THEATRE 3 sem. hrs.

Trends in dramatic literature and theatrical productions in England from the Restoration period to the present time.

436 THE AMERICAN THEATRE 3 sem. hrs.

Development of the theatre, its dramatic literature and its arts and crafts, in America from its beginning to the present time.

438 DRAMA THEORY AND CRITICISM 3 sem. hrs.

An examination of aspects of theatre practice from the point of view of a contemporary aesthetic. The subject of investigation will change from semester to semester. Recent seminars have studied "Comedy and Tragedy" and "Existentialism in the Theatre."

439 DRAMA FORM 3 sem. hrs.

An examination of theories of drama as a basis for developing a contemporary aesthetic. Aesthetic will then be applied to the works of major contemporary dramatists.

440 SELECTED STUDIES IN DRAMA AND THEATRE 1-5 sem. hrs.

The field of study will vary each semester according to interests and needs of students. Units include: aspects of drama form and their application to modern and traditional theatre practice, drama theory and criticism, theatre history, and special problems in dramatic production.

441 DIRECTED READINGS IN SPEECH PATHOLOGY 1-3 sem. hrs.

For the student who would benefit from specialized independent study which can be adapted to his background and needs. Permission to enroll should be secured from the student's adviser and the instructor involved. May be repeated with a maximum of 3 hours credit. Prerequisite: Evidence of substantial background in speech pathology.

443 SYMPOSIUM IN AUDIOLOGY OR SPEECH PATHOLOGY 1-6 sem. hrs.

For the experienced professional person in speech pathology and/or audiology or for advanced graduate students. May be repeated up to 6 hours. Prerequisite: Consent of the director of the symposium.

444 NEUROPATHOLOGIES OF SPEECH 3 sem. hrs.

The nature and types of neuropathologies that have an effect on speech production, with particular emphasis given to cerebral palsy. Content intended to familiarize the student with evaluation and treatment of speech disorders arising from neurological impairment. Prerequisite: Speech 316 or equivalent.

445 ORO-FACIAL ANOMALIES AND ASSOCIATED SPEECH DISORDERS 2 sem. hrs.

Embryological growth and development and the etiologies, diagnostic, and habilitative procedures for cleft lip and palate and associated congenital anomalies. Prerequisites: Speech 215 and Speech 316 (Introduction to Organic Disorders of Speech) or equivalent.

450 CLINICAL EVALUATION OF HEARING 3 sem. hrs.

The rationale, application, and interpretation of advanced testing procedures; evaluation of research. Students may acquire up to approximately 50 clock hours of laboratory experience in addition to the academic requirement above. Prerequisite: Speech 350 or equivalent.

451 SEMINAR IN AUDIOLOGY 2-6 sem. hrs.

Specific topics selected by the student with approval of the instructor, or assigned topics will be explored. In general, library resources will be employed; however, some experimental procedures may be approved. The student may repeat the seminar for credit provided that the subject matter is not duplicated and the total credit earned does not exceed six semester hours.

452 COMMUNICATION DISORDERS OF THE HEARING IMPAIRED 3 sem. hrs.

The examination of the theories and principles underlying the clinical management of communication disorders resulting from and related to hearing impairment, with emphasis on speech audiometry and hearing aids. Prerequisite: Speech 350 or equivalent.

455 PATHOLOGIES OF HEARING IN CHILDREN 3 sem. hrs.

A review and study of the literature in audiology and otology of the etiology, loci, and effects of pathology in the auditory system of children. Prerequisite: Consent of the instructor.

456 AUDITORY FUNCTIONS 3 sem. hrs.

Anatomy of the ear; function of the auditory mechanism as evidenced by various methods of investigation; theories of hearing; implications from pathological conditions; anatomical and physiological. Prerequisite: Consent of the instructor.

457 PSYCHOLOGICAL IMPLICATIONS OF HEARING IMPAIRMENT 3 sem. hrs.

The effects of hearing loss on behavior, the tests of intelligence and personality suitable for use with the hearing impaired; and study of counseling for the hearing impaired as well as parents of children with hearing loss. Prerequisite: Speech 350 or equivalent.

458 PRACTICUM IN AUDIOLOGY 1-4 sem. hrs.

Supervised experience in all aspects of audiology. Emphasis in one or more aspects will be permitted to suit the objectives of the student. The student may enroll more than once if the subject matter is not duplicated and the total credit earned does not exceed six semester hours. Prerequisite: Speech 350 or similar experience.

461 SELECTED STUDIES IN RADIO AND TELEVISION 3 sem. hrs.

The field of study will vary according to student needs and interests. Areas to be considered will include broadcasting criticism, audience formation and reaction to educational and commercial broadcasting, problems posed by the media.

471 EXPERIMENTAL PHONETICS 2 sem. hrs.

Laboratory course in the study of phenomena prevailing in and accompanying the production of spoken language.

481 SEMINAR IN SPEECH EDUCATION 2 sem. hrs.

491 INTERNSHIP-SEMINAR IN COLLEGE TEACHING IN SPEECH 3 sem. hrs.

Credit for the course is given in Education (see Education 491).

497 RESEARCH SEMINAR   1-6 sem. hrs.

Introduction to bibliography, methods of scholarly research and the critical evaluation of research in the field. Must be taken by first year graduate students unless the department requires Education 475. May be repeated by more advanced students who desire direction and constructive criticism as they pursue special research problems.

499 INDEPENDENT RESEARCH FOR THE MASTER'S THESIS   1-6 sem. hrs.

A student electing the thesis option must take from four to six hours of 499. A proposal for research must be on file before registration for this course is approved by the student's adviser. While registration beyond six hours may be permitted for the convenience of the student, he may not count more than a total of six hours of 499 among the 32 required for the master's degree.

Western European Studies

Coordinator: David L. Wheeler.   Office: Hovey Hall 310

The Western European Studies program is offered by the College of Arts and Sciences and the College of Business and leads to the degree of Master of Arts. The program is designed for students who wish to pursue international careers in business or in the foreign service as well as for those who want a deeper understanding of Western European affairs. The program consists of intensive training in a modern European language and course work in business, economics, geography, history, and political science.

Zoology

(See Biological Sciences)

General Courses

389 SELECTED STUDIES   1-6 sem. hrs.

Course work not offered within the framework of existing departmental courses. The topic to be covered will be identified in the class schedule booklet each semester. Experimental courses and courses cutting across departmental lines may be offered as selected studies.

393 WORKSHOP   1-6 sem. hrs.

Advanced workshop for juniors, seniors, and graduate students. Credit will be given by the department offering the workshop.

397 INSTITUTE IN .... 1-9 sem. hrs.

Federal and state sponsored institutes or similar short term programs requiring treatment of subject matter of a special nature or for special groups.

399 ARTS AND SCIENCES MULTI-DISCIPLINARY SEMINAR   3 sem. hrs.

Intensive study in selected topics of a multi-disciplinary nature to be offered cooperatively by two or more departments.

400 INDEPENDENT STUDY 1-4 sem. hrs.

Independent work under a qualified member of the faculty, in areas not available through regular courses. Prerequisites: Permission of the faculty member, the student's adviser and the heads of the departments involved.

489 ADVANCED STUDY 1-6 sem. hrs.

Advanced course work not offered within the framework of existing departmental courses. The topic to be covered will be identified in the class schedule booklet each semester. Experimental courses and courses cutting across departmental lines may be offered as advanced studies.

The Graduate Faculty

Henry H. Adams (1965)
Head of the Department of English, Professor of English
Ph.D., Columbia University

Richard E. Allen (1963)
Associate Professor of English
Ph.D., Washington University

Robert M. Anderson (1967)
Associate Professor of Special Education
Ed.D., University of Pittsburgh

Edward A. Andreasen (1967)
Associate Professor of Theatre
M.A., Michigan State University

William D. Ashbrook (1947)
Professor of Industrial Technology
Ph.D., University of Pittsburgh

Eric Baber (1965)
Director of Research Services and Grants, Professor of Education
Ed.D., Michigan State University

Paul J. Baker (1965)
Associate Professor of Sociology
Ph.D., Duke University

G. Bradford Barber (1944)
Professor of Speech
Ph.D., Ohio State University

George Barford (1947)
Associate Professor of Art
M.A., Teachers College, Columbia University

Buford H. Bass (1951)
Associate Professor of Health and Physical Education for Men
Ed.D., Louisiana State University

Claude A. Bell (1956)
Associate Professor of Industrial Technology
Ed.D., University of Missouri

Dennis D. Bell (1968)
Assistant Dean of the College of Education, Associate Professor of Educational Administration
Ph.D., The Ohio State University

Ralph A. Bellas (1965)
Associate Professor of English
Ph.D., University of Kansas

Francis B. Belshe (1948)
Associate Dean of Faculties, Director of Summer Session, Professor of Education
Ph.D., Yale University

Charles R. Berger (1968)
Assistant Professor of Psychology
Ph.D., Michigan State University

Kenneth N. Berk (1969)
Associate Professor of Mathematics
Ph.D., University of Minnesota

Douglas R. Bey (1944)
Professor of Mathematics
Ph.D., University of Illinois

Allie Ward Billingsley (1949)
Professor of Spanish
Ph.D., University of Illinois

Dale E. Birkenholz (1962)
Professor of Ecology
Ph.D., University of Florida

Ferman Bishop (1960)
Professor of English
Ph.D., University of Wisconsin

Lawrence E. Bitcon (1965)
Associate Professor of Health and Physical Education for Men
Ed.D., University of Arkansas

Alton J. Bjork (1968)
Professor of Education
Ed.D., Teachers College, Columbia University

E. Scott Blankenship (1956)
Professor of Education
Ph.D., Ohio State University

Roger D. Blomgren (1949)
Professor of Industrial Technology
Ed.D., University of Illinois

Joseph T. Bombelles (1968)
Associate Professor of Economics
Ph.D., Case Western University

James W. Bommarito (1967)
Associate Professor of Special Education
Ed.D., Wayne State University

Arthur D. Bond (1966)
Associate Professor of Chemistry and Biological Sciences
Ph.D., University of Oregon

Richard R. Bond (1966)
Vice President of the University and Dean of Faculties, Professor of Zoology
Ph.D., University of Wisconsin

Harold J. Born (1961)
Head of the Department of Physics, Professor of Physics
Ph.D., Iowa State University

Harold E. Boyd (1965)
Assistant Professor of Art
M.F.A., University of Kansas

Samuel E. Braden (1967)
President, Professor of Economics
Ph.D., University of Wisconsin

Robert J. Brake (1968)
Associate Professor of Speech
Ph.D., Michigan State University

Paul J. Brand (1958)
Professor of Geography
Ed.D. in Geography, Teachers College, Columbia University

Benton K. Bristol (1965)
Associate Professor of Agriculture
D.Ed., The Pennsylvania State University

Herman E. Brockman (1963)
Professor of Genetics
Ph.D., Florida State University

Francis R. Brown (1949)
Director of University Extension and Field Services, Assistant Director of Summer Session, Professor of Mathematics
Ed.D., University of Illinois

Lauren E. Brown (1967)
Assistant Professor of Vertebrate Zoology
Ph.D., The University of Texas

R. Elizabeth Brown (1955)
Professor of Psychology
Ph.D., Northwestern University

Walter H. Brown (1955)
Professor of Botany
Ph.D., University of Illinois

Leonard A. Brubaker (1964)
Associate Professor of Elementary Education
Ph.D., The Ohio State University

Clinton R. Bunke (1967)
Associate Professor of Education
Ph.D., University of Iowa

Cecilia P. Bunney (1945)
Director of Museums and Professor
Ph.D., State University of Iowa

Roger K. Bunting (1966)
Associate Professor of Chemistry
Ph.D., The Pennsylvania State University

Wesley C. Calef (1970)
Professor of Geography
Ph.D., University of Chicago

George R. Canning, Jr. (1958)
Professor of English
Ph.D., University of Wisconsin

R. Jerry Cantlon (1962)
Associate Professor of Education
Ed.D., University of Colorado

Lessie Carlton (1955)
Professor of Education
Ed.D., The University of Houston

Dorothy H. Carrington (1961)
Assistant Dean of Students, Associate Professor of Psychology
Ed.D., Florida State University

Valjean M. Cashen (1961)
Professor of Psychology
Ed.D., Colorado State College

Helen M. Cavanagh (1946)
Professor of History
Ph.D., University of Chicago

Merritt M. Chambers (1966)
Visiting Professor of Educational Administration and Professional Consultant in Higher Education
Ph.D., Ohio State University

Roger J. Champagne (1960)
Chairman of the Department of History, Professor of History
Ph.D., University of Wisconsin

Robert M. Chasson (1965)
Associate Professor of Botany
Ph.D., University of Missouri

Patricia A. Chesebro (1963)
Associate Professor of Psychology
Ph.D., University of Illinois

Tsan-Iang Chuang (1967)
Assistant Professor of Botany
Ph.D., University of California at Berkeley

Faith Clark (1958)
Associate Professor of Health and Physical Education for Women
Ph.D., Florida State University

Herbert E. Clark (1966)
Associate Professor of Psychology
Ph.D., Purdue University

James E. Collie (1957)
Professor of Health and Physical Education for Men
P.E.D., Indiana University

Thomas E. Comfort (1965)
Head of the Department of Foreign Languages, Professor of French
Ph.D., University of Illinois

Arnold C. Condon (1964)
Professor of Business Education
Ph.D., New York University

Carrol B. Cox (1961)
Assistant Professor of English
Ph.D., University of Michigan

Virginia R. Crafts (1967)
Associate Professor of Health and Physical Education for Women
Ed.D., Teachers College, Columbia University

John C. Cralley (1963)
Assistant Professor of Zoology
Ph.D., University of Illinois

John E. Crew (1963)
Professor of Physics
Ph.D., University of Illinois

Robert L. Crist (1962)
Professor of Psychology
Ph.D., Purdue University

Gary L. Cronkhite (1967)
Associate Professor of Speech and Psychology
Ph.D., State University of Iowa

John H. Crotts (1968)
Associate Professor of Elementary Education
Ed.D., University of Missouri

Norton B. Crowell (1969)
Professor of English
Ph.D., Harvard University

Richard D. Crumley (1962)
Associate Professor of Mathematics
Ph.D., University of Chicago

Alfred A. Culver (1961)
Associate Professor of Agriculture
Ph.D., Purdue University

DeVerne H. Dalluge (1947)
Professor of the Teaching of Physics in University High School
Ed.D., University of Kentucky

William L. Daniel (1967)
Assistant Professor of Genetics
Ph.D., Michigan State University

Lillian S. Davies (1963)
Associate Professor of Elementary Education
Ph.D., University of Minnesota

C. Richard Decker (1968)
Assistant to the Dean of the College of Business, Acting Chairman of the Department of Business Administration, Assistant Professor of Business Administration
Ed.D., Indiana University

Richard L. Desmond (1967)
Assistant Dean of Faculties, Acting Dean of the College of Fine Arts, Associate Professor of Educational Administration
Ph.D., University of Michigan

Louise E. Dieterle (1969)
Supervisor of Off-campus Student Teaching, Professor of Education
Ed.D., Loyola University

Eleanor Dilks (1952)
Professor of Zoology
Ph.D., University of Wisconsin

Pasquale DiPasquale, Jr. (1969)
Professor of English
Ph.D., University of Pittsburgh

Paul F. Dohrmann (1961)
Professor and Supervising Teacher of Health and Physical Education in Metcalf
Ph.D., State University of Iowa

Pauline S. Drawver (1956)
Associate Professor of English
Ph.D., University of Illinois

George M. Drew, Jr. (1962)
Acting Chairman of the Department of Elementary Education, Professor of Elementary Education
Ph.D., University of Iowa

Robert L. Duncan (1961)
Associate Professor of English
Ph.D., Indiana University

Joseph T. Durham (1968)
Associate Dean of the College of Education, Professor of Education
Ed.D., Teachers College, Columbia University

Robert C. Duty (1963)
Professor of Chemistry
Ph.D., State University of Iowa

Leo E. Eastman (1954)
Chairman of the Department of Education, Professor of Education
Ed.D., University of North Dakota

Alice L. Ebel (1934)
Professor of Political Science
Ph.D., University of Illinois

Dorathy Eckelmann (1945)
Professor of Speech Pathology
Ph.D., University of Iowa

Charles W. Edwards (1964)
Associate Professor of Educational Administration
Ph.D., University of Iowa

Thomas F. Edwards (1957)
Associate Professor of Chemistry
Ed.D., Michigan State University

Elwood F. Egelston (1962)
Professor of Educational Administration
D.Ed., University of Oregon

Lawrence C. Eggan (1968)
Associate Professor of Mathematics
Ph.D., University of Oregon

Ray E. Eiben (1967)
Assistant Professor of Education
Ph.D., The Ohio State University

Alice M. Eikenberry (1945)
Professor of the Teaching of History in University High School
Ed.D., Teachers College, Columbia University

Ralph A. Elliot (1963)
Medical Director of the University Health Service, Professor
M.D., Northwestern University Medical School

Raymond W. Esworthy (1949)
Head of the Department of Accounting, Professor of Accounting
Ph.D., University of Illinois

G. Harlowe Evans (1946)
Professor of Chemistry
Ph.D., University of Michigan

John M. Ewing (1969)
Associate Professor of Elementary Education
Ed.D., The University of Nebraska

Lloyd W. Farlee (1962)
Associate Professor of Music
Ph.D., University of Iowa

Dorothy E. Fensholt (1951)
Professor of Botany
Ph.D., Northwestern University

Geraldine K. Fergen (1969)
Professor of Special Education
Ed.D., University of Missouri

A. Gordon Ferguson (1964)
Associate Professor of Spanish
Ph.D., University of Nebraska

John W. Ferrell (1961)
Professor of Music
Ph.D., State University of Iowa

Howard I. Fielding (1944)
Professor of English
Ph.D., University of Wisconsin

Kenneth L. Fitch (1963)
Associate Professor of Anatomy
Ph.D., University of Michigan

Eugene D. Fitzpatrick (1965)
Associate Professor of Psychology
Ed.D., Colorado State College of Education

D. Franklin Fox (1967)
Assistant Professor of Mathematics
Ph.D., University of Nebraska

Charles P. Frahm (1968)
Assistant Professor of Physics
Ph.D., Georgia Institute of Technology

Wolfgang F. Freese (1969)
Assistant Professor of German
Ph.D., University of Tubingen, Germany

John L. Frehn (1962)
Professor of Physiology
Ph.D., The Pennsylvania State University

Bernice G. Frey (1930)
Professor of Health and Physical Education for Women
Ph.D., University of Iowa

Ruth M. Freyberger (1951)
Professor of Art
Ed.D., The Pennsylvania State University

Walter H. Friedhoff (1958)
Chairman of the Department of Psychology, Professor of Psychology
Ph.D., State University of Iowa

William Frinsko (1961)
Professor of Elementary Education
Ed.D., Wayne State University

William D. Fuehrer (1963)
Associate Professor of the Teaching of German in University High School
Ph.D., University of Michigan

Frederick W. Fuess (1963)
Professor of Agriculture
Ph.D., Michigan State University

Vytas V. Gaigalas (1965)
Associate Professor of French
Ph.D., University of Colorado

Leo O. Garber (1967)
Professor of Educational Administration
Ph.D., University of Chicago

Harold E. Gibson (1950)
Special Assistant to the President, Director of the Bureau of Appointments, Professor of Education
Ed.D., University of Missouri

Arley F. Gillett (1944)
Head of the Department of Men's Physical Education, Health, and Athletics; Professor of Health and Physical Education for Men
P.E.D., Indiana University

Victor E. Gimmestad (1948)
Professor of English
Ph.D., University of Wisconsin

William J. Gnagey (1961)
Professor of Psychology
Ph.D., Wayne State University

Joseph L. Grabill (1968)
Associate Professor of History
Ph.D., Indiana University

Miriam Gray (1946)
Professor of Health and Physical Education for Women
Ed.D., Teachers College, Columbia University

Milton Greenberg (1969)
Dean of the College of Arts and Sciences, Professor of Political Science
Ph.D, University of Wisconsin

Ivo P. Greif (1961)
Professor of Elementary Education
Ed.D, Wayne State University

Audrey J. Grupe (1968)
Associate Professor of Psychology
Ph.D, University of Illinois

Stanley E. Grupp (1957)
Associate Professor of Sociology
Ph.D., Indiana University

Kwang-Chul Ha (1967)
Associate Professor of Mathematics
Ph.D., The University of North Carolina

Dean S. Hage (1959)
Professor of Special Education
Ph.D., State University of Iowa

Donald R. Hakala (1969)
Associate Professor of Finance
Ph.D., Indiana University

Barbara C. Hall (1957)
Professor of Health and Physical Education for Women
Ed.D., Teachers College, Columbia University

James A. Hallam (1966)
Assistant Dean of the College of Business, Associate Professor of Accounting
Ph.D., University of Iowa

Warren R. Harden (1954)
Coordinator of Academic Planning, Director of Institutional Research, Professor of Economics
Ph.D., Indiana University

Clarence W. Hardiman (1964)
Associate Professor of Physiology
Ph.D., Florida State University

Richard R. Hart (1961)
Associate Professor of Geology
Ph.D., State University of Iowa

W. Douglas Hartley (1954)
Assistant Professor of Art
M.F.A., Kansas City Art Institute

Mostafa F. Hassan (1968)
Associate Professor of Economics
Ph.D., University of Wisconsin

John M. Heissler, Jr. (1961)
Professor of English
Ph.D., University of Illinois

Arlan C. Helgeson (1951)
Dean of the Graduate School, Professor of History
Ph.D., University of Wisconsin

Robert E. Hemenway (1964)
Associate Professor of Special Education
Ed.D., Boston University School of Education

Robert P. Hendon (1967)
Associate Professor of Education
Ph.D., University of Oklahoma

Ruth Henline (1926)
Professor of English
Ph.D., Northwestern University

Henry J. Hermanowicz (1959)
Dean of the College of Education, Professor of Education
Ed.D., Teachers College, Columbia University

Howard R. Hetzel (1962)
Professor of Zoology
Ph.D., University of Washington

Charles R. Hicklin (1960)
Professor of Education
Ed.D., University of Illinois

G. Alan Hickrod (1967)
Associate Professor of Educational Administration
Ed.D., Harvard University

Jerry G. Higgins (1968)
Assistant Professor of Chemistry
Ph.D., University of Arizona

Eugene L. Hill (1930)
Professor of Health and Physical Education for Men
Ed.D., Colorado State College of Education

John S. Hill (1962)
Professor of English
Ph.D., University of Wisconsin

William R. Hodgson (1969)
Associate Professor of Speech
Ph.D., Ohio University

Robert A. Hogan (1963)
Professor of Psychology
D.Ed., Western Reserve University

Frank J. Holmes (1962)
Professor of Psychology
Ph.D., New York University

M. Paul Holsinger (1969)
Associate Professor of History
Ph.D., University of Denver

Gerlof D. Homan (1968)
Associate Professor of History
Ph.D., University of Kansas

Joseph C. Honan (1968)
Associate Professor of Political Science
Ph.D., University of Missouri

F. Louis Hoover (1944)
Professor of Art
Ed.D., New York University

Charles E. Howard (1967)
Associate Professor of Theatre
M.F.A., Carnegie Institute of Technology

Quinn L. Hrudka (1962)
Supervisor of Off-campus Student Teaching and Associate Professor of Education
Ed.D., Indiana University

Lucy Jen Huang (1967)
Associate Professor of Sociology
Ph.D., University of Chicago

Benjamin C. Hubbard (1961)
Chairman of the Department of Educational Administration, Professor of Educational Administration
Ed.D., University of Alabama

Harry W. Huizinga (1967)
Assistant Professor of Parasitology
Ph.D., The University of Connecticut

Richard E. Hulet (1956)
Vice President of the University and Dean of Student Services, Professor of Education
Ed.D., University of Illinois

Raymond H. Hunt (1965)
Associate Professor of Chemistry
Ph.D., University of Illinois

Mary M. Huser (1966)
Supervisor of Off-campus Student Teaching and Associate Professor of Education
Ed.D., University of Illinois

Barbara B. Hutchinson (1966)
Associate Professor of Speech Pathology
Ph.D., University of Utah

Virgil R. Hutton (1968)
Associate Professor of English
Ph.D., University of Michigan

Thaddeus C. Ichniowski (1961)
Professor of Chemistry
Ph.D., Purdue University

Eugene R. Irving (1969)
Associate Professor of Elementary Education
Ed.D., University of Illinois

Leslie M. Isted (1940)
Professor of Music
Ph.D., Indiana University

Irving Jacks (1968)
Associate Professor of Psychology
Ph.D., New York University

Teddy R. Jackson (1969)
Associate Professor of Speech
Ph.D., University of Wisconsin

Jeannie H. James (1959)
Associate Professor of Home Economics
D.Ed., Pennsylvania State University

Kenneth E. James (1962)
Associate Professor of Agriculture
Ed.D., University of Missouri

Edward B. Jelks (1968)
Professor of Anthropology
Ph.D., University of Texas

D. Reed Jensen (1966)
Associate Professor of Physiology
Ph.D., Utah State University

Wayne H. Jepson (1969)
Director of Allied Health Professions, Professor of Health Science
Ph.D., Stanford University

Kenneth E. Jesse (1967)
Assistant Professor of Physics
Ph.D., Arizona State University

Milford C. Jochums (1948)
Professor of English
Ph.D., University of Illinois

Blossom Johnson (1945)
Acting Chairman of the Department of Home Economics, Professor of Home Economics
Ed.D., University of Missouri

Eric H. Johnson (1958)
Vice President of the University and Dean of Administrative Services, Professor of Educational Administration
Ed.D., University of Illinois

James J. Johnson (1966)
Assistant Professor of Psychology
Ph.D., Northwestern University

John L. Johnston (1956)
Professor of Industrial Technology
Ed.D., University of Missouri

H. Twyman Jones (1967)
Assistant Professor of Education
Ed.D., University of Missouri

Margaret L. Jones (1956)
Professor of Health and Physical Education for Women
Ph.D., University of Wisconsin

Frederick D. Kagy (1965)
Professor of Industrial Technology
Ed.D., University of Wyoming

Jacqueline Q. Karch (1957)
Associate Professor of Home Economics
Ed.D., Washington University

Benjamin J. Keeley (1952)
Adviser for Social Science Majors, Professor of Sociology
Ph.D., University of Nebraska

Ellen D. Kelly (1957)
Professor of Health and Physical Education for Women
Ph.D., State University of Iowa

Francis C. Kenel (1961)
Associate Professor of Industrial Technology
Ed.D., Michigan State University

Kenneth C. Kennard (1968)
Chairman of the Department of Philosophy, Professor of Philosophy
Ph.D., Northwestern University

Betty J. Keough (1955)
Professor of Health and Physical Education for Women
Ph.D., State University of Iowa

John H. Kirchner (1964)
Associate Professor of Psychology
Ph.D., Northwestern University

John W. Kirk (1966)
Director of University Theatre, Associate Professor of Theatre
Ph.D., University of Florida

Homer T. Knight (1957)
Professor of Education
Ed.D., Teachers College, Columbia University

James V. Koch (1967)
Assistant Professor of Economics
Ph.D., Northwestern University

Robert W. Koehler (1961)
Assistant Professor of Health and Physical Education for Men
Ed.D., University of Utah

Harold F. Koepke (1934)
Professor of Management
Ph.D., University of Iowa

Frederick W. Kohlmeyer (1964)
Associate Professor of History
Ph.D., University of Minnesota

Walter S. G. Kohn (1956)
Professor of Political Science
Ph.D., New School for Social Research, New York, New York

Joe W. Kraus (1966)
Director of Libraries, Professor of Library Science
Ph.D., University of Illinois

Frederick P. Kroeger (1968)
Acting Director of Freshman English, Associate Professor of English
Ph.D., University of Michigan

Brigitta J. Kuhn (1961)
Professor of French
Ph.D., Sorbonne, University of Paris

Clarence H. Kurth (1951)
Associate Professor of Education
Ed.D., Indiana University

Michael E. Kurz (1968)
Assistant Professor of Chemistry
Ph.D., Case Institute of Technology

Theodore W. Laetsch (1968)
Assistant Professor of Mathematics
Ph.D., California Institute of Technology

Arthur H. Larsen (1935)
Distinguished Professor of Higher Education, Consultant for Institutional Studies
Ph.D., University of Wisconsin

Cecilia J. Lauby (1949)
Head of the Department of Professional Laboratory Experiences, Professor of Education
Ed.D., Indiana University

Joseph L. Laurenti (1962)
Professor of Spanish and Italian
Ph.D., University of Missouri

Ronald L. Laymon (1965)
Associate Professor of Elementary Education
Ed.D., Indiana University

Kenneth L. Leicht (1967)
Assistant Professor of Psychology
Ph.D., Northwestern University

Elmer A. Lemke (1965)
Associate Professor of Psychology
Ph.D., University of Wisconsin

Anthony E. Liberta (1961)
Professor of Mycology
Ph.D., University of Illinois

William R. Linneman (1964)
Associate Professor of English
Ph.D., University of Illinois

Harry A. Little (1964)
Associate Professor of Special Education
Ed.D., Indiana University

Robert D. Liverman (1969)
Associate Professor of Health and Physical Education for Men
Ph.D., University of Illinois

David L. Livers, Jr. (1962)
Professor of Education and Psychology
Ph.D., State University of Iowa

Harry D. Lovelass (1946)
Director of University High School, Professor of Education
Ed.D., University of Illinois

Marvin L. Luther (1966)
Associate Professor of Physics
Ph.D., Virginia Polytechnic Institute

G. Laurene Mabry (1960)
Associate Professor of Health and Physical Education for Women
Ph.D., University of Iowa

Normand W. Madore (1961)
Associate Professor of Elementary Education
Ed.D., Wayne State University

Thomas E. Malone (1969)
Assistant Professor of Art
M.S., University of Wisconsin

Henry R. Manahan (1961)
Professor of Latin
Ph.D., Northwestern University

J. Louis Martens (1947)
Professor of Botany
Ph.D., Indiana University

Jose L. Martin (1968)
Associate Professor of Spanish
Ph.D., Columbia University

Thomas B. Martin (1962)
Professor of Business Education
Ed.D., Indiana University

Stanley S. Marzolf (1937)
Distinguished Professor of Psychology
Ph.D., Ohio State University

Paul F. Mattingly (1962)
Associate Professor of Geography
Ph.D., The Pennsylvania State University

James L. McBee (1970)
Chairman of the Department of Agriculture, Professor of Agriculture
Ph.D., University of Missouri

Bernard J. McCarney (1958)
Associate Professor of Economics
Ph.D., University of Pittsburgh

Clyde T. McCormick (1944)
Head of the Department of Mathematics, Professor of Mathematics
Ph.D., Indiana University

George F. McCoy, Jr. (1962)
Professor and School Psychologist in Metcalf
Ph.D., University of Illinois

James C. McCroskey (1969)
Associate Professor of Speech
D.Ed., Pennsylvania State University

J. H. McGrath (1968)
Associate Professor of Educational Administration
Ph.D., University of Iowa

John V. Meador (1969)
Associate Professor of Finance
Ph.D., State University of Iowa

Loren W. Mentzer (1957)
Professor of Botany
Ph.D., University of Nebraska

Arthur W. Merrick (1968)
Professor of Physiology
Ph.D., University of Missouri

Ralph A. Meyering (1961)
Professor of Education and Psychology
Ph.D., State University of Iowa

E. Joan Miller (1962)
Associate Professor of Geography
Ph.D., University of North Carolina

Murray Lincoln Miller (1950)
Associate Professor of Education
Ph.D., University of Pittsburgh

Wilma H. Miller (1968)
Associate Professor of Education
Ed.D., University of Arizona

Frederick V. Mills (1968)
Chairman of the Department of Art, Professor of Art
Ed.D., Indiana University

Robert V. Mitchell (1968)
Dean of the College of Business, Professor of Business Administration
Ph.D., University of Illinois

Orrin J. Mizer (1947)
Associate Professor and Supervising Teacher of Biological Sciences in Metcalf
Ph.D., State University of Iowa

Edward L. Mockford (1960)
Professor of Entomology
Ph.D., University of Illinois

Clarence L. Moore (1961)
Professor of Agriculture
Ph.D., South Dakota State University

Robert H. Moore (1952)
Adviser of General Students, Professor of Education
Ph.D., Ohio State University

Mark R. Moran (1966)
Associate Professor of Social Work in the Department of Sociology-Anthropology
Ph.D., The Ohio State University

Lal M. Mukherjee (1969)
Associate Professor of Chemistry
Ph.D., University of Minnesota

Stanley A. Murrell (1968)
Assistant Professor of Psychology
Ph.D., University of Kansas

Mathew J. Nadakavukaren (1964)
Associate Professor of Botany and Electron Microscopy
Ph.D., Oregon State University

Helen M. Nance (1954)
Professor of Elementary Education
Ph.D., Ohio State University

Edwin E. Niemi (1958)
Associate Professor of Art
M.S., University of Wisconsin

Burton L. O'Connor (1937)
Professor of Health and Physical Education for Men
Ed.D., The Pennsylvania State University

Phares G. O'Daffer (1968)
Associate Professor of Mathematics
Ph.D., University of Illinois

Albert D. Otto (1969)
Associate Professor of Mathematics
Ph.D., State University of Iowa

Virginia S. Owen (1964)
Assistant Professor of Economics
Ph.D., University of Illinois

David J. Parent (1968)
Associate Professor of German
Ph.D., University of Cincinnati

Kelvin M. Parker (1967)
Associate Professor of Spanish
Ph.D., University of Chicago

James E. Patterson (1957)
Professor of Geography
Ph.D., University of Illinois

Harlan W. Peithman (1937)
Professor of Music
Ed.D., Teachers College, Columbia University

Ralph M. Perry (1967)
Associate Professor of French
Ph.D., University of Illinois

Warren S. Perry (1955)
Head of the Department of Business Education, Associate Professor of Business Education
Ed.D., University of Colorado

Harold R. Phelps (1958)
Chairman of the Department of Special Education, Professor of Special Education
Ph.D., Ohio State University

David D. Pittman (1966)
Associate Professor of Microbiology
Ph.D., Southern Illinois University

Mark A. Plummer (1960)
Professor of History
Ph.D., University of Kansas

Douglas Poe (1959)
Acting Head of the Department of Economics, Professor of Economics
Ph.D., Indiana University

Vernon C. Pohlmann (1955)
Professor of Sociology
Ph.D., Washington University

Charles B. Porter (1961)
Dean of the College of Applied Science and Technology, Professor of Industrial Technology
Ed.D., University of Illinois

David G. Poultney (1968)
Assistant Professor of Music
Ph.D., University of Michigan

William C. Prigge (1963)
Coordinator of Audiovisual Programs, Associate Professor of Education
Ed.D., Indiana University

Calvin L. Pritner (1966)
Associate Professor of Theatre
Ph.D., University of Illinois

Gary C. Ramseyer (1965)
Associate Professor of Psychology and Education
Ph.D., University of Iowa

Taimi M. Ranta (1959)
Professor of English
Ph.D., University of Minnesota

H. Earle Reese (1958)
Professor of Insurance
Ed.D., George Peabody College for Teachers; C.L.U.; C.P.C.U.

Earl A. Reitan (1954)
Professor of History
Ph.D., University of Illinois

Richard C. Reiter (1964)
Associate Professor of Chemistry
Ph.D., Purdue University

Max R. Rennels (1968)
Assistant Professor of Art
Ed.D., Indiana University

Vernon L. Replogle (1950)
Director of Metcalf Elementary School, Professor of Education
Ed.D., University of Illinois

Kenneth A. Retzer (1959)
Associate Professor of Mathematics
Ph.D., University of Illinois

Dent M. Rhodes (1965)
Associate Professor of Education
Ph.D., Ohio State University

E. Ione Rhymer (1954)
Professor of Bacteriology
Ph.D., University of Illinois

John H. Rich (1964)
Associate Professor of Accounting
Ed.D., Indiana University

R. Omar Rilett (1958)
Head of the Department of Biological Sciences, Professor of Biological Sciences
Ph.D., University of Wisconsin

Stanley G. Rives (1958)
American Council on Education Intern in the Office of the Dean of Faculties, Professor of Speech
Ph.D., Northwestern University

Frederick J. Roberts (1968)
Assistant Professor of Political Science
Ph.D., Princeton University

Hibbert R. Roberts (1968)
Acting Chairman of the Department of Political Science, Associate Professor of Political Science
Ph.D., University of Washington

James L. Roderick (1956)
Professor of Music
Ed.D., University of Illinois

Jose A. Rodriguez (1961)
Associate Professor of Spanish
Ph.D., Universidad de la Habana, La Havana, Cuba

Kurt K. F. Rothmann (1969)
Assistant Professor of German
Ph.D., University of Cincinnati

Robert E. Rumery (1964)
Assistant Professor of Psychology
Ph.D., University of Illinois

Bernard L. Ryder (1956)
Professor of Chemistry
Ph.D., University of Illinois

Howard H. Rye (1957)
Professor of Music
Ed.D., Teachers College, Columbia University

Theodore Sands (1950)
Associate Dean of Faculties for Special Programs, Professor of History
Ph.D., University of Wisconsin

Edward L. Schapsmeier (1966)
Associate Professor of History
Ph.D., University of Southern California

Jean Scharfenberg (1966)
Associate Professor of Theatre
Ph.D., University of Wisconsin

Else A. Schmidt (1958)
Professor of Geography
Ph.D., University of Munich, Germany

Raymond L. Schmitt (1968)
Associate Professor of Sociology
Ph.D., University of Iowa

Virginia Schnepf (1967)
Associate Professor of Elementary Education
D.Ed., University of Illinois

Jurgen M. Schroeer (1969)
Associate Professor of Physics
Ph.D., Cornell University

Keith L. Scott (1960)
Associate Dean of Administrative Services, Associate Professor of Educational Administration
Ed.D., University of Colorado

Phebe M. Scott (1966)
Acting Assistant Dean of the College of Applied Science and Technology, Chairman of the Department of Health and Physical Education for Women, Professor of Health and Physical Education for Women
Ph.D., State University of Iowa

Thomas K. Searight (1959)
Associate Professor of Geology
Ph.D., University of Illinois

Thomas G. Secoy (1968)
Associate Professor of Accounting
Ph.D., University of Illinois; C.P.A.

Mary C. Serra (1951)
Director of Reading Laboratory, Professor of Special Education
Ed.D., Temple University

Kyle C. Sessions (1967)
Associate Professor of History
Ph.D., The Ohio State University

Sol Shulman (1969)
Head of the Department of Chemistry, Professor of Chemistry
Ph.D., North Dakota State University

Stanley B. Shuman (1969)
Assistant Dean of the College of Arts and Sciences, Professor of Geography
Ph.D., University of Illinois

L. Moody Simms, Jr. (1967)
Associate Professor of History
Ph.D., University of Virginia

Edwin B. Smith (1965)
Dean of Students, Assistant Professor of Psychology
Ph.D., Kent State University

Gwen K. Smith (1946)
Professor of Health and Physical Education for Women
Ph.D., University of Iowa

Ralph L. Smith (1959)
Director of Radio and Television, Professor of Radio-Television-Film
Ph.D., University of Wisconsin

Robert C. Smith (1969)
Associate Professor of Music
Ed.D., University of Illinois

George A. Soderberg (1959)
Professor of Speech Pathology
Ph.D., Ohio State University

Irwin Spector (1948)
Professor of Music
Ph.D., New York University

Christopher Spencer (1962)
Professor of English
Ph.D., Yale University

William C. Starrett (1961)
Research Associate of Aquatic Biology
Ph.D., Iowa State University

C. Louis Steinburg (1959)
Assistant Professor of Art
M.S. in Ed., Southern Illinois University

C. Edward Streeter (1967)
Associate Professor of Education
Ph.D., Michigan State University

Hugh W. Stumbo (1969)
Associate Professor of Art
Ph.D., Ohio State University

Conrad B. Suits (1962)
Associate Professor of English
Ph.D., University of Chicago

Robert D. Sutherland (1964)
Associate Professor of English
Ph.D., State University of Iowa

Joe E. Talkington (1962)
Chairman of the Department of Industrial Technology, Associate Professor of Industrial Technology
Ed.D., Colorado State College

Patrick Tarrant (1963)
Professor of French
Ed.D., Teachers College, Columbia University

Lucy L. Tasher (1935)
Professor of History
Ph.D., University of Chicago

Glenn J. Taylor (1950)
Professor of Audiology
Ph.D., University of Southern California

Isabelle Terrill (1949)
Director of University Auditorium, Associate Professor of Music
D.Ed., Teachers College, Columbia University

Clayton F. Thomas (1964)
Professor of Educational Administration
Ph.D., University of Iowa

Shailer Thomas (1969)
Chairman of the Department of Sociology-Anthropology, Associate Professor of Sociology
Ph.D., Michigan State University

James T. Thompson (1966)
Associate Professor of Agriculture
Ph.D., University of Kentucky

Herman R. Tiedeman (1946)
Acting Director of Test Service, Professor of Psychology
Ph.D., University of Iowa

Jim N. Tone (1963)
Associate Professor of Physiology and Anatomy
Ph.D., Iowa State University

Naomi W. Towner (1965)
Assistant Professor of Art
M.F.A., Rochester Institute of Technology

John E. Trotter (1956)
Head of the Department of Geography-Geology, Professor of Geography
Ph.D., University of Chicago

Wayne O. Truex (1957)
Associate Professor of Health and Physical Education for Men
Ed.D., University of Utah

Joseph C. Tsang (1968)
Assistant Professor of Chemistry and Biological Sciences
Ph.D., University of Oklahoma

Robert T. Tussing (1968)
Associate Professor of Accounting
Ph.D., The University of Texas; C.P.A.

Charles L. Vanden Eynden (1969)
Associate Professor of Mathematics
Ph.D., University of Oregon

Steven W. Vargo (1965)
Associate Professor of Audiology
Ph.D., Indiana University

Wilbur R. Venerable (1963)
Dean of Admissions and Records, Associate Professor of Education
Ph.D., Southern Illinois University

Joel G. Verner (1967)
Assistant Professor of Political Science
M.A., University of Kansas

Walter M. Vernon (1963)
Associate Professor of Psychology
Ph.D., Washington University

Dale B. Vetter (1941)
Professor of English
Ph.D., Northwestern University

Virginia H. Vint (1967)
Associate Professor of Art
Ed.D., Stanford University

Morton D. Waimon (1961)
Professor of Education
Ed.D., Teachers College, Columbia University

Lawrence D. Walker (1969)
Associate Professor of History
Ph.D., University of California, Berkeley

Jack A. Ward (1965)
Associate Professor of Ethology
Ph.D., University of Illinois

David F. Weber (1967)
Assistant Professor of Genetics
Ph.D., Indiana University

Robert D. Weigel (1959)
Professor of Vertebrate Zoology and Paleontology
Ph.D., University of Florida

Milton E. Weisbecker (1963)
Director of Athletics, Professor of Health and Physical Education for Men
Ed.D., Syracuse University

David L. Wheeler (1961)
Associate Dean of the Graduate School, Associate Professor of Geography
Ph.D., University of Michigan

Charles A. White (1957)
Assistant to the President, Professor of Speech
Ph.D., University of Wisconsin

Ray Lewis White (1968)
Assistant Professor of English
M.A., University of Arkansas

Edwin R. Willis (1962)
Professor of Entomology
Ph.D., The Ohio State University

Joseph M. Wilson (1967)
Chairman of the Department of Music, Professor of Music
D.Ed., Teachers College, Columbia University

Emory E. Wiseman (1963)
Assistant Professor of Industrial Technology
Ed.D., University of Illinois

Harvey S. Woods (1957)
Professor of Agriculture
Ph.D., University of Illinois

William C. Woodson (1968)
Assistant Professor of English
Ph.D., University of Pennsylvania

Donna Jo Workman (1959)
Associate Professor of Health and Physical Education for Women
Ph.D., State University of Iowa

Lyle M. Young (1952)
Professor of Music
Ed.D., Columbia University

Martin A. Young (1968)
Acting Chairman of the Department of Speech, Director of Speech Pathology and Audiology and Director of the Speech and Hearing Clinic, Professor of Speech
Ph.D., University of Iowa

Robert D. Young (1967)
Assistant Professor of Physics
Ph.D., Purdue University

Harvey G. Zeidenstein (1965)
Associate Professor of Political Science
Ph.D., New York University

William D. Zeller (1963)
Professor of Education
Ph.D., Michigan State University

Herman L. Zimmermann (1967)
Assistant Professor of Latin
Ph.D., St. Louis University

Wayne H. Zook (1968)
Assistant Professor of Industrial Technology
Ph.D., Iowa State University

ASSOCIATE MEMBERS OF THE GRADUATE FACULTY

Donald J. Armstrong (1966)
Assistant Professor of Music
D.M.A., University of Texas

William N. Blake (1968)
Assistant Professor of Education
Ph.D., University of Alberta, Canada

Lynn H. Brown (1960)
Assistant Professor of Mathematics
Ph.D., The University of Iowa

James D. Clemmons (1967)
Supervisor of Off-campus Student Teaching, Assistant Professor of Education
Ph.D., Southern Illinois University

Barry J. Cronin (1968)
Assistant Professor of Radio-Television-Film
Ph.D., University of Missouri

L. Dale Cruse (1967)
Assistant Professor of Health and Physical Education for Men
Ed.D., University of Southern Mississippi

Thomas W. Dunfee (1968)
Assistant Professor of Business Law
J.D., New York University

David C. Eaton (1969)
Assistant Professor of Sociology
Ph.D., University of Texas

Clifford H. Edwards (1968)
Assistant Professor of Education
Ed.D., University of Utah

Duane D. Edwards (1968)
Assistant Professor of English
Ph.D., University of Wisconsin

Donald H. Ericksen (1969)
Assistant Professor of English
Ph.D., University of Illinois

Alan D. Fletcher (1969)
Associate Professor of Marketing
Ph.D., University of Illinois

Ronald Foreman (1969)
Assistant Professor of Speech and English
Ph.D., University of Illinois

John T. Goeldi (1967)
Assistant Professor of Elementary Education
Ph.D., Michigan State University

Ronald S. Halinski (1968)
Assistant Professor of Education
Ph.D., University of Iowa

Ruby A. Hauseman (1967)
Assistant Professor of Theatre
Ph.D., University of Illinois

Kenneth A. Holder (1969)
Assistant Professor of Art
M.F.A., School of the Art Institute, Chicago

Robert E. Holdridge (1965)
Assistant Professor of Education
Ed.D., University of South Dakota

James E. House (1966)
Assistant Professor of Chemistry
M.A., Southern Illinois University

Samuel Hutter (1955)
Assistant Professor of Psychology
M.S., University of Illinois

E. Carmen Imel (1964)
Assistant Professor of Health and Physical Education for Women
Ph.D., University of Iowa

Arnold J. Insel (1969)
Assistant Professor of Mathematics
Ph.D., University of California

Steven E. Kagle (1969)
Assistant Professor of English
Ph.D., University of Michigan

Won-Mo Kim (1969)
Associate Professor of Music
D. of M., Florida State University

Keith P. Knoblock (1967)
Instructor in Art
M.F.A., Ohio State University

Ralph L. Lane (1968)
Associate Professor of Speech
Ph.D., Northwestern University

Marjorie L. Lewis (1951)
Associate Professor of Psychology
Ph.D., University of Illinois

Timothy W. Mather (1967)
Instructor in Art
M.F.A., Ohio University

John P. Mees (1968)
Supervisor of Off-campus Student Teaching, Assistant Professor of Education
Ed.D., Indiana University

William W. Morgan (1969)
Assistant Professor of English
Ph.D., University of Tennessee

Robert L. Oppelt (1968)
Professor of Music
A. Mus.D., University of Rochester

Alan H. Peters (1967)
Assistant Professor of Music
D.M.A., University of Iowa

Mildred S. Pratt (1969)
Assistant Professor of Social Work in the Department of Sociology-Anthropology
Ph.D., University of Pittsburgh

Theodore A. E. C. Pratt (1969)
Assistant Professor of Physics
Ph.D., Carnegie-Mellon University, Pennsylvania

Samuel T. Price (1968)
Associate Professor of Special Education
Ed.D., University of Pittsburgh

John T. Rehm (1969)
Assistant Professor of Music
M.M., Indiana University

Evelyn J. Rex (1958)
Assistant Professor of Special Education
M.A., Northwestern University

Don J. Scalamogna (1969)
Assistant Professor of Business Education
Ed.D., University of Houston

Harvey J. Schmidt, Jr. (1969)
Assistant Professor of Mathematics
Ph.D., University of Oregon

Charles E. Sherman (1969)
Associate Professor of Education
Ed.D., Northern Illinois University

Tai S. Shin (1968)
Assistant Professor of Finance
Ph.D., University of Illinois

Arnold A. Slan (1967)
Associate Professor of Elementary Education
Ed.D., Indiana University

Robert W. Small (1969)
Assistant Professor of Art
M.Ed., St. Lawrence University, New York

Michael T. Stack (1967)
Instructor in Art
M.F.A., University of Florida

Robert H. Steinkellner (1968)
Associate Professor of Elementary Education
Ed.D., University of Missouri

Arthur W. Sweet (1969)
Assistant Professor of Art
M.S. in Art Ed., Florida State University

Rodger L. Tarr (1969)
Assistant Professor of English
Ph.D., University of South Carolina

Robert H. Walsh (1964)
Assistant Professor of Sociology
M.A., State University of Iowa

D. Gene Watson (1968)
Assistant Professor of Educational Administration
B.S. in Ed., Illinois State University

Macon L. Williams (1968)
Assistant Professor of Psychology
Ph.D., The Ohio State University

Index

Academic advisers 20, 23, 27
Accounting 39
Accreditation 6
Administration, Educational 63
Admission................. 7, 11, 22, 24
Admission to candidacy...... 21, 24, 26
Alumni 16
Anthropology 122
Art 30
Assistantships 14
Auditor 29

Biological sciences 34
Board of Regents................. 4
Botany 39
Business 39
Business Administration 41
Business Education 44

Calendar 3
Candidacy, admission to...... 21, 24, 26
Chemistry 46
College teaching 19
Commencement 29
Counseling services 15
Course numbering system 30
Credit transfer................. 20, 23
Curricula 17

Degrees 17
Doctoral dissertations 26
Doctoral program......... 6, 9, 10, 24

Economics 50
Education 53
Educational media 54
Elementary Education 66
Employment 14
English 73
Evening, late afternoon, and Saturday
    classes 7
Examinations.............. 22, 24, 27
Extension 7, 20

Faculty 133
Fees 11, 29
Foreign languages............. 25, 79
French 80

General courses 132
Geography 85
German 81
Grading system 27
Graduate council 5
Graduation fee 29

Guidance 54
Health and Physical Education...... 89
Health Service 15
History 93
Home Economics 97
Housing 13

Incompletes 28
Industrial Technology 99

Latin 82
Library 6
Loans 14

Master's program.............. 9, 18
Mathematics 102
Microbiology 108
Music 108

Non-degree students 8

Officers of the University.......... 5

Physical sciences 112
Physics 112
Placements 16
Political science 114
Professional Laboratory Experiences.. 69
Psychology 117

Reading 54
Refunds 13
Residence requirements....... 20, 23, 25

Scholarship requirements 28
Scholarships 14
School psychology 117
Secondary education 55
Social sciences..... 50, 93, 114, 121, 122
Sociology 122
Spanish 83
Special education 70
Specialist programs........... 10, 22
Speech 125
Summer sessions 7
Supervision 55

Thesis 21

University Foundation 16

Veterans 16

Western European Studies......... 132
Withdrawal 27
Workshop 132

Zoology 132

CPSIA information can be obtained
at www.ICGtesting.com
Printed in the USA
BVHW041347070119
537204BV00013B/621/P